Windjammers

Windjammers

Songs of the Great Lakes Sailors

BY

IVAN H. WALTON

WITH

JOE GRIMM

Illustrated by Loudon G. Wilson
Musical scores by Lee Murdock

WAYNE STATE UNIVERSITY PRESS   DETROIT

GREAT LAKES BOOKS

A complete listing of the books in this series can be found at the back of this volume.

PHILIP P. MASON, EDITOR
Department of History, Wayne State University

DR. CHARLES K. HYDE, ASSOCIATE EDITOR
Department of History, Wayne State University

Copyright © 2002 by Wayne State University Press,
Detroit, Michigan 48201. All rights are reserved.
No part of this book may be reproduced without formal permission.
Manufactured in the United States of America.

Library of Congress Control Number: 2001098997
ISBN 0-8143-2996-9 (alk. paper)
ISBN 0-8143-2997-7 (pbk: alk. paper)

This volume was published with the assistance of a fund established by
Thelma Gray James of Wayne State University
for the publication of folklore and English studies.

CONTENTS

Introduction 9
    Sailing Songs 9
    The Collector: Ivan H. Walton 12
    The Artist: Loudon G. Wilson 18
    An Unusual Collaboration 20

Acknowledgments 23

PART 1. WORK CHANTEYS 29

Chapter 1 Capstan Chanteys 33
    Sally Brown 33
    The Rio Grande 34
    Shenandore 36
    A-Roving 36
    Banks of Sacramento 39
    Santa Anna 40
    The Ward Line 41
    Heave Her Up and Bust Her 45
    Good-bye, My Lover, Good-bye 46
    Leave Her, Johnny, Leave Her 48
    Homeward Bound 50
    Rolling Home 52

Chapter 2 Halyard Chanteys 57
    Blow the Man Down 57
    Blow, Boys, Blow 60
    Roll the Cotton Down 62
    Reuben Ranzo 63
    Whiskey, Johnny 64
    Hanging Johnny 65

Tommy's Gone to Hilo   67
A Long Time Ago   68
The Drunken Sailor   70
In a Handy Four-Master   71

Chapter 3 **Short-Drag Chanteys**   75

Haul on the Bowline   75
Haul Away, Joe!   76
Boney   78

PART 2. AMUSEMENT SONGS   81

Chapter 4 **Songs of Everyday Life**   85

It's Me for the Inland Lakes   85
Up Anchor   86
The Stomach Robber   87
The Sailor's Alphabet   89
Scrubber Murphy   92
We Leaves Detroit Behind Us   96
The *Sephie*'s First Trip   96
The *Dreadnaught*   97
The Schooner *John Bentely*   98
The Flash Packet *Worts*   100
You Pretty Girls of Michigan   101
Bonnie Highland Laddie   103
The *Three Bells*   103
James Bird   104
The Dredge from Presque Isle   107
On Gravelly Bay   109
The *Darius Cole* and *Mackinac*   110
On the Schooner *Africa*   111
The Steamer *Wyoming*   112
The *Fayette Brown*   112
The Seamen's Union   114
The Buffalo Whore   114
The Smugglers of Buffalo   116

Chapter 5 **Songs of the Iron Ore Trade**   119

The Red Iron Ore (The *E. C. Roberts*)   119
Bound Away on the *Twilight*   122

A Trip on the *George C. Finney*   124
The Old Mont Line   125
Loss of the *City of Green Bay*   127

Chapter 6   Songs of the Lumber Trade   129

The Timber Drogher *Bigler*   129
The Stone Scow   135
The Mules That Walked Our Fo'c'sle Deck   135
The *Jennie P. King*   137
A Trip on the *Lavindy*   139
On the Schooner *Hercules*   142
The Old Barge *Oliver Cromwell*   144
A Trip on the Schooner *Kolfage*   147
The Crew of the *Clara Youell*   149
The Jam on Gerry's Rocks (The Foreman John Monroe or Young Monroe)   152

Chapter 7   Scow and Canalboat Songs   155

The Wood Scow *Julie Plante*   155
Legend of the *Rosie Belle Teeneau*   158
De Scow *Jean La Plante*   161
De Scow *Look 'n' See*   162
De Scow *Nettie Fly*   164
The Good Scow *Alice Strong*   165
Yim Yonson (The Scow *Sam Patch*)   166
The E-ri-o Canal   167
The Canaller's Lament   168

Chapter 8   Songs of Beaver Island   171

Lost on Lake Michigan (The Gallagher Boys)   172
The Gallant Tommy Boyle   175
The Ill-Fated *Vernon*   176
The *Pere Marquette 18*   177
The *Clifton* Tragedy   179
The Seaman's Lament   180
The *Clifton*'s Crew   181
The *Clifton*   184
The *U.S. Lightship 98*   185
The Fisherman Yankee Brown   187

Chapter 9 **Disaster Songs**   191

    Lake Huron's Rockbound Shore
    (The Ill-Fated *Persian*)   191
    Loss of the *Maggie Hunter*   194
    The Schooner *Thomas Hume*   196
    The Loss of the *Gilcher*   197
    Lost on the *Lady Elgin*   199
    The Shores of Michigan (The *Antelope*)   202
    Cruel Waves of Huron   205
    The Foundering of the *Asia*   208
    The Dismasting of the *Cummings*   209
    The Fierce *Alpena* Blow   211
    The Loss of the *Gilbert Mollison*   213
    Let the Lower Lights Be Burning   214
    The Schooner *Oriole*   216
    The Steam Tug *Olson*   217
    The Wreck of the *Julia Dean*   219
    The Schooner *Jenkins*   220
    The Wreck of the *Belle Sheridan*   221
    The Car Ferry *Marquette and Bessemer No. 2*   223
    The Loss of the *Souvenir*   224
    The Old *Bay State*   225
    The *Carter* and the *Erie Belle*   226
    The Steamer *Idaho*   228

The Final Chapter   231

    The Crack Schooner *Moonlight*   231

Glossary   237
Notes on Sources and Informants   245
Bibliography   249
Index of First Lines   251
Name and Subject Index   255

INTRODUCTION

> If ever I follow the ships again
>   To gather my spuds and cakes,
> I'll not be workin' a deep-sea hack,
>   It's me for the inland Lakes.
> —"It's Me for the Inland Lakes," opening stanza

SAILING SONGS

Life under sail is a swirl of observations, fancies, conjecture, jokes, and gibes. Sailors' collective knowledge of weather, the ways of the sea, and shipboard life is crystallized in story, song, and rhyme. Most evocative of all is the chantey. Spelled *chantey* or *shanty*, but always pronounced with the softer "sh" sound, the term applies to songs for work.

The origin of the chantey is lost in antiquity, but by the time American waterborne commerce reached noticeable proportions the chantey had achieved a high state of development. On the Great Lakes, the golden age of sail ran from the close of the Civil War through the 1880s. The industrial boom of those decades inflated waterborne commerce, particularly in bulk freight, which sailing vessels could carry much more economically than could the steamers. In the year after the war, more than 1.5 million tons of grain traveled east to Buffalo harbor and about 400,000 tons of lumber went west to Chicago, while Cleveland and other ports took delivery of 300,000 tons of ore from the north. Fifteen years later, lumber shipments had increased greatly, grain traffic had doubled, and ore shipments had increased sevenfold.

Shipyards around the Lakes built hundreds of barks, barkentines, fore-and-afters, three- and four-masted schooners, and various combination rigs. These sailing vessels obtained a near monopoly of the bulk freight traffic and held it for decades until, near the end of the century, steam-powered commerce swept them from the Lakes. Big shipping corporations had not yet developed, so most wind-driven bulk cargo boats were individually owned family rigs. The larger ones carried a captain, a mate or two, eight to twelve crewmen, a cook, and the ship's boy. In the 1870s there was enough business to employ eighteen hundred vessels under American registry and several hundred more under Canadian.

Men did most of the heavy work on Great Lakes vessels, and chanteys freed them from boredom or bound them together in all kinds of labor, from hauling the anchor off the bottom to furling royals and skysails to the tops of swaying masts. Under stormy skies or clear, at midnight or noon, the chanteys had the same effect on sailors under command that martial music has upon soldiers under march. Work chanteys possess few of the characteristics of finished poetry common to most songs. But then, they are not sung to express sentiments or tell stories. Work chanteys unite the muscle and sinew of laboring men into a concerted effort. The melody is the thing, and it is marked by the slow, steady rhythm of men at work. A good chanteyman could wrap up a chantey, essentially an improvisation, whenever the men finished the job, or extend it indefinitely without repeating a rhyme.

Deep-water sailors brought their skills, songs, and stories to the Lakes, so some standards, sung the world over, echoed in Great Lakes ports just as they were heard in Liverpool or around the Great Cape Horn. Lakesmen localized others, replacing ocean ports with the names of more familiar lake towns. For a few songs, lakesmen stripped off the saltwater lyrics and re-outfitted the melodies from stem to stern for freshwater. The Great Lakes in the 1800s rang with the sounds of maritime nations and the twang of American innovation.

In the summer of 1932, Captain Fred Nelson, age seventy-three, said that most Great Lakes crews were only six to ten or twelve men forward, but with some deep-water men and a permissive mate aboard, they would chantey while working, though they couldn't make as much noise as the larger ocean crews. Some mates thought chanteying made the work go too slowly, "but ten men singing a lively chantey could outhaul twenty with no song."

Nelson said he had written down a lot of the songs in a book, but he lost them when the *Our Son* went down in a gale on Lake Michigan on September 20, 1930. Nelson was master of the vessel, one of the last commercial schooners that sailed the Great Lakes. He mourned the loss of his book and of real sailors. "There used to be damn good sailormen. . . . Now it's all steamboats and they ship any harbor rat that comes along and leave the real sailormen without any jobs. What you think this country's coming to?"

The following summer, former schooner captain A. N. Conkey recalled: "Some of them schooners was as pretty a sight as—well, there ain't a goddamn thing as pretty on this earth as a ship carryin' all her canvas before a good breeze! Crowds of people used to gather along the river right here in Port Huron to watch a tow of schooners comin' up an' all a'makin' sail an' crews a'singin', an' as soon as they'd let go they'd square away for a race up the lake. They'd never stop for any kind of weather." A Captain Adams, speaking later that summer at Ashtabula, Ohio, concurred: "Chanteying puts life into a crew, and a man can pull twice as much to a good song and not even know he's working."

This forced fraternity of city men and their country cousins working, living, and socializing in close confines spawned a folk tradition with its own customs, stories, and songs. Besides singing to lighten their work, they sang for fun.

Amusement songs, unlike the work chanteys, did not coordinate their labor, but liberated them from it. Great Lakes sailors sang amusement songs to while away leisure hours in forecastles aboard vessels and at gathering places ashore. They sang popular land songs as well as ocean songs such as "The Bold *Princess Royal,*" "The Stately *Southerner,*" "The *Flying Cloud,*" and "The *Dreadnaught.*" They made up others about their own lives. They sang of the girls they left behind, the peril of their work, their derision for landlubbers, and their contempt for tightfisted vessel masters. They made up their own songs, often on the spur of the moment, then passed them along, changing them to suit the situation. In a relatively short time, a song might have several incarnations, each one spinning off derivatives of its own. Many of these songs had no standard—or several—and relied on the oral tradition to keep them moving, ever-changing, from port to port, boat to boat, and throat to throat.

Captain William R. Dunn of Cleveland, reminiscing on September 17, 1933, said: "Life around the old schooners was a dog's life. In fact, no one now would make a dog live in the quarters we had nor eat the food we ate. And often we had only snatches of sleep day after day during bad weather, but, by God, I'd do it again if I had the chance! A vessel under canvas is alive—you feel it, an' how we'd drive 'em! But these damn steamboats are just lifeless machines with no personality."

The songs that have come down to us from the lore-building era of the "great white wings" on the Lakes give a colorful glimpse of the unique life that once thrived but is now forever gone. Steel, bulk-carrying freighters, the characteristic vessels on the Lakes today, brought efficiency and dispatch to Great Lakes commerce, and industry and respectability to the sailors, but they have taken most of the romance that filled the sails of the old sailing vessels.

Interviewed at St. Clair, Michigan, On July 14, 1933, "Major" Charles Leach said: "There ain't no more real sailors no more. Hell, anybody who can drive a horse can drive one of them steamboats up and down here. B'god, they've got every little bend and bump in the bottom of the whole damn string of lakes and rivers marked for 'em and they carry electric range finders and radio an' every damn thing they can think of to help 'em; still, they run aground, have collisions and founder in storms. B'god, when I started there wasn't a range or buoy or a damn thing the length of the rivers and damn few along the lake shores, and we went out in all kinds of weather and in late and early season. I've been out on Lake Huron day and night when it was snowing and freezing and the wind blowing a gale, and we'd fetch up where we wanted to go.

"Them fellows on them freighters ain't sailors. Hell, they'll take any damn farmer or coal heaver that comes along and call him a sailor when he doesn't know his ass from a hatch, and couldn't splice a line to save his damn soul. In my day you had to know every damn thing about a boat, an' it took you years to learn it."

The chanteyman's rhymes may have been forced, and his verses may have been doggerel, but as poet and spokesman for his mates his words told of their sentiments and longings.

Professor Ivan H. Walton. Courtesy of the Michigan Historical Collections at the Bentley Library, University of Michigan.

THE COLLECTOR: IVAN H. WALTON

Born in the days of steam, Ivan H. Walton was called by the earlier age of sail. Although he heard the call faintly in his youth, he didn't understand it clearly until it was almost too late. Once he understood, though, Walton worked feverishly to save the songs of the schooner age. And then, one day, he curiously walked away from the work to which he had dedicated more than thirty years of his life. His desperate race is unique in the history of the Great Lakes. It is also as ordinary as the story of anyone who, realizing that the years, the friends, or the autumn leaves are so swiftly fleeing, races about to scoop up the remaining few.

Sails brought Walton's grandfather to the shores of North America, and a storm stranded him here. As Lynn H. Walton, Ivan's only son, tells the family story, Nicholas Walton was an English farmer who used to sail across the Atlantic to sell cattle in Canada. On one such trip, a storm blew up and threatened to sink the ship. The crew, trying to lighten the load and save themselves, drove the cattle, representing a good deal of Walton's fortune, into the sea. The crew survived, but Nicholas Walton, broke and lucky to be alive, never returned to England. It is quite likely that Nicholas heard, or even sang, some of the songs his grandson would later chase.

Ivan Walton's intense interest in Great Lakes chanteys suggests that he spent most of his life within earshot of the Lakes. Not so. Ivan grew up in the Michigan woods and died in the mountains of the Southwest. In between, he visited most significant port towns on the Lakes. Born on August 10, 1893, Ivan grew up on his family farm outside Rosebush, a tiny town north of Mount Pleasant in Michigan's Isabella County, about sixty miles north of the state capital of Lansing. The Lakes, although forty miles away, called to him at an early age. On February 26, 1931, as he stood on the brink of the search that would take him to old seamen's homes and watering holes around the Lakes, Walton wrote to poet and folklore collector Carl Sandburg: "When I was a boy in north central Michigan, a roving cousin made his home with us during the intervals between his winters in the lumber woods and his summers on the Lakes, and would frequently while with us provide considerable entertainment with songs of lost boats, ore-carriers, storms, etc., and with Paul Bunyan yarns and accounts of practical jokes played upon inexperienced men in camp. I would give much (if I had it) for a source of such material now." Walton heard the call again in the popular sailing song "The Red Iron Ore," which one of his father's hired men sang while working one winter in between summers on the Lakes. And again, at the Lake Michigan port of Ludington where Walton lived for about a year while in his early twenties, he had heard "a group of men down in their quarters sing by the hour to the accompaniment of an accordion after they had loaded a shipment of fruit aboard. I don't know what they sang; I wasn't interested in the subject then."

Naturally, Walton's Mount Pleasant youth led to the local institution of higher learning, the Central Michigan College of Education. In 1913, though, after three years at Central, he left school to be a reporter and wrote for several newspapers, including the *Detroit News,* the *Toledo Blade,* and the *Grand Rapids Herald.* Walton finished college at the University of Michigan in Ann Arbor, graduating in 1917, and joined the Army Signal Corps during World War I. Achieving the rank of second lieutenant in the pilot training program, he returned to the University of Michigan in 1919 as a lecturer in the English department of the university's College of Engineering. He stayed for forty-three years, earning his master's degree in 1921 and advancing to full professorship in 1947. At the university, Walton met Mildred D. Hallett, and they were married in 1922.

As a professor of American literature, Walton mixed work and pleasure freely and nurtured his interest in folklore with studies at the University of Chicago and the University of Illinois. In the 1920s, Walton decided to compile a bibliography of the extensive body of Great Lakes literature. By the early 1930s his collection was growing explosively. During 1931 alone his bibliography grew from eight hundred items to three thousand, and he wrote that he planned to publish an anthology of literature and poetry in the spring or summer of 1932. Often sitting at the typewriter until well past midnight, he tapped out single-spaced requests to libraries, publishers, newspapers, and sailors throughout the Great Lakes region. Lynn Walton said that his father practiced typical reporter typing of his era, using as many as, but rarely more than, four fingers.

The thousands of literary works piled around him were like the pieces to an ever-expanding jigsaw puzzle of indefinite size and shape. And Walton kept looking for more. He wrote that he wanted to gather as many as he could to ensure that he could cull his collection from the best. As he gathered, a nagging buzz grew louder. Some of the literature contained references to singing. Walton recognized perhaps half a dozen of the pieces as sailor songs. The pieces began to arrange themselves into a new puzzle. The cousin of his youth . . . the hired man's songs . . . the singing men at Ludington . . . the scraps of song in this mountain of verse. It seemed that there must have been a considerable body of song, a vast and colorful tradition he was only glimpsing. Across the nation at this time, folklorists were publishing songs and stories of "the folk": cowboys, mountain people, hoboes, loggers. These encouraged Walton's hunch. Was he onto something similar? Was it already too late?

Just about the time Walton was coming to this realization, one of the last commercial sailing vessels on the Great Lakes, the fifty-five-year-old *Our Son*, was destroyed in a gale on September 26, 1930. In 1931, Captain James McCannell of the SS *Assinibois* wrote to Walton: "My people were telling me about your calling and sorry to have missed you. I have taken a good deal of interest in matters concerning the Great Lakes, having sailed for over 40 years on steamboats, but I am afraid I can not help you out very much about the songs etc. as during all my experience I have not heard many on board steamboats. Years ago I used to hear some of the old-time barnacles humming snatches about the famous clipper ship *Dreadnaught*, the schooner *Bigler*'s crew, Loss of the *Lady Elgin*, and the Wreck of the Steamer *Antelope*. On board schooners the crews often sang as they hoisted sails, anchors, etc. As a very small boy I often heard my brother-in-law and his brother (former sailors) singing short chanteys, but do not remember any of them." Collector-author Frank Shay, to whom Ivan also wrote for help in 1931, advised: "In my own experiences as a sailor I found many salt-water men who had been on the Lakes and it is my belief that if many got that far they took the songs current on the Atlantic with them. I doubt if you will find many singers of the old songs . . . I know that on the Atlantic today were the order given to 'heave and chantey' the bosun would be rewarded with blank stares. The real place to find old sea songs is in the shore-side gin mills and you'll do a lot better if you find a place where you can set up the drinks for Lake men too far gone to get a job."

Despite this gale of discouragement, Walton wheeled his search over onto a new tack. In 1932, the year he had planned to publish his anthology, he was instead packing his car with a collapsible bed and writing paper. With five hundred dollars in university money and some of his own, he drove off in search of songs that had been dying since before his birth almost forty years earlier. From June 23 until September 8 of that summer, Walton drove twenty-two hundred miles around Lake Michigan, the one he knew best, mildly cursing the foldaway bed and his bad luck in not having started sooner. On the first night of his trip, he wrote: "May the man who invented automobile folding beds be condemned to an eternity of setting one of them up in a car loaded for a summer trip."

Seeking out lighthouse keepers, librarians, and, especially, retired lakesmen, Walton turned up several key informants—and many disappointments. One of his most extraordinary successes came in South Haven, Michigan, on the first day of the trip. Rose and Arthur Gallagher told him of the rich and colorful song life on remote Beaver Island in northern Lake Michigan. He visited the island many times over the years, and it became the most important of his many sources. Walton made similar trips around Lakes Erie and Ontario in 1933. Less extensive trips followed, and in 1938 he began making field recordings on wax platters with a primitive, suitcase-sized recorder.

But disappointment littered the trail. Death, old age, alcohol, and the ephemeral nature of songs that were passed along orally from singer to singer conspired to confound Walton's quest. Late one night at the Muskegon harbor a man, elderly and poorly dressed, asked Walton for twenty-five cents. Walton questioned the man and learned that he had been a sailor, so he asked about songs. The ex-mariner claimed to know "every damn . . . [song] any sailor ever sang." When Walton offered the man a quarter in exchange for a song, the shabbily dressed man couldn't recall even one. At a Chicago sailors' union hall, Robert Collen seemed to be a much more reliable source. Walton gave Collen money to secure a second interview the following day. When Collen failed to show, the union hall business agent told Walton, "You gave him too much. He'll not be around now for several days." And at Mackinaw City, an old ex-lakesman sniffed that he had known "no end of that kind of stuff," but had "put all them worldly and sinful songs" out of his life forever when he had "found the Lord" in 1893, the very year Walton had been born.

Despite dead ends and disappointments, Walton found many men who recalled hundreds of songs, in part or in whole. Collen eventually did come back and became one of Walton's best informants. He was an ex-seaman of uncertain advanced age whose remaining bleached and sandy hair encircled a considerable bald space. He walked with a pronounced starboard list, and had big, reddish freckles on his face, neck, and forearms, faded eyes, and an underjaw that was slightly off center. In a voice with a pleasant Irish flavor, Collen said he had earned his nickname, "Brokenback," while working in a Cleveland shipyard when a scaffolding gave way under a vessel, consigning him to the hospital for twenty-one months. At one of his first meetings with Walton in 1932, he arrived at the union hall, as agreed, and apologized for not having more material. He then extracted from his coat pocket a handful of notes on assorted pieces of paper. Thumbing through them, he half talked and half sang a number of old songs, some from the shore and some from the sea. Some, he said, he had learned in 1880 during his first trip on the ocean as an apprentice seaman. He had, as a boy, run away from home and shipped on an outward-bound Liverpool square-rigger. In the late 1880s he had worked his way on an Erie Canal boat from New York to Buffalo and then sailed on the Lakes until the schooner days ran out. "Steam-boatin' ain't no fit work for a real sailorman," he said.

Collen stated that he sometimes acted as chanteyman on old Lakes schooners "when der wan't no better one aboard." He explained in some detail that chanteys "ain't no regular songs," that crews sing the same regular choruses on all ships, but the chanteyman "just makes up the rest of 'em as he goes along," and he added that he couldn't sing one twice the same if he wanted to, "so der ain't no way to write 'em down."

In meetings like this, Walton collected hundreds of songs and scraps. Ocean songs, work chanteys, disaster songs, legends, and lore came spilling or trickling out of his informants' fading memories. Walton followed their leads, asked them to review or rearrange one another's recollections, and reconstructed the songs as best he could. As much as the gaps in his collection frustrated him, Walton built a rich assemblage of Great Lakes songs.

Is Walton's collection a complete registry of Great Lakes singing? No. Many likely were lost before he arrived, just as Captain McCannell had predicted. Also, Walton's search was focused on the waters that bordered his home state. Fortunately, Michigan is bordered by four of the five Great Lakes, so its location may have provided a more varied collection than other starting points.

In establishing himself as a leading authority on Great Lakes folklore, Walton became colleague and guide to some of the foremost folklorists of the day. As a man who loved people and naturally attracted them, his home became a meeting place for students, teachers, and some of the giants in folklore. Gatherings at the Waltons' home featured plenty of singing and storytelling. Guests included Carl Sandburg, singer Burl Ives, and folklorists Stith Thompson and Alan Lomax. Collectors, including Sandburg and Lomax, asked Walton for sources and examples of Lakes lore, and he freely shared with them. Trading with Lomax, Walton had some of his recordings placed in the Library of Congress. Working with Michigan folklorists, including Earl Clifton Beck, who collected among former Michigan lumberjacks, Walton helped found a folklore interest group in 1938. It evolved into the Michigan Folklore Society in 1940.

On radio shows, in journals, and before clubs, Walton kept the songs of sailing alive. At night he continued to work over his collection, refining, typing, sifting, and reorganizing. Those closest to him say he was working on a book, and his correspondence agrees. In a December 21, 1941, Christmas card to Lomax, assistant in charge of the Archive of American Folk Songs at the Library of Congress, Walton wrote: "I'm working on mine . . . and it doesn't go very fast, particularly with a full time Univ. job and now extra duties. Some day I'll reach the end—I hope. Got some real background last summer when assisting two other men bring a 33-foot sloop down from the western end of L. Superior, to Charlevoix, on L. Mich. We had the darndest weather, three weeks of it, and the last day of it we battled a stiff north-wester for five hours about 10 miles off Charlevoix until the Coast Guard sighted us and came out after us. You should try these Lakes some time when they're really performing."

Whenever Walton wrote about the lakes, he capitalized Lakes.

Walton left a handwritten outline, four folders of typescript songs with descriptions, and a ninety-one-page manuscript intended to be Chapter 22 in a collaboration called "Regional American Folklore." Stith Thompson of Indiana University tried to pull the book together, but he couldn't get it published and gave up on it in 1952 after it was declared "commercially unfeasible." In the 1955–56 academic year, building heavily on his collection of Lakes lore, Walton established the first folklore course at the University of Michigan, and perhaps in the state.

Retirement came in 1963, and with it, presumably, all the time Walton would need to finish his book. But then he followed a calling that was louder than the sounds of the Great Lakes under sail: that of family. His son, Lynn, and daughter-in-law, Sue, had moved to Arizona ten years earlier, and the good-byes after their too-infrequent visits had always been extraordinarily tough on Ivan. The elder Waltons decided to retire to Arizona. Once there, Ivan fell in love with his new home. Sue said, "The day they moved in Mother said to me, 'Where's Ivan?' I said, 'I don't know.' I heard something and I said, 'Oh, he's out in back.' He was up a tree, chopping it down because it disturbed his view of the mountain range from his study. I don't think Mother was too happy." Ivan Walton was so smitten by the beauty and culture around him that he immediately threw himself into Southwest culture. His work on Great Lakes chanteying was over.

On Easter, April 14, 1968, Ivan Walton died. In accordance with his wishes, his ashes were scattered over the mountains he had come to love. His collection of Great Lakes songs nearly met a similar fate. Confronted with his mountain of handwritten and typed notes, shelves of books and record albums, and accumulation of clutter, Mildred Walton began giving some things away and destroying others. Lynn and Sue Walton feared that Ivan's collection might be broken up or lost and pulled it together so that it could be preserved. Within weeks of Ivan's death, Mildred turned his collection over to the Bentley Historical Library at the University of Michigan. There the transcripts, field diaries, notes, and recordings have been preserved and are open to researchers. But what of the book? University of Michigan colleague and friend George M. McEwen wrote: "I am convinced that what Ivan wanted to do was too much to be embraced in one publication. A comparison of the little he was able to include about the songs in the preserved manuscripts and the wealth of songs among his recordings and his listings of titles makes me believe that Ivan was overwhelmed by the quantity of his material. I suspect, moreover, that he was not satisfied to publish an anthology of the songs and that he wanted to communicate the unique qualities and the immense vitality of the life under sail as well as to reflect the individuality and the lustiness of the lakesmen who took part. He had come to know both the reality and the romance of the era of commercial sailing through his intimate associations over the years with many former sailors. If I am correct in my surmise, what he wanted to do can probably never be accomplished and yet, from Ivan's point of view, anything less probably seemed empty."

It is hoped that this collaboration, though it may fall short of Ivan Walton's vision, is in harmony with his mission of preserving and spreading the songs of the Great Lakes under sail.

Loudon G. Wilson. Courtesy of Craig Wilson.

THE ARTIST: LOUDON G. WILSON

Parallels between the lives of Ivan Walton and Loudon Wilson abound. Both men had ancestors who emigrated from Great Britain to Canada. Both families came by ship, of course, and both men were exposed to sea lore as youths. Walton and Wilson spent most of their lives in Michigan, became fascinated with Lakes lore around 1930, and spent the next several decades filling their hours by visiting Great Lakes ports, interviewing ex-sailors, and compiling information about the Lakes under sail. Late in their lives they moved to the American West, where they died, leaving their unfinished legacies amid thousands of pages of notes and plans. This volume is meant to reflect Walton's vision, supported by Wilson's artwork.

Loudon Guthrie Wilson was born on September 29, 1903, in the coal-mining town of Kilsyth, Scotland. The Wilsons lived near the River Clyde and the Forth and Clyde Canal, which carried vessels loaded with goods bound across Scotland from the estuaries of those great rivers. Wilson credited his mother, Agnes Loudon Dykes, with imbuing him with a sense of awe and admiration for the fast, colorful side-wheel excursion steamers. He wrote that her favorite was the *Jeanie Deans* and said that she came by her interest naturally, descended as she was from Dutch forebears. Writing in 1970, this is how he told his story: "Our large family all seemingly liked 'boats' and football (soccer). My oldest brother was apprenticed to John Brown & Co. shipbuilders at Clyde Bank, and trips down the Clyde to Rothesay and Dunoon were a highlight of early days. When trouble came, my father was a bewildered man whose farm and dairy background were little help in a business venture which folded and was preceded by our mother's death. Father took we two youngest boys for long walks as he mulled over his problems and entertained us with sweets and a much interrupted discussion on the sights along the Forth and Clyde Canal, the horse-drawn barges, the wee buffers and the trim excursion steamers all moving through the locks and traversing that lovely Scottish countryside with its heather and hills, its bluebell woods, shady barns and glens. Then came the closing and selling and the trip to Canada on the meager resources left. Memorable was that trip on an immigrant ship third class. The *Cassandra* took seven days and nights through ice fields that covered the whole visible world . . . water, ice and iceberg . . . I was not told then that it was then less than a month after the loss of the unsinkable *Titanic* on the same passage, the reason for the fear and misery of the crossing in that small, more fragile, elderly ship. Hard times and long, cold winters were the features of the first years on the Manitoba prairie, where depression was the deterrent to high hopes. The endless miles of sun-baked or snow-blanketed prairie were a harsh substitute for Scotland."

It was there, near the Red River, that the teen Wilson began sketching vessels. He moved to Detroit, Michigan, in 1923 and began his career as an advertising artist. He married Grace Florence Harrington in 1926, and they raised four sons: Craig, Alan, Gary, and Thomas. Around 1930, Loudon Wilson began his project in earnest, setting out to capture the evolution of sailing vessels on the Great Lakes into their unique design. In a January 13, 1936, letter to fellow Great Lakes lover Herman Runge, Wilson wrote: "I have been interested in the lakes ever since I was a boy and in the last five years or so have become more enthusiastic about the sailing vessels. My old notes on steamers lie almost forgotten. From old sailors I have gleaned considerable data on the general construction and rigging of all the outstanding types of schooners."

A perfectionist, Wilson pursued several avenues to get his drawings right. He sketched, photographed, examined artwork, collected articles, interviewed retired vessel masters repeatedly, studied models, built models, and even constructed a twelve-foot scow in his basement. Wilson was interested in the nature of rigging, the length of bowsprits, the sheer of masts, and a thousand other little details that went into the vessels. He filled notebooks, graph paper, and writing paper with notes, sketches, and drawings. His vision was a book, or pair of volumes, that would go over Great Lakes vessel architecture and rigging from masthead to keel. In his quest, Wilson swapped notes, observations, and photos with a circle of Great Lakes scholars. A. J. Fisher, who operated a small business selling parts to ship model builders, read an October 8, 1933, article in the *Detroit Free Press* about Ivan Walton's quest and on October 16 wrote to tell Walton about Wilson, who lived just a block away and who illustrated his catalogs.

Walton and Wilson met by mail and agreed on a collaboration in which Wilson's illustrations would accompany Walton's collection of songs. On December 28, 1949, Wilson opened a sheaf of notes and examples from Walton. It included a title page on which Walton had typed: "Windjammers on the Great Lakes, by Ivan H. Walton, illustrated by Loudon Wilson." Wilson roughed out several sketches and even completed a few, but most, like Walton's book, were never finished. Through the early 1950s, the co-conspirators wrote to each other, asking for forgiveness and patience as they described how work and other obligations kept them from completing their respective ends of the project. The illustrations in this book reflect all stages of Wilson's work, from working sketches to finished artwork. Most were not even intended for the book. Loudon Wilson, ever the perfectionist, would not have deemed them worthy of publication. They are included, despite their inconsistency and his presumed objections, to preserve the partnership and to convey his vision, though interrupted, of the Great Lakes under sail.

Wilson's interest in Great Lakes marine architecture followed him into his retirement in Santa Paula, California, but illness prevented him from working on his book in the last few years before his death on November 19, 1988. The following March, his family donated the Loudon G. Wilson Collection to the Institute for Great Lakes Research at Bowling Green State University in Ohio (now the Historical Collections of the Great Lakes). The collection of notes, photographs, artwork, and clippings traces the genealogy of marine architecture from spare Viking ships of 1000 A.D. through the thousand-foot freighters of Wilson's lifetime. Among those thousands of pages is a sketch on which Wilson wrote, in the lower righthand corner, "for unpublished book for Ivan Walton." It is on page 21.

An Unusual Collaboration

People who collaborate on books generally get to meet each other. Circumstances prevented that in this case. Ivan Walton completed virtually all of his collecting and writing by 1952, two years before I was born. His wife, Mildred, their son, Lynn, and daughter-in-law, Sue, saw that his huge collection was shipped off to the University of Michigan's Bentley Historical Library to reside as a bounty for researchers and scholars. I became one of those researchers.

Like Ivan, I grew up in Michigan and was called at an early age by the Great Lakes and their storied romance. Since childhood, I have walked the shores of Lakes Huron and Michigan. Growing up during the folk revival of the 1960s, it is only natural that I am drawn to the music Walton collected. I happened across a recording of Great Lakes songs and years later wanted to include its flavor in a history series I was writing for the *Detroit Free Press* to mark Michigan's 150th birthday. Running down the origins of those songs, I found that most roads led to the Ivan Walton Collection. Once immersed in his notes and transcripts, I saw his world of largely forgotten songs. Ivan's correspondence showed that he had intended to write a book all along, but never did. An interview with his son and a paper by his friend and teaching colleague George McEwen confirmed that Ivan never realized his dream. I resolved to help him finish his book.

Hours of searching and reading his collection turned up key pieces of the puzzle. A chapter he wrote for a never-published collection of folk songs showed his

"I love to see a schooner when getting underway," for unpublished book for Ivan Walton. Courtesy of the Historical Collections of the Great Lakes.

arrangement and observations about the work chanteys. A four-page, handwritten outline showed an arrangement for the amusement songs. He had typed out arrangements for most of the songs, along with stories of their origin, discovery, or meaning.

Passages in the introductory section "Sailing Songs" are straight out of "Michigan Lore," the chapter Ivan wrote for the Work Projects Administration's 1941 Michigan guidebook, and "Sailors on Lakes and Sea," his chapter for the never-published anthology that Stith Thompson gave up on in 1952. Ivan's notes indicate he did not envision a separate Beaver Island chapter, but it was such a vital and rich source for his collecting that one seemed appropriate. Portions of the chapter come from "Folk Singing on Beaver Island," his article in the *Midwest Folklore* magazine published in the winter of 1952. Walton's field notes reflected his journalistic training and provided good quotes for several parts of the book.

While the written material was essentially a cut, paste, and edit job, the musical scores and artwork were more challenging. In his letters, Ivan said that he felt musical scores were essential to the book, but his notes contained little more than chicken-scratch scores. Fortunately, he spent a great deal of time making field recordings. Those scratchy recordings, along with his notes and other sources, provided a treasure trove of material for singer-songwriter Lee Murdock of Kaneville, Illinois, who incorporated many traditional songs and ballads in his work. In creating the scores, Murdock's familiarity with the collection and with Ivan Walton meant every bit as much as his ear for music and eye for historical authenticity. He gently suggested improvements in the text, pointed out better versions of songs, and, using equal parts inspiration and serendipity, seems to have reunited some of the lyrics with long-lost melodies.

Artwork was the final hurdle. The Walton Collection contains almost no useful art, so I relied on a collection of artwork done by Walton contemporary Loudon G. Wilson. He and Ivan had corresponded, but the letters in the Walton Collection didn't clue me in to the partnership. The clues were in *Michigan History Magazine,* in an article by Robert Graham of the Institute for Great Lakes Research. He wrote an article about the Wilson Collection, and an accompanying sketch of sailors enjoying an amusement song on deck looked like a good fit for the Walton Collection. A few minutes with the Wilson Collection showed that it had the depth and breadth to serve as a source of artwork for this book. A couple of hours turned up letters showing that the men had intended a collaboration, and that artwork published in the magazine had been meant for that book.

I have tried to let Ivan Walton's spirit guide me as I assembled his notes and writing into the book-length manuscript he intended to leave us. In some places, the writing is all his; in others, it is mine. In most places, it is a bit of each of us, though I have tried to make it speak with one voice: Professor Walton's. The result, I hope, is true to his vision and a faithful reflection of how he came to understand the life of the Great Lakes sailor. It has been my pleasure to serve some small part in this collaboration. I only wish we could have talked things over.

Joe Grimm

ACKNOWLEDGMENTS

This book would not exist except for the understanding support of Mildred Walton, who put up with Ivan's summertime sojourns and midnight writing. It was she who, with son Lynn and daughter-in-law Sue, put his life's work into the capable stewardship of the people at the University of Michigan's Bentley Historical Library. There, it was preserved, organized, cataloged, and cataloged again. Some of the principals in those efforts have been directors Robert M. Warner and Fran Blouin, archivist Nancy Bartlett, 1979 catalogers Wil Rollman, Cheryl Baker, Glen Hendrix, and May Davis Hill, as well as Melinda Babcock, who reworked the collection in 1989. For insurance, a copy of the Walton Collection was placed in the Wayne State University Folklore Archives, where director Janet Langlois and archivists Wendy Flanagan and Suzanne Kent helped with the research. That material is now in the Michigan State University Museum's archives. Some copies also reside at the Library of Congress, where folklore specialist Jennifer A. Cutting helped make the most of a visit there.

Loudon G. Wilson's family—his wife, Grace Florence Harrington, and their sons, Craig, Alan, Gary, and Thomas—put up with easily as much obsession as Walton's family did. Wilson's artwork came spilling out of his collection at the Historical Collections of the Great Lakes in Bowling Green, Ohio, with the assistance of archivists Robert Graham and Susan Riggs.

Debbie Bedard Grimm became another "schooner widow" as the manuscript took its final form, and sons Dan and Steve lived in mortal fear that Dad would play tapes of the dread "Dad music" in the presence of friends.

The role of singer-songwriter-historian Lee Murdock cannot be overstated. In addition to pulling the manuscript off the rocks by agreeing to score music from a collection he knew so well, he offered invaluable insight that helped bring this book closer to what Professor Walton envisioned. Beyond being a musical historian, Murdock is part detective and part preservationist. While he has, in his role as a performer, written modern music for Walton Collection lyrics such as "De Scow *Nettie Fly*" and "The Mules That Walked Our Fo'c'sle Deck," the only scores presented in this book appear on the say-so of a Walton informant.

Murdock's work was informed by archivist and folksinger Joseph C. Hickerson, who worked for thirty-five years at the Library of Congress's Archive of Folk Song, later the Archive of Folk Culture. Edward J. Soehnlen, with a doctorate in musicology from the University of Michigan and who teaches at Saginaw Valley

State University, went over the scores after meeting Murdock on a cruise where Lee was performing.

    Members of the folklore community cheered on the book and offered suggestions and direction. They include Yvonne Lockwood, LuAnne Gaykowski Kozma of the Michigan State University Museum, and ethnomusicologist Laurie Sommers, a regular visitor to Walton's mother lode, Beaver Island.

    Several others who, like Walton and Wilson, are drawn to the Lakes generously shared expertise, energy, and encouragement. They include Dossin Great Lakes Museum director John Polacsek, whose voluminous vessel files are exceeded only by the ones in his head. Historian, author, and St. Clair Shores Library director Arthur Woodford helped, as did Cynthia Bieniek, who works at both the library and the Dossin. Author and bibliophile Larry Massie, diver/historian Jeri Baron Feltner, and newspaper editor/song buff Jean Thompson lent their hands, too. Thanks to *Detroit Free Press* artist Fred Fluker for the map.

    Several people at Wayne State University Press made invaluable contributions. They include Arthur Evans, director of the press, and members of the Great Lakes Books advisory board. Jonathan Lawrence, the copy editor with a musician's background, sweated the details in the text and the scores and made some great contributions. Others who helped were acquisitions editor Jane Hoehner, project editor Kristin Harpster, and production coordinator Danielle DeLucia. One more Wayne State University supporter was Thelma James, a contemporary of Walton's. An English professor, ethnic folklorist, and archivist at Wayne State, James cofounded the Michigan Folklore Group with Walton. They were its first two chairs. James made a bequest to Wayne State to support the publication of books like this one, and part of her bequest has been used to bring her colleague's work to light.

    Finally, there are the hundreds of lakesmen, lighthouse keepers, librarians, and others who talked about, wrote about, or searched for the material that made the vast collection from which this book comes. Many of their names are between these covers; many more are not. Regrettably, Ivan was not here to ensure their proper credit or to see this volume.

WINDJAMMERS

PART 1
Work Chanteys

The typical work chantey has two distinct parts: the solo lines sung out by the chanteyman, and the group choruses. In hoisting a yard, for example, the men available for the work would "tail on" the appropriate halyard, apprentice seamen taking their places behind the old hands. On an officer's order to "heave and chantey," the chanteyman would take a position where he could be seen and heard by all. To wind up the anchor or heavy lines, men tramped around a barrel-like capstan, pushing before them the wooden bars that radiated from it like spokes. The chanteyman might sit atop the capstan head and announce a song simply by singing the first line of a familiar couplet. As his final syllable hung in the air, the crew sang out with the second line. The chanteyman broke in on the last word of the chorus to start the second couplet, and the men gathered breath and strength for their next effort. The chanteying continued until the work was done and the officer in charge ordered "Belay."

The choruses, their mouth-filling vowels accentuating the points of united effort, were standard, and experienced sailors knew them by heart. But verses, aside from a few more or less customary opening couplets, were up to the chanteyman. A good chanteyman with a reputation to uphold would improvise verses without repeating any for as long as the work required, embellishing the melody with grace notes and various tricks of vocalization. Striking lines and images seem to have been wedded to certain songs, but the chanteyman was free within the theme to introduce current events, experiences ashore, lines from other songs, comments on the boat, its food, crew, and officers, or any other subject that struck his fancy. Not all the lines are printable. The singer who could surprise a laugh from his mates encouraged a hearty chorus and lightened the work.

There are three families of work chanteys, each suited for a different type of work, but used interchangeably at the whim of the sailors. Capstan chanteys accompanied men at the steady, even work of weighing anchor, warping the ship, or hoisting heavy canvas. Halyard chanteys unified men in the long, hard task of pulling on lines to hoist heavy sails and other loads. Short-drag chanteys, the third family, encouraged the comparatively light work of furling or reefing sails, "sweating up" halyards, and boarding tacks and sheets. In the music—even in the lyrics alone—one can feel the rhythm of the work. Capstan chanteys in particular lent themselves to all kinds of mechanical work, including the windlass and pumps, which had some chanteys of their own. Collectively, capstan, windlass, and pump chanteys can be called heaving chanteys.

A. E. Baker of Dunkirk, New York, a former schoonerman and commercial fisherman, said in 1933: "There was no harder work in the world than that on the old windjammers and I swore off many times, but always went back. There's nothing in this world like being to leeward of a big sailboat as her canvas is filling and she's beginning to move off from her anchorage and the crew is still bellowing some old song as they set the last sails."

Work chanteys practically disappeared from the Lakes in the late 1880s with the advent of the donkey engine, which did most of the heaving formerly done by men and mules. They breathed their last in the closing years of the schooner era, when the largest of the wind-driven vessels were converted into undignified barges and dragged by the nose behind steamboats.

Off-duty sailors pose on this vessel at Port Dalhousie. At work, they would push wooden bars to turn the capstan drum, on the deck at lower left. Dossin Great Lakes Museum.

Notes on this rough sketch indicate that Wilson planned to use it to illustrate Walton's section on work chanteys. Courtesy of the Historical Collections of the Great Lakes.

CHAPTER 1

Capstan Chanteys

British sailor-poet John Masefield called capstan chanteys the most beautiful of the sailors' work songs, and no wonder. They are characterized by a steady, measured rhythm and generally have a stateliness not found in other work chanteys. Capstan work is smoother than other shipboard tasks and doesn't require the heave-rest-heave of tasks such as hoisting sails. A capstan is a drum, mounted vertically to revolve on a spindle. A heavy line attached to the drum, or capstan barrel, is wound up as men turn the capstan by tramping around it, two or three abreast on big vessels, pushing chest-high wooden capstan bars before them. The cable or line winds around the capstan, raising the anchor, hoisting canvas, or doing other heavy work. Pawls—stout iron bars mounted to the barrel on pins at deck level—catch the capstan, also called a pawl post, should it start to rewind. As men pushed the capstan around, the clanking pawls punctuated their singing. Some capstan chanteys had but one chorus of several lines, while others had the traditional group parts, the second line being longer than the first. Given the steady work required at the capstan, the men found that almost any type of song helped relieve the drudgery of the work. Capstan chanteys also lent themselves well to work on the windlass and some types of pumps.

Sally Brown

Sally Brown seems to have been the work chantey's chief heroine. Her name and easy ways have been sung in ports all over the world. This song has a good marching rhythm for hoisting the lighter sails, and it was a favorite for a "capstan walkaround" as an outbound ship left the pier.

Captain William E. "Billy" Clark of Buffalo, who had long known the song and sung it for many seasons on Lakes vessels, said that it was one of the most popular chanteys used on capstan hauls. His neighbor, Captain Thomas Hylant, recalled that it was mostly used on halyards. It was well known and used on the big grain carriers in 1870s when both men began their careers as Lakes sailors. This version came from Harry and George Parmalee in 1932.

Sally Brown

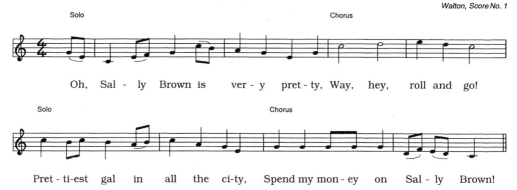

Oh, Sally Brown is very pretty,
    Way, hey, roll and go!
Prettiest gal in all the city,
    Spend my money on Sally Brown!

Sally Brown, she's a bright mulatto,
She drinks rum and chews tobacco.

Seven long years I courted Sally,
But she was always a dilly dally.

Oh, Sally Brown, I long to see you,
Oh, Sally Brown, I'll n'er deceive you.

The Rio Grande

The capstan chantey "The Rio Grande" seems to have been unusually popular among Great Lakes sailors. A dozen ex-schoonermen living in ports from Chicago to Oswego recalled its use more than three decades after the big grain schooners were gone from the Lakes, and half of them still remembered stanzas to it. Its beautiful melody, the slow and graceful amplitude of its rhythm, the clear, idealized imagery, and the mouth-filling vowels in the choruses added to its popularity and enjoyment.

    The men who sang "The Rio Grande" said it was used only on the larger outbound vessels when the full crew was available for duty. Men walked the capstan to its rhythm while warping the vessel out of its loading dock, getting the main anchor, and setting the heavy sails next above the main deck. Sailors, of course, always pronounced the word "Rio" to rhyme with "good-bye-O." The music of the name of the South American river that "flowed down golden sands" helped make the region a sort of sailor's Elysian Fields and invited full support in the singing. The incongruity of reaching this faraway happy land on board a Great Lakes grain carrier didn't seem to bother anybody. At least the singers were going away.

    This is a composite, with verses recalled by Captain William Clark, Carl Joys of Milwaukee, Ben Peckham of Oswego, and Robert "Brokenback" Collen. All had sailed in the grain freighters between Chicago, Milwaukee, and Buffalo.

The Rio Grande

Walton, Score No. 2

Oh, say, was you ev-er in R-i-o Grande? A-way you, Ri-o!

It's there that the ri-ver runs down gold-en sand, And we're bound for the Ri-o Grande.

And a-way, haul a-way, a-way, you Ri-o! It's fare you well,

my bon-nie young gal, We're bound for the Ri-o Grande!

Oh, say, was you ever in Rio Grande?
    Away you, Rio!
It's there that the river runs down golden sand,
    And we're bound for the Rio Grande.
    And away, haul away, away, you Rio!
    It's fare you well, my bonnie young gal,
    We're bound for the Rio Grande!

Oh, man the good capstan and run it around
We'll heave in the anchor, for we're outward bound.

Oh, man the good capstan, heave steady and strong,
And sing a good chorus for 'tis a good song.

Our anchor we'll weigh, and the sails we will set
And the girls in Chicago we'll never forget.

Oh, the town of Chicago is no place for me,
I'll pick up my dunnage and go off to sea.

Oh, good-bye to Sally, and good-bye to Sue
And you who are listening, it's good-bye to you.

It's good-bye, fair ladies, it's good-bye all 'round
We've left enough cash to buy half this town.

In Rio Grande I'll take my stand,

Oh, Rio Grande is a happy fair land.

It's there that the Portugee girls can be found

And they are the girls to waltz sailors around.

We'll ride in a carriage and live high and free.

Oh, that happy strand is the right place for me.

Away Rio, away you Rio!

Before launching into the traditional stanzas and improvisations about the fabled country to the south of England, some chanteymen opened the song with some stanzas from an old English nursery song beginning "Oh, where are you going, my pretty fair maid?"

Shenandore

Few, if any, work songs are so hauntingly beautiful as this one. Once heard, it will not soon be forgotten. The stanzas tell no story, nor do they present any clear glimpse or vignettes of sea life, as many chanteys do. Its strong appeal to sailors seems to stem very largely from its melancholy melody, which is contrary to most chanteys.

"Shenandore" was one of the most widely used of the capstan chanteys on both American and British ships. In *Ships, Sea Songs, and Shanties,* W. B. Whall presents a pre–Civil War version that recounts a trader's courtship of the daughter of an Indian chief, Shenandoah, and of his taking her "across the wide Missouri." David W. Bone's version in his *Capstan Bars* is that of a sea wanderer longing for his native Shenandoah Valley in Virginia. In still other versions, Shenandoah—or "Shenandore," as the sailors pronounced it—is a packet sailor and a bright mulatto. The word itself seems to have a strong appeal to seamen's imagination.

The Great Lakes version given here dates back to the 1870s and seems to be closer to Bone's version than to any other. The wide distribution of ex-sailors who mentioned "Shenandoah" suggest it was well known among early Lakes schoonermen. All of them pronounced it "Shenandore."

John S. Parsons sang this rendition in the marine museum-office of his ship chandlery on the Lake Ontario waterfront of Oswego, New York, during the summer of 1933. Parsons said he learned it from some shellbacks in the 1880s when he sailed the Great Lakes as a boy.

A-Roving

In the days of sail, the Amsterdam maid, like Sally Brown, was known by British and American sailors everywhere. Masefield states that the air is an old Elizabethan tune and that some of the solo couplets are identical with those in a song in act 4, scene 6 of Thomas Heywood's play *The Rape of Lucrece,* which dates from 1640. Great Lakes sailors used it widely as a capstan chantey in working the larger grain vessels into position for loading and unloading, hoisting heavy canvas, or any other

Shenandore

Walton, Score No. 3

Oh, Shenandore's a rolling river,
    Away, you rolling river!
Oh, Shenandore's a rolling river,
    Away, we're bound to go, 'crost the wide Missouri!

Oh Shenandore, I long to hear you
    (Repeat after chorus)

Oh Shenandore, I long to see you
    (Repeat after chorus)

Oh Shenandore, I'm bound to leave you
    (Repeat after chorus)

Oh Shenandore, I'll never grieve you
    (Repeat after chorus)

Oh Shenandore, I'll love you ever
    (Repeat after chorus)

capstan work. The chanteyman's amorous adventures ashore always had a good audience about the capstan, and the song could be made to last any length of time. Lakes sailors sometimes effected a local setting by substituting "Buffalo" for "Amsterdam" in the opening line.

    Collen recalled the air and first three stanzas in the summer of 1932. Like other saltwater men, he adapted ocean songs to fresh water and sang them to lighten labor on the Great Lakes and to win free drinks in the taverns along its shores. The last two stanzas came from Captain William Clark in 1933. Clark had begun sailing as a boy in Buffalo grain schooners in the late 1870s and "followed the Lakes" continuously from then on.

A - Roving

Walton, Score No. 4

In Amsterdam, there lived a maid,
    Mark well what I do say! In
        Amsterdam there lived a maid,
And she was mistress of her trade.
    I'll go no more a-roving with you,
        fair maid.
    A-rovin', a-rovin', since rovin's been
        my ru-i-in,
    I'll go no more a-roving with you,
        fair maid.

Her cheeks were red, her eyes was
    brown,
Her hair like glowworms hangin' down.

Her eyes was like the stars at night,
Her face was fair, and she was white.

I put my arm around her waist,
Says she, "Young man, you're in great
    haste!"

She swore that she was true to me,
And spent my cash all fast and free.

Banks of Sacramento

You'll immediately recognize this tune and some of the phrases as being very close to those of Stephen Foster's minstrel song "Camptown Races," which dates from 1850. The song was taken to sea and widely used on clippers sailing around the Horn to California in the boom days of the gold rush. But which came first, the minstrel song or the chantey? In her book *Roll and Go: Songs of the American Sailormen*, Joanna Colcord speculated that Foster picked up the song on the New York waterfront, though it is more likely, she wrote, that "it was taken to sea and fitted to new words."

By the time the chantey reached the Great Lakes, probably in the 1870s, verses descriptive of a horse race had been lost and others telling of a clipper's voyage around the Horn to California, a more familiar subject to sailors, had taken their place.

In this version, the first two stanzas, the chorus, and the tune are from Captain M. J. Bonner of Charlevoix, Michigan, who did most of his sailing in the Lake Michigan lumber trade. Bonner recalled learning these lines from sailors walking capstans on their vessels in the Chicago harbor. He added that there were many more verses telling of an ocean trip to San Francisco Bay, but he was unable to recall any of them. The third and fourth stanzas were obtained from ex-sailor John S. Parsons, but he could not recall where he had learned them.

Banks of Sacramento

Walton, Score No. 5

Oh, heave my lads, oh heave and sing, To me, hoo-dah! To me, hoo-dah! Oh,

heave and make those oak sticks spring, To me, hoo-dah, hoo-dah day! Oh, it's

blow, my bul-ly boys, blow, for Cal-i-for-ni-o, There's

plenty of gold, so I've been told, on the banks of Sac-ra-men-to!

Oh, heave, my lads, oh heave and sing,
    To me, hoo-dah! To me, hoo-dah!
Oh, heave and make them oak sticks
    spring,
    To me, hoo-dah, hoo-dah day!
    Oh, it's blow, my bully boys, blow,
For Cal-i-for-ni-o,
    There's plenty of gold, so I've been
    told,
    On the banks of Sac-ra-men-to!

A bully ship and a bully crew,
A bully mate and a captain, too.

Our money all gone, we shipped to go,
Around Cape Horn, through ice and snow.

Around Cape Horn in the month of May,
With storm winds blowing every day.

The oak sticks referred to are, of course, the capstan bars the men pushed on as they walked around the capstan.

Santa Anna

The Mexican general Santa Anna has, no doubt, been much more of a hero to sailors than to historians. But then, the chanteymen were less concerned with historical facts than with songs that had a good rhythm and some vowels in the right places. To the chanteyman it mattered little whether credit for the victory went to Santa Anna or General Taylor, later President Zachary Taylor. The song has a good swing and was popular with seamen for nearly half a century. Many Great Lakes sailors said they recalled the song, but these four verses were the only ones that any of them could remember. This may indicate that the song was of limited popularity, or that it didn't make it over to the Lakes until late in the schooner period, after the events for which the hero was known were forgotten. Enough of a memory survived, however, for chanteymen to use the song in sublimating some otherwise monotonous work.

    Captain Thomas Hylant of Buffalo supplied the tune and the first two stanzas. Captain Charles Millard of Sarnia, Ontario, contributed the others.

Santa Anna

Oh, Santa Anna gained the day,
    Hooray, Santa Anna!
He lost it once but gained it twice,
    All on the plains of Mexico!

Oh Santa Anna won the day,
He won the day in Monterey.

Old Santa, he was brave and bold,
An' won many battles, I'm told.

Oh, many battles Santa won,
But now old Santa's day is done.

The Ward Line

There is mystery in this song—or at least in its recovery—and the mystery reveals the strange lives and turns these songs took. Throughout the Upper Great Lakes, sailors knew the Ward Line and the work chantey of the black men who trucked the iron ore and copper pigs that filled the boats' holds. Captain Eber Brock Ward became Michigan's richest man with his ventures in steelmaking, glass making, real estate, and banking. Ward's wealth was rooted in shipping, the family business started by his uncle Sam at Marine City, Michigan, in 1820. Although E. B. Ward dropped dead on the streets of Detroit in 1875, his shipping business survived, as did this song about one of the most prominent Ward Line vessels, the *Sam Ward*. Nicknamed the "Old Black Sam" for its distinctive paint job, the side-wheeler steamed between Michigan's Lake Superior copper country and the ports of Detroit, Cleveland, and Buffalo. Captain Harvey Kendall of Marysville, Michigan, claimed to have served as mate for several seasons on the "Old Black Sam." The mystery is that the vessel was lost in 1861, making it unlikely that Kendall had ever served on it. And why should verses mention vessels that were not around while the *Sam Ward* sailed? The explanation might be that the song long outlived its namesake, and grew with additions and embellishments.

    Kendall said that the steamer would stop at Detroit on its upbound trip and ship a team of twenty or more black men to load the copper pigs waiting at the Keweenaw Peninsula on Lake Superior. The men would stay on until after they had unloaded the pigs at their destination, received their substandard wages (about fifty cents a day), and been put off at Detroit. The deckhands loaded and unloaded the "Old Black Sam" with hand trucks or wheelbarrows. Pushing their heavy loads in an endless loop between vessel and warehouse, the men worked continuously with only brief time-outs. It took two or three laborious days to load a cargo of copper this way. During the long, tedious work and for similar chores, the men sang. They preferred chanteys for their steady rhythm, improvisation, and group choruses. When the work slowed, an officer would try to pick up the pace by tapping out a quicker rhythm on the ship's bell. If there was a musician in the group, he might be called up to play a lively tune on the upper deck, above the gangway where the copper-wheeling circle looped into and out of the boat. On at least one occasion, the officers served the men a tub of "suds"—liquor that had been watered down and doped up with hot pepper. "Then," said Kendall, "you ought to see the copper come aboard."

Kendall said that the song had no particular beginning, order, or end, that choruses generally didn't make much sense, but that the tune invariably had a good, marked, and relatively slow rhythm. "The Ward Line" stuck with Kendall long after other songs had passed out of his memory. "I probably remember it because of the choruses," he said. "Even they knew they weren't goin' anywhere on the wages they received and the kind of life they led." Hence the chorus:

Who's on de way, boys, who's on de way?
Tell me, whar yo' goin'!

Most of these verses come from Captain Harvey Kendall and his son, Earl, and other Ward Line officers. They included John E. Hayes of the propeller *Wm. H. Stevens,* Grafton McDonald of Marine City, and C. D. Secord, interviewed on September 15, 1933, at Cleveland. This song was retold in dialect, much as the scow songs later in this book are told in French or Scandinavian. This song is included at length, despite some offensive lyrics, as testimony to an African American presence on the Lakes and a reminder of the working conditions.

Kendall recalled that soloists who came up with original couplets were great crowd pleasers and that humor was highly prized. One Sunday morning as chanteying filled the air above the Houghton waterfront, Kendall recalled, a delegation from a waterfront church approached the vessel to ask that the men be quieted so that services could continue. As the delegation approached, a new couplet rang out:

Der come mister parson in his long black coat,
    Who's on de way, boys, who's on de way?
He'll go t' Heav'n, a'ridin' on a goat!
    Tell me whar yo' goin'!

The couplet drew a hearty laugh, but Kendall quieted the men, who pushed their trucks in silence for a few minutes as the delegation made its request and

The Ward Line

Murdock, Score No. 7

De cap'n's in de pilot house ringin' de bell,
    Who's on de way boys, who's on de way?
'N' de mate's down 'atween decks giv'n de niggas hell!
    Tell me, whar yo' goin'!

When I sign on de cap'n say,
"On dis fine ship, no wo'k, all play."

De mate he say, "no wo'k on de ship,
Jes' lay aroun' an' enjoy de trip."

De mate he say, "one trip up de Lake,
Jes' set yo' up like a plutocrate."

Ah'd rudd'r be daid 'n' a'lyin' in de san',
Dan make a'nudda trip on de "Old Black Sam."

Her smokestack's black 'n' her whis'l's brown,
'N' ah wish de Lawd ah'd a'stay'd in town.

Ah don' min' wo'kin' by de light o' de moon,
If de cap'n giv' us a half-hour noon.

"Git along der, Mose, yo' feet ain't stuck,
Jes' hump yo' back an' push dat truck."

"Git along der Mose, push dat truck,
By 'n' by yo' dead, 'n' yo' have good luck."

Takes tons o' coppa t' fill dat hol',
"Step along, der, nigga, damn yo' soul."

It's wo'k all night an' wo'k all day,
An' all yo' get am not half pay.

De mate say, "Sam, I'se raise yo' pay,
Yo' now git fifty cents a day!"

Roll 'em up dat long gangplank,

It make yo' thin 'n' lean 'n' lank.

City folks, dey's gon' to bed,
But we push coppa till we's dead.

De cap'n he give us a tub o' suds,
It burn yo' belly 'n' rot yo' guts.

Jes' one drink fum de cap'n's tin,
'N' it makes yo' feel like commit'n sin.

Black boy, tick'l dat ol' banjo,
It lif' yo' heels an' make 'em go.

It mak' me think o' ma Liza Lou,
When she hear music, man! What she do!

Lake Superior's col'er 'n' ice,
Fall in jes' once, freeze all yo' lice.

Lake Superior's big 'n' rough,
'N' fo' dis nigga, one trip's enough.

It mus' be hours pas' dinna time,
'N' boss, ah's sho' da eat'n kind.

De *Ward*'s boun' up, de *Moran*'s boun' down,
'N' de *John M. Nichol* am hawd agroun'.

De *Wm. H. Stevens* is a'lyin' roun' de ben',
'N' all she's doin' is a'killin' good men.

Now I'se goin' back to Detrite,
'N' no more wo'k both day 'n' night.

'N' ah's goin' way down to Mobile
Whar white man bring de nigga's meal.

'N' ah's goin' down to Baltimore,
'N' ah ain't goin' to wo'k at all no more.

then headed back to church. Then the men raised their voices to the heavens in a traditional hymn that stirred his heart.

Kendall recalled a late-season trip that gave birth to another couplet. One night, ice closed in on a loaded vessel downbound through Mud Lake, now Munuscong Lake, in the St. Marys River. At first light, Kendall took the deck crew over the side to cut the ice and free the boat. The temperature was exhilarating in the extreme, but the work was tedious and the men soon struck up "The Ward Line." Kendall remembered these lines from that frozen autumn morning:

I'se a'goin' back whar de shugga' cane grow,
 Who's on de way, boys, who's on de way?
I'se a'goin' far away from dis ice an' snow.
 Tell me, whar yo' goin'!

Frank Mahaffey of Port Colborne, Ontario, recalled teams of black men with wheelbarrows who used to "coal up" steamboats and tugs at Amherstburg, Ontario, and other ports and who sang the same chantey. One day, a worker with a squeaky wheelbarrow had asked Mahaffey for some grease. "I told him where the grease was," Mahaffey said, "but he didn't want to be bothered, and so continued without using any. Shortly afterward at a break in the song when, of course, he was near enough so I would have to hear him, he sang":

Dis one-wheeled buggy is cryin' cuz she's ol'
 Who's on de way boys, who's on de way?

By 'n' by she's flop, spill all de coal.
    Tell me, whar yo' goin'!

Another old sailor, Frank Murphy, recalled seeing a crew of black men pushing wheelbarrows loaded with wood at a fueling dock at Amherstburg, where the Detroit River enters Lake Erie. He recalled little except the oft-repeated line:

Beech an' maple, beech an' maple,
Shove dat co'd wood long's you's able.

Heave Her Up and Bust Her

The verses of this anchor-weighing chantey reflect several themes popular among sailors. The first jokes about sailing ships being pulled around at the end of a towline; there is the familiar gibe at smoke-belching tugs; the sailor's image of himself as a ladies' man and the dig at soft landlubbers who had better chow and easier lives than the hardworking sailors. A couple definitions are in order. The Flats are the wide, shallow areas at the north end of Lake St. Clair. To "heave" a vessel up and "bust" her meant to wind in the anchor chain so as to draw the vessel directly up over the anchor, and then to pull it free of the mud holding it.

This is a collaboration by Jim McCarthy, J. Sylvester "Ves" Ray, and William J. Small, all of Port Huron, Michigan.

The St. Clair River is thirty miles long,
    HEAVE 'er up lads, HEAVE 'er high!
An' we'll set our canvas to this merry song.
    HEAVE 'er up and BUST her.

Up the river we sail on a towline breeze,
Astern the Flats, ahead the big seas.

The wind is strong from the nor'west,
An' Lake Huron's seas we soon will test.

The tug is belching fire and smoke,
The line holds firm on the towing post.

The wind's nor'west and holding strong.
Sheet 'er close, send her along.

The girls are list'ning from both shores,
Their welcome smiles we do adore.

The girls, they wish we'd come ashore,
An' it breaks their hearts when we pass their doors.

The landlubbers sleep in their soft beds,
While sailors are hauling to earn their bread.

The landlubbers fill up on beefsteak and pie,
While the grub they give sailors would make a saint die.

Soon we'll leave the Lake Huron light,
The stormy winds and sea to fight.

Good-bye, My Lover, Good-bye

This chantey was used frequently on grain boats in Chicago or Milwaukee when all hands worked the capstan kedging a vessel out of her loading dock or raising anchor preparatory to towing out of the harbor for a down trip to Buffalo. It expressed none too subtly the professional sailor's contempt for landlubbers and, like all other chanteys, could be extended as long as the chanteyman could think of new rhymes. The general idea seems to be that the greenhorn sailor will be a wiser man when he reaches port.

This is collected from Captain Thomas Hylant of Buffalo and George Leach of St. Clair, Michigan.

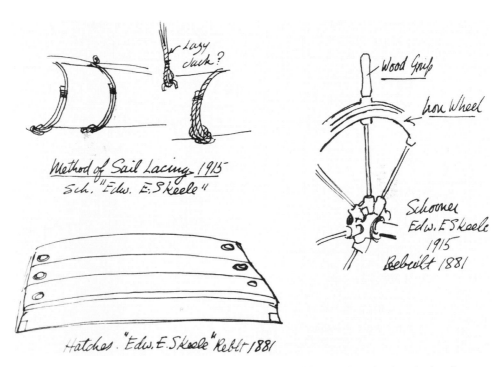

Details from the schooner *Edward E. Skeele,* including sail lacing, the wheel, and a hatch. Courtesy of the Historical Collections of the Great Lakes.

Good-bye, My Lover, Good-bye

Murdock, Score No.16

A farmer boy stands on the deck,
  Good-bye, my lover, good-bye.
He's eatin' peanuts by the peck,
  Good-bye, my lover, good-bye,
  Good-bye, aye, good-bye, my lads,
  Good-bye, my lover, good-bye.

He came on board in his Sunday clothes,
In his Sunday hat an' his Sunday hose.

He should a'stayed with his mules, and plow,
He thinks the rudder's in the bow.

He walks the deck with farmer's feet.
He don't know a halyard from a sheet.

He thinks himself a hell of a tar,
As he pushes around a caps'n bar.

He thinks himself the old ship's match,
He don't know his stern from the after hatch.

He thinks from evenin' till morning light,
In his warm bed he'll dream all night,

The mate will say, "Wow, mister Jack,
This chair'll be easier on your back!"

When the night winds blow and the seas they roar,
He'll curse the day he left the shore.

When the green seas roll across our deck,
He'll pray the Lord for to save his neck.

When the old ship rolls all day 'n' night,
It'll turn him green and blue and white.

When he has to go aloft at night,
He'll soil his drawers in his awful fright.

At him the Old Man looks so grim,
He thinks his eyes is a'gettin' dim.

He'll know aloft from down below,
Before we sight old Buffalo.

Leave Her, Johnny, Leave Her

Itinerant sailors seldom, if ever, shipped on the same vessel for two consecutive trips, and many Great Lakes sailors followed the same practice. At the end of a trip they were paid off and spent their time in waterfront sailor hangouts until they shipped out on another vessel to repeat the process. Before they were permitted to leave the vessel, however, they were required to prepare for it to be unloaded, and the final task was pumping the hold.

In the 1890s, when competition of the new bulk-carrying steam freighters on the Great Lakes made the old wooden sailing vessels less and less profitable, some were allowed to deteriorate to the extent that they required frequent and long pumpings. The final pumping out at the end of the trip was the least-liked work aboard the ship, and the sailors had a special chantey, "Leave Her, Johnny, Leave Her," reserved for this work. "Johnny" was often substituted with "Bullies" or "Laddies." In the song, the men about to leave the vessel, and therefore no

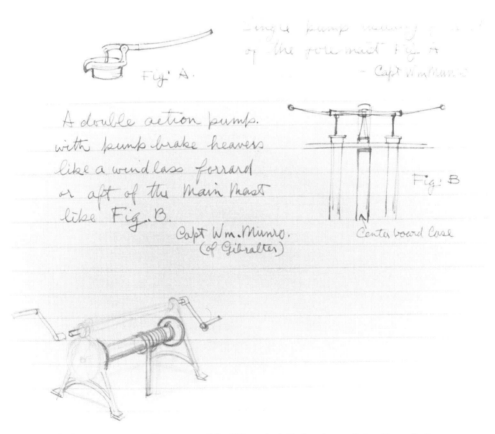

Details of schooner pumps. Courtesy of the Historical Collections of the Great Lakes.

48 　✳　WORK CHANTEYS

longer at the mercy of the officers, express their accumulated grouses and pay their compliments to the vessel, food, officers, owners, and anyone else who they thought deserved it. The tune and some of the stanzas date back to the days of the Atlantic immigrant packets.

Captain Henry Ericksen of Milwaukee provided these lines in 1932. He learned them on salt water in the early 1880s and said he often heard them on the Great Lakes.

Leave Her, Johnny, Leave Her

Walton, Score No. 9

I thought I heard the Old Man say, Leave her, John-ny, leave her!

"Just pump her out and draw your pay," It's time for us to leave her!

I thought I heard the Old Man say,
    Leave her, Johnny, leave her!
"Just pump her out, then draw your pay."
    It's time for us to leave her!

There was a ship that went to sea,
She was not the ship that she might be,

The times are hard, the ship is old,
And there's six feet of water in her hold.

Our hands are sore, our backs are humped,
And half the Lakes went through her pumps.

We pumped all night, we pumped all day,
We pumped and pumped the whole damn way.

We pumped all day, we pumped all night,
And her pump rods shine just like a light.

The ship is old and would not stay
She shipped it green both night and day.

The Old Man's cross-eyed and cannot see,
The mate was drunk and on a spree.

The cook's best meat was old and tough,
And of his stew, none was enough.

The ship's a sieve, both fore and aft,
    Leave her, Johnny, leave her,
And no, by God, we've pumped our last!
    Leave her, damn her, leave her!

A timber drogher in tow to the sounds of "We'll crack on the canvas" from "Homeward Bound." Courtesy of the Historical Collections of the Great Lakes.

Homeward Bound

Collen recalled this Great Lakes version of the saltwater capstan chantey. He said that he learned this and other songs in 1880 during his first trip on the ocean as an apprentice seaman. Sailors always liked to hear new lines, he said, especially about themselves, their vessel and trip, and what they did ashore, so "when a chanteyman fetched 'em in, they'll really yell out the choruses." Collen was embarrassed that he couldn't "think up a hundred more parts" of "Homeward Bound," and for his final appraisal he added, "Dat's the best goddamn chantey dat was ever lifted over a ship!"

Former sailors from Milwaukee to Oswego remembered the song, especially those who had sailed in the grain trade. Crews on larger vessels sang this chantey when they were weighing anchor or hoisting the heavy sails just above the deck in preparation for towing out of the loading harbor. As for all capstan chanteys, the tempo is slow and measured, that of straining men pushing the capstan bars around and around on the forecastle deck.

The vessel envisioned by the chanteyman is loaded with prairie wheat, probably in Chicago, and bound for Buffalo for transshipment eastward. A good sailing wind is blowing out of the northwest, and if it holds the crew can sail a port tack all the way to the Straits of Mackinac, with little work to do changing sails.

"Down the long Lakes" is, of course, toward the Niagara River. A vessel with a "bone in 'er teeth" is making speed enough to produce a foaming bow wake. Racing among the Lakes schooners was common practice, and the stakes were prestige and the preferred unloading docks at their destination. A vessel sailing into the wind and heeled over enough to put "her lee rail under" would be making maximum speed. The last stanza is a hint to the officer in charge that the work at hand has progressed far enough.

Homeward Bound

Walton, Score No. 8

Oh, fare you well, we're home-ward bound, Good-bye, fare you well;

good-bye, fare you well! Oh, fare you well, 'tis a joy-ful sound,

Hur-rah, my boys, we're home-ward bound!

Oh, fare you well, we're homeward bound,
    Good-bye, fare you well; good-bye, fare you well!
Oh, fare you well, 'tis a joyful sound,
    Hurrah, my boys, we're homeward bound!

We're homeward bound, the Old Man did say,
We're homeward bound this very day.

Come man the good caps'n, heave hearty and strong,
Come sing a good chorus, for 'tis a good song.

This anchor we'll weigh, and the sails we will set,
And the friends we are leaving we leave with regret.

Though we leave with regret, it's happy I be,
For a lass in Buffalo is a'waiting for me.

Oh, fare you well, we're outward bound,
We're outward bound for Buffalo town.

We're outward bound with wheat in her hold,
'N' we'll crack on the canvas and then let 'er roll.

The wind is nor'west, an' it's steady and strong,
We'll reach to the Straits as we send 'er along.

Oh, down the long Lakes with a bone in 'er teeth,
With her lee rail under, we'll lead the whole fleet.

Oh, Buffalo town is the right town for me,
In Buffalo town we'll go on a spree.

Oh, I think that I heard the Old Man say,
I think that I heard the command to "belay."

Rolling Home

This capstan chantey is more formal than most, telling as it does the chronological story of a vessel's passage. The names of port towns might easily be changed—and often were—to suit the particular voyage at hand. This is a localized version of a song imported from deep water. It was recalled by Collen.

"We'll weigh the anchor cheerily" from "Rolling Home." Courtesy of the Historical Collections of the Great Lakes.

Rolling Home

Hugill, Score No. 1

When the Mate calls up all hands
To man the capstan, Walk 'er 'round!
We'll heave 'er up, lads, with a will,
For we are homeward bound!

    Rolling home, rolling home,
    Rolling home across the sea;
    Rolling home to old Chicago,
    Rolling home, old town, to thee.

We'll leave the ladies now, my lads,
Them and our money both forsake.
We'll weigh the anchor cheerily,
And steer for the open lake.

Oh, we'll steer for the rolling lake
And lads, we'll set the flowing sail,
And to the town of Buffalo
We'll show the old ship's tail.

Then we'll gather in the fo'c'sle
Then "off watch" we plough along;
We'll have 'er going smoothly, lads,
And sign a jolly song.

Oh, we'll beat the length of Erie,
With Long Point on our lee;
We'll hail a tug 'neath Passage Light
Or tow from Point Pelee.

Up the river on a towline,
Past the city of Detrite;
The cinders fall upon the deck
All day and half the night.

We'll drag the length of steep St. Clair,
And at Port Huron we'll let go;
Hoist the canvas on the forestick,
On the main and mizzen, too.

Up the length of old Lake Huron
With all our canvas at her best;
We'll drive across the pounding bay
With a wind from out of the west.

Through the straits, a beat to windward,
Far astern, the Isle Bob-Lo;
Then southward down Lake Michigan
To the town of Chicago.

Soon, my friends, our trip is over,
And I got no more to say;
We'll go to Old Black Pete's, my lads,
And spend our whole trip's pay!

Men haul together to make sail aboard the *Lyman Davis* on Lake Huron in 1912. Ivan H. Walton Collection, Bentley Historical Library, University of Michigan.

Raising the halyard. Courtesy of the Historical Collections of the Great Lakes.

CHAPTER 2
Halyard Chanteys

Sailors sang halyard chanteys more often than any other work songs. They were best for hauling on a line, usually in the long, hard task of hoisting topsails or topgallant yards. Typically, the halyard ran down from the sail, through pulleys and blocks so that the haul very often might be a horizontal one. The halyard chantey's rhythm is that of a slow hauling motion. Halyard chanteys are simply made, built of stanzas with two solo verses, each followed by a chorus of the same length to provide for one or two strong pulls.

Blow the Man Down

Probably the most popular halyard chantey was "Blow the Man Down." A breezy, swinging song, the good, loud vowels of its choruses marked the pulls sailors used to make sail the world over. The rhythm of the song was as constant as the work it accompanied, and choruses were constant too, but at least three distinct sets of solo lines developed over the half century of its heaviest use. The first celebrates the Black Ball Line of Atlantic packets.

The Black Ball Line, established directly after the War of 1812, quickly became famous for fast passages between New York and Liverpool. Thousands of immigrants arrived in the New World aboard the line's vessels, identified by their crimson swallow-tailed pennants and the large black ball painted on their foretopsails.

The *Flying Fish* mentioned in this first version was a world-ranging clipper. The singer, if a "packet rat," was assuming a higher caste by trying to pass as a member of the clipper's crew. If he actually was what he claimed, he felt himself insulted by being considered a packet sailor. "Blow" is used here in the sense of "knock."

The first two versions here came from Carl M. G. Becker of Cleveland in 1933. He had sailed on the oceans as well as the Great Lakes and included both versions in one song. Captain William E. "Billy" Clark of Buffalo recalled the third version in 1933.

Hauls on the halyard in this and the following chanteys are indicated by capitalized words or syllables.

Blow the Man Down

Walton, Score No.11

Oh, blow the man down, bul-lies, blow the man down! To me

WAY, hey, BLOW the man down! Oh, blow the man down for

Liv-er-pool town, GIVE me some time to BLOW the man down!

Oh, blow the man down, bullies, blow the man down!
    To me WAY, hey, BLOW the man down!
Oh, blow the man down for Liverpool town,
    GIVE me some time to BLOW the man down!

As I was a-walking down Paradise Street,
A saucy young p'liceman I happened to meet.

Says he, "You're a Black-Baller by the cut of your hair,
You are a Black-Baller by the clothes that you wear."

"You've sailed in a packet that flies the Black Ball,
You've robbed some poor Dutchman of boots, coat and all."

Oh, p'liceman; Oh, p'liceman, you do me much wrong;
I'm a *Flying Fish* sailor, just home from Hong Kong!

They gave me six months in Liverpool town
For booting and kicking and blowing him down.

    To keep the Black Ball Line's advertised schedule in all kinds of weather, vessel masters enforced rigid discipline and drove both their ships and their crews without mercy. As a consequence, the line acquired a bad reputation among seamen and was forced at times to draw its crews from the dregs of the New York and Liverpool waterfronts. The following version speaks to shipboard conditions and the composition of the crew.

>Come all ye young fellows who follow the sea,
>   To me WAY, hey, BLOW the man down!
>Now please pay attention and listen to me,
>   GIVE us some time to BLOW the man down.
>
>'Twas in a Black-Baller I first served my time,
>And in that Black-Baller I wasted my prime.
>
>'Tis when a Black-Baller's preparing for sea,
>You'd split your sides laughing, the sights you would see,
>
>For the tinkers and tailors, shoemakers, and all,
>Who sign as prime seamen aboard the Black Ball!
>
>'Tis when a Black Baller is clear of the land,
>That the bosun bawls out the word of command.
>
>Aye, first it's a fist and then it's a fall,
>When you're a sailor aboard a Black Ball.
>
>"Lay aft," is the cry, "to the poop you will go,"
>"Or I'll help you along with the tip of my toe."
>
>"Pay attention to orders, now you one and all,
>For see, right above you, there flies the Black Ball."
>
>To larboard and starboard on deck they will sprawl,
>For Kicking Jack Williams commands the Black Ball.

    In the third version, the sailor has picked up a doxy—a neat little craft—who has steered him into a grogshop on a notorious street and shanghaied him onto an outbound packet. The street is usually Liverpool's well-known Paradise Street, but the chanteyman could tailor it to whatever port he liked. If it was Ratcliffe Highway, the port was London. If it was New York's Broadway, the second verse was changed to "I chanced for to spy" in order to make it rhyme. On the Great Lakes, chanteymen sang out with "a Buffalo street."

>Oh, blow the man down, bullies, blow the man down!
>   To me WAY, hey, BLOW the man down!
>Oh, blow the man down, bullies, blow him right down.
>   GIVE me some time to BLOW the man down!

As I was a-walking down Paradise Street,
A neat little craft I chanced for to meet.

She was round in the counter, and bluff in the bow,
So I took in all sail and cried, "Way enough now."

I hailed her in English, she answered me clear,
"I'm from the Black Arrow to the Shakespeare."

So I tailed her my flipper, and took her in tow,
And yardarm to yardarm away we did go.

Says she, "My dear Jack, now, will you stand treat?"
"Delighted," says I, "for a charmer so sweet."

And as we were walking she said unto me,
"There's a spanking full-rigger just ready for sea."

That spanking full-rigger to New York was bound,
She was very well manned and very well found.

But soon as that packet was clear of the bar,
The mate knocked me down with the end of a spar.

As soon as that packet was out on the sea,
'Twas cruel hard treatment of every degree.

So I give you my warning before we belay,
Don't never take heed of what pretty girls say.

A chantey similar to that one and to "Roll the Cotton Down" began:

I wish I was in Mobile Bay
WAY, hey, KNOCK a man down!
A-rolling cotton night and day
THIS is the time to KNOCK a man down.

In this one, the chanteyman continued wishing he were in New Orleans, Boston, New York, or any other port about which he could make up rhymes.

Blow, Boys, Blow

An endless variety of stanzas followed the traditional opening of this chantey. The nature of the ship, its cargo, its destination, and the character and ancestry of the captain, the mate, and the cook gave the chanteyman ample opportunity to demonstrate his originality. Most of these verses are from David W. Bone's *Capstan Bars*, published in 1932, but some were written for the Lakes.

Blow, Boys, Blow

Walton, No. 12

Oh, blow ye winds, I long to hear you,
  BLOW, boys, BLOW!
Oh, blow ye winds, I long to hear you,
  BLOW, my bully boys, BLOW!

A Yankee ship's comin' down the river,
Her masts and spars, they shine like silver.

An' how d'ye know she's a Yankee clipper?
By the Stars and Stripes that flies above 'er.

An' who d'ye think is captain of 'er?
Oh, Bully Haines, the hoodlum scoffer.

An' who d'ye think's the mate aboard 'er?
A bowery tough that's never sober.

An' what d'ye think they had for dinner?
Hot water soup, but a little thinner.

Oh, blow today and shine tomorrow.
Oh, blow today and shine tomorrow.

Another pull, oh rock and shake 'er
Oh, go she must, and go we'll make 'er.

An alternate introductory verse was:

Blow, my bullies, I long to hear you,
Blow, my bullies, I long to hear you.

The song almost always contained at least one stanza that began: "And what do you think they had for dinner?" Among the answers:

Scupper soup and donkey's liver.
Why, handspike hash, or I'm a sinner.

A stanza referring to a tow of vessels on the Detroit and St. Clair Rivers goes:

A tow of ships came down the river,
And what are the tubs you think was in her?

Roll the Cotton Down

It is generally agreed that at least the choruses and possibly some of the verses of this halyard chantey originated with African American workers in the South. New Orleans and Mobile were important ports for the exportation of baled cotton, and stevedores doing the loading received relatively high pay for this strenuous work. Since the cotton was light and bulky, the bales were packed into the ships' holds with powerful jackscrews and the stevedores lightened their labors with song. The call-and-response form was very similar to the halyard shanty form.

It is not known whether sailors aboard the vessels acquired the pattern for this and other chanteys from black stevedores or from stevedores turned sailors. However, there is a pronounced African American influence on chanteys. Like others, this song makes reference to a two-tiered wage structure based on race.

This rendition comes from the memory of Cleveland's Carl M. G. Becker. Other versions had five additional stanzas in which the singer sails around "Cape Stiff" to Mandalay, where he jumps ship and learns to talk like "furr'nerrs do."

Roll the Cotton Down

Walton, Score No. 13

Oh, roll the cot - ton down, my boys, Oh, ROLL the cot - ton DOWN!

Oh, roll the cot - ton down, my boys, Oh, ROLL the cot - ton DOWN!

Oh, roll the cotton down, my boys,
    Oh, ROLL the cotton DOWN!
Oh, roll the cotton down, my boys,
    Oh, ROLL the cotton DOWN!

I'm bound to Alabama,
I'm bound to Alabama.

Away down south in Mobile Bay,
I signed on a Yankee ship one day.

A pleasant place is Mobile Bay,
A rollin' cotton all the day.

A dollar a day is a white man's pay,
And four bits a day is a nigger's pay.

I thought I heard the first mate say,
Just one more pull and then belay.

Reuben Ranzo

Mercifully, the original identity of poor, unfortunate Reuben Ranzo, like that of most chantey characters, has been forgotten. He represents the hapless farmer who happens to find himself working as a sailor. Poor Reuben Ranzo can do no right, and with each of his misadventures he reaffirms the talent and superiority of the chanteying sailors. They may be overworked, underpaid, and poorly fed, but at least they are better off than poor old Reuben Ranzo.

In the choruses, the "r" in Ranzo was rolled to prompt maximum efforts on the hauls. Like many other work songs, this one gave the chanteyman good opportunity to criticize any seafaring deficiencies on the part of the officers. In the waning days of sail, the chanteyman used it to express his contempt for steamships by having Reuben learn his trade aboard the "cinder tubs." His name was sometimes given as "Randso" or "Rauzo."

The sources are Harry and George Parmalee, 1932.

Reuben Ranzo

Walton, Score No. 14

Oh, poor old Reu-ben Ran-zo, RAN-zo, boys, RAN-zo!

Oh, poor old Reu-ben Ran-zo, RAN-zo, boys, RAN-zo!

Oh, poor old Reuben Ranzo,
    RANZO, boys, RANZO!
Oh, poor old Reuben Ranzo,
    RANZO, boys, RANZO!

Oh, Ranzo came up to the Lakes,
Where sailors live on prime beefsteaks.

Now, it's a widespread rumor,
That he shipped aboard a schooner.

But Ranzo was no sailor,
For Ranzo was a tailor.

The Old Man set him wheeling,
For Ranzo was appealing.

But he could not rock or shake her,
For Ranzo was no sailor.

His course was up Lake Erie,
But he grounded on Point Pelee.

The Old Man loud did curse him,
Oh, how the Old Man cursed him.

He kicked him to the galley,
With pots and pans to dally.

When they came into a grain port,
The Old Man cut his sailin' short.

But old Ranzo became the owner,
And the Old Man now works for him.

Whiskey, Johnny

This halyard chantey has been called one of the oldest used on deep-water square-riggers, and as Frederick Pease Harlow wrote in *The Making of a Sailor,* "Every deep-water sailors knew it as he knew his A, B, C's." Some wandering sailors brought the song inland in the early 1860s, and in the following two decades it was carried the length of the Lakes by men working at the halyards of the larger schooners. Its marked rhythm and easy and bland treatment of a nearly universal sailor weakness seem to have made it a favorite.

Robert "Brokenback" Collen and several unemployed friends at the sailors' union hall in Chicago pieced the first six stanzas together in the summer of 1932. Collen sent stanzas seven and eight in a letter a few weeks later. Stanza nine was obtained from David McLoud of Port Colborne, Ontario. Captain William Clark supplied the remainder of the verses and the tune.

Whiskey, Johnny

Walton, Score No. 15

Oh, whis-key is the life of man, Oh, WHIS-key, JOHN-ny! It

al-ways was since time be-gan, Oh, WHIS-key for my JOHN-ny!

Oh, whiskey is the life of man,
    Oh, WHISkey, JOHNny
It always was since time began,
    Oh, WHIskey for my JOHNny.

Oh, whiskey here and whiskey there,
Oh, whiskey almost everywhere.

If whiskey comes too near my nose,
I tip her up and down she goes.

Oh, whiskey made me pawn my clothes,
And whiskey gave me a broken nose.

Oh, whiskey killed my poor old dad,
And whiskey drove my mother mad.

Oh, whiskey gave me much abuse,
And whiskey put me in the calaboose.

If whiskey was a river and I was a duck,
I'd dive to the bottom and never come up.

Oh, whiskey straight and whiskey strong,
We'll hoist the sail to this old song.

Oh, whiskey puts the mate to bed,
Oh, whiskey goes straight to his head.

Here comes the cook with the whiskey can,
And a glass brim-full for every man.

Oh, a glass brim-full for every man,
And a dipper full for the chanteyman!

Oh, I thought I heard the Old Man say,
Just one more pull and then belay.

Hanging Johnny

The halyard chantey "Hanging Johnny," like many others sung on Great Lakes vessels, was an import from salt water, where it was widely used. Ocean sailor Frederick Pease Harlow described it this way: "Next morning had all the earmarks of a pleasant day, and the men, while setting the main topsail, were so elated over the prospects of finer weather that . . . no one could help putting his entire strength into the pull of this chantey, for not only were the men's voices unusually good, but the chantey was sung with a jerk and a swing. . . . It was a great favorite with us and sung nearly every time the topsails were hoisted."

The song was evidently brought to the Lakes shortly after the Civil War. Captain Timothy Kelly of Manitowoc, Wisconsin, reported hearing sailors sing it while making sail in Buffalo harbor in the late 1860s when he was a boy and first "went to sea." Carl Joys and Captain W. A. Ashley, both of Milwaukee, recalled stanzas they had learned aboard big Milwaukee grain schooners in the early 1870s when each began more than a half century on Great Lakes vessels.

Joys explained that "hanging Johnny" did not refer to a sheriff's hangman, but instead to nimble young sailors who, when a topsail was to be hoisted, would climb to the masthead and "swing out" on the proper halyard. They would then ride to the deck as the men at the foot of the mast brought them down by their successive pulls. Joys recalled one chanteyman who would always tell the boys when to swing out by shouting up at them, "Hang, you bastards, hang!" Then, while the boys were hanging on the halyard fifty feet or more above the deck, he'd start his song and the crew would make two pulls on each chorus. When the boys hit the deck, they would tail on behind the other men and pull with them until the work was finished. Joys added that the word "hang" was "the best goddamn pullin' word in the language, especially on a down haul."

Ashley said the tune was "a bit mournful, but a good one for hoisting light canvas," noting that the words enabled the sailors to find fault, good-naturedly, with all their real and fancied enemies, "if the work lasted long enough." He said that the line about Johnny hanging for money was supposed to be humorous because Johnny, as an apprentice seaman, didn't make more than ten dollars a month.

A "boarding boss" was manager of a waterfront rooming and boarding house. A "Jon-er" was a namesake for the biblical Jonah who was credited with most of the bad luck aboard ship. A "rigger" was a man who equipped a vessel with its standing and running rigging (shrouds, braces, sheets, halyards, blocks, etc.). Should they fail under the stress of bad weather, sailors had to make their own repairs, so they had no love for a careless rigger who caused them this extra work. A "buck-o-mate" was an old-time ship's officer who enforced his orders by brute strength. A "soger" (soldier) was a malingering sailor who in various ways got out of doing his share of the work.

The following is a compilation as recalled by Joys (first four stanzas), Kelly (fifth stanza), and Ashley (last six stanzas and his version of the melody). When Collen was shown these stanzas, his remark was, "Yep, yep, but dere's lots more."

Hanging Johnny

Walton, Score No. 16

They call me "Hang-ing John-ny,"   Hoo-RAY, boys, hoo-RAY!

Oh, they call me "Hang-ing John-ny,"   So HANG, boys, HANG!

They call me "Hanging Johnny,"
    HOORAY, boys, hooRAY!
Oh, they call me "Hanging Johnny,"
    So HANG, boys, HANG!

Oh, hang and haul together,
Oh, hang for better weather.

We'll sway and hang together,
Like seabirds of a feather.

They call me "Hanging Johnny,"
They say I hang for money.

They say I hung my mother,
An' then I hung my brother.

I'd hang all boardin' bosses,
Who nicked us for their losses.

I'd hang all scrimpin' owners,
The same as any Jon-ers.

I'd hang a careless rigger,
Who couldn't plan or figger.

I'd hang all buck-o-mates,
All on the Devil's gates.

I'd hang a lazy soger,
The same as any other.

I'd hang 'em all together,
I'd hang 'em all together.

Tommy's Gone to Hilo

Tommy's wanderings to distant seaports the world over paralleled those of the old-time sailor. A fluent chanteyman could send Tommy off to as many ports as were necessary to masthead the yard. As in any chantey, a surprise rhyme was always welcome. When stuck for a rhyme, however, the chanteyman could make the second verse of a couplet the same as the first.

The identity of Hilo (always pronounced HIGH-low) is unclear, though David Bone suggests in *Capstan Bars* that it was the Peruvian port of Ilo, from which nitrates were shipped. This song is slower and less vigorous than most other halyard songs and is used frequently in hoisting light sails hand over hand.

Notice the verses that make references to the capstan chantey "The Rio Grande" and the halyard chantey "Roll the Cotton Down."

Stanzas one through seven and eleven were recalled by Collen in 1933. William Clark recognized them and readily followed them with the remainder.

Oh, Tommy's gone, what shall I do?
   AWAY to HILO!
Oh, Tommy's gone and I'll go too,
   My TOMMY's gone to HILO!

Oh, Tommy's gone to New York town
The Bowery girls to dance around.

Oh, Tommy's gone to Baltimore,
To live upon that happy shore!

Oh, Tommy's gone to Mobile Bay
The cotton bales to load all day.

Oh, Tommy's gone to New Orleans
Where rum is free and the maidens queens.

Oh, Tommy's gone to London town,
Where skysail ships go up and down.

Oh, Tommy's gone to Liverpool,
Oh, Tommy's gone to Liverpool.

Oh, Tommy's gone to Buffalo,
To live at ease and make some dough.

Oh, Tommy's gone to the Rio Grande,
Where the seas wash over golden sand.

Oh, Tommy's gone around the Horn
An' Tommy'll wish he'd not been born!

Oh, Tommy's gone to Singapore
Oh, Tommy's gone for evermore!

I think I heard the captain say,
Just one more pull and then belay.

The Old Man's asleep, or he would say,
"She's high enough, belay, belay!"

A Long Time Ago

This chantey, like all others, has many variants. In one version, the ship concerned is bound westward, not to the east, around Cape Horn:

Around Cape Horn we've got to go,
Around Cape Horn to Callao.

And in another:

Around Cape Horn with frozen sail,
Around Cape Horn to fish for whale.

In others it is "a small Yankee packet" or a "lime-juicer," and is even identified with Noah's ark.

This song, traded back and forth between logging camps and lakeborne decks, also had a cousin in the woods, "The Little Brown Bull."

Despite variations in the nautical strain, the second chorus has remained quite constant, both in rhyme and in words, but the first one can be found as "To the way, hey, hey, hee," "To me way, hey-i-oh," "To me, way, hey Ohio," and the version given here. The woods-to-water cycle of seasonal labor is evident in another version, recalled by sailors, with references to bulls, often used for work in logging camps, and two prominent loggers.

Carl M. G. Becker of Cleveland provided the words in 1933; the air came from William Clark.

A Long Time Ago

Walton, Score No. 18

A long, long time and a very long time,
  To me WAY-hey-hey YAH!
A long, long time and a very long time,
  It's a LONG time AGO.

Oh in Frisco Bay a clipper ship lay,
Oh in Frisco Bay a clipper ship lay.

The crew came on board and they all were drunk,
The whiskey they had a ship would have sunk.

She sailed away on a summer's day,
She was decked with flags like a bride so gay.

She rounded Cape Horn with her royals set,
She was driving bows under, the sailors all wet.

Around Cape Horn where wild winds blow,
Around Cape Horn through sleet and snow.

The wind from the sou'west a-blowin' a gale,
The clipper ship was a-crowdin' sail.

She was leaning right over from even keel,
And the captain was logging the man at the wheel.

On a night at the Cape I shall never forget,
She was running sixteen, the main skysail set.

Oh I had a letter from a Yankee girl,
Oh I had a letter from a Yankee girl.

She promised that she would marry me.
She promised that she would marry me.

That's a long, long time and a very long time,
That's a long, long time and a very long time.

The Drunken Sailor

This chantey, possibly more popular ashore than on board ship, accompanied the hoisting of lighter canvas above the topsails. Only crews that were large enough to "walk away with a halyard"—that is, walk along the deck, stomping to the rhythm—used the song. Smaller crews had to stay in one place and take a new hold, hand over hand, for each haul. In the song, "Early" is pronounced "Earl-eye."

This is the collaboration of about a dozen men, including several former schoonermen, in a convalescent ward of the Chicago Marine Hospital in 1932.

The Drunken Sailor

Walton, Score No.20

What shall we do with a drunken sailor (3 times)
Early in the morning?
    Way, hey, and up she rises (3 times)
    Early in the morning.

Put him in the long boat and make him bale her. (3 times)
Early in the morning.

What shall we do with a drunken skipper? (3 times)
Early in the morning.

Lock him in the cabin and stop his liquor. (3 times)
Early in the morning.

What shall we do with a drunken bosun?
Early in the morning.

Put him in the slop chest 'til he's sober.
Early in the morning.

Succeeding stanzas dealt with men aboard the ships, friends ashore, and enemies, too.

In a Handy Four-Master

The Great Lakes saw a wide variety of vessel types, both wind-driven and mechanical. Marine architecture became increasingly specialized to perform specific tasks and meet certain local conditions. While four-masters were far less common on the Great Lakes than sailing vessels with two or three masts, they were not unheard of, and there were a very few with five. This was collected from Captain Henry Ericksen, Milwaukee, 1932.

In a handy four-master I once took a trip,
    Hooray boys, heave 'er down,
An' I thought that I was aboard a good ship,
    Way down, laddies down.

But when on the lake to my sorrow I found,
    Hooray boys, heave 'er down,
That she was a workhouse and that I was bound
    To be down, laddies down.

We left with a fair wind, a mere little breeze,
    Hooray boys, heave 'er down,
But, somehow, the old man was not at his ease,
    Way down, laddies down.

We looked at the sky, and he said, "Mr. Brown—"
    Hooray boys, heave 'er down,
"Just clew up those tops'ls and then reef 'er down,"
    Way down, laddies down.

We reefed up and we furled from dark to daylight,
    Hooray boys, heave 'er down,

You never in your life did see such a sight,
    Way down, laddies down.

The mate was a shellback from way down below,
    Hooray boys, heave 'er down,
He'd rave and he'd roar as he walked to and fro,
    Way down, laddies down.

The galley was dirty, the cooking was bad,
    Hooray boys, heave 'er down,
Fresh meat was a thing that we never had,
    Way down, laddies down.

But now we are bound down the long Lakes once more,
    Hooray boys, heave 'er down,
An' this old wagon I'll ship never more.
    Way down, laddies down.

Belay.

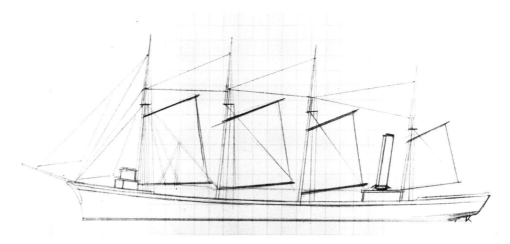

A rough sketch on graph paper of the four-master *V. H. Ketcham*. Courtesy of the Historical Collections of the Great Lakes.

Decades of hard work on the Lakes show in this portrait taken at St. Ignace, Michigan. Clarke Historical Library, Central Michigan University.

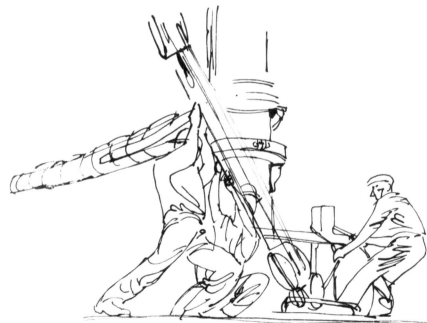

Sweating home the mainsheet required a few short, strong pulls. Courtesy of the Historical Collections of the Great Lakes.

CHAPTER 3
Short-Drag Chanteys

The short-drag chantey is undoubtedly the oldest of the sailors' work songs. Dating back nearly five hundred years, short-drag chanteys are close cousins of the old cries and the "yo-heave-ho" combinations that preceded them. As the oldest type of chantey, it then follows, as clearly as chorus follows verse, that short-drag chanteys are also the simplest in construction. A stanza consists of a relatively short solo verse and a standardized chorus with a well-marked rhythm that builds to a strongly emphasized word upon which the singers unite in a haul or push. Sung less frequently than capstan or halyard chanteys, short-drag chanteys generally were reserved for the last few hauls in "sweating home" a yard or furling a rebellious sail on a yard in a heavy wind.

Haul on the Bowline

In the sixteenth century, "Haul on the Bowline" encouraged work on English vessels. By the nineteenth century, the bowline (pronounced bo-lin) was little used, but British and American sailors still sang this chantey as they trimmed heavy sails. On Great Lakes grain and ore carriers, "Haul on the Bowline" accompanied the work of controlling a large, square running sail carried on the foremast in a fair and following wind. It also was favored when the men were "sweating home" any of the heavy sails and only a few extra-strong pulls on the halyard would stretch all the slack out of a sail.

The slow, stately melody builds to a single, powerful pull on the final word: haul. John S. Parsons recalled this at Oswego, New York, in 1933.

Haul on the Bowline

Walton, Score No. 21

Haul on the bow-lin', our bul-ly ship's a-rol-lin'!

Haul on the bow-lin', the bow-lin' HAUL!

Haul on the bowlin', our bully ship's a-rollin'!
    Haul on the bowlin', the bowlin' HAUL!

Haul on the bowlin', the Old Man is a-growlin'.

Haul on the bowlin', the first mate is a-sleepin'.

Haul on the bowlin', the second mate's a-heavin'.

Haul on the bowlin', oh Kitty, she's my darlin'.

Haul Away, Joe!

Singing to encourage their work on tasks requiring a few short pulls, sailors used "Haul Away, Joe!" to sheet home courses, topsails, and topgallant sails. "Haul Away, Joe!" bears close similarities to "Haul on the Bowline." Verses were contributed by John S. Parsons of Oswego, New York, Captain William E. Clark of Buffalo, and Robert "Brokenback" Collen of Chicago.

Haul Away, Joe!

Walton, Score No. 22

Solo

A - way, haul a - way, we'll haul a - way to - geth - er,

Chorus

A - way, haul a - way, we'll haul a - way, JOE!

Solo

A - way, haul a - way, we'll haul for sun - ny weath - er,

Chorus

A - way, haul a - way, we'll haul a - way, JOE!

Away, haul away, we'll haul away together,
    Away, haul away, we'll haul away, JOE!
Away, haul away, we'll haul for sunny weather,
    Away, haul away, we'll haul away, JOE!

In Buffalo, I met a maid as trim as any daisy,
In Bonny's bar I lost my coin and also mistress Mazie.

A mate came in to Bonny's bar and bawled out loud and long,
"Ten able men come follow me, we're sailing with the dawn."

Away, haul away, our good ship is a-rollin',
Away, haul away, the Old Man is a-growlin'

Oh, once I sailed the oceans wide to earn my rum and 'taties,
But now I'm on a Great Lakes tub as fat as any lady.

Oh, once I sailed the oceans wide for China silks and spices,
But now our hold is full of coal, my bunk with hungry lices.

Oh, once I had a German girl, but she was fat and lazy,
And then I had an Irish girl, she damn near drove me crazy.

Away, haul away, I'll sing to you of Nancy,
For now I have a New York girl, she's just my cut and fancy.

Oh, Nancy is my New York girl and I must sing her praises,
She love but me, she waits for me, oh yes she does, like blazes.

Boney

Why Napoleon should appeal to sailors' fancy is a mystery, but men working light canvas celebrated the French emperor's exploits wherever wind-driven vessels sailed. A staysail, for example, would be run up to a hand-over-hand rhythm and call, but the final stretching required slower, stronger pulls, and at such a time a chanteyman would line out with "Boney."

Brothers Harry and George Parmalee of Waukegan, Illinois, said they used the song frequently as a rowing chantey when becalmed on Lake Michigan with their ex-sailor-singer father in his fishing boat. The pulls came on the final stressed word of each chorus. Captain A. E. Baker, a commercial fisherman from Dunkirk, New York, recalled using it the same way on his early fishing boats, and added that when he was young and sailed on the big grain schooners, they frequently sang this song when setting a raffee, the triangular foretopsail carried on many vessels. Captain William E. "Billy" Clark, former chanteyman of Buffalo, also recalled the song's use in setting the light sails on Lakes schooners.

"Franswor" appears to be a corruption of the French name Francois, leading some to believe that "Boney" is derived from the French hauling song "Jean Francois de Nantes."

Harry and George Parmalee in 1932 supplied all but the last stanza, which came from Clark.

Boney

Walton, Score No. 23

Bon - ey was a war - ri - or, A - WAY, ay, YAH!

A war - rior and a ter - ri - er, JOHN Fran - SWOR!

Boney was a warrior,
    AWAY, ay, YAH!
A warrior and a terrier,
    JOHN Franswor!

Boney was the king of France,
Boney made the Prooshians dance.

Boney fought at Moscow,
Across the plains of ice and snow.

Boney fought at Waterloo,
An' there he met his overthrow.

He was sent to St. Helen's Isle,
There to spend a long exile.

Boney could not there abide,
Boney broke his heart and died.

Boney fought the Roo-shi-ans,
Boney fought the Proo-shi-ans.

Boney never hit New York,
Boney's life was cut too short.

PART 2
Amusement Songs

Not all the songs that merchant seamen sang on the Great Lakes were for working. Far from it. During the comparative freedom of the early-evening dogwatches between 4 and 8 P.M., the whole crew was on deck and "dogged" (changed tours of duty). For the men off watch and free to amuse themselves, singing was popular entertainment. Hopefully, one of the crew had a strong voice and a good repertoire, some other might come up with an accordion, another a harmonica, and someone else a pipe or other instrument. If another vessel was anchored nearby, the Old Man might let the crews visit with each other to exchange news and boasts and compete in story and song. Amusement songs recounted the exploits of a particular vessel or individual members of its crew, the conditions of shipboard life, and—very often—tragedies. Sailors raised voice and glass in waterfront gin mills, and any man who couldn't sing a song, play a tune, dance, or provide some other entertainment had to buy drinks for those who could.

The crew and, presumably, a cook on deck during the dogwatch for some entertainment. Courtesy of the Historical Collections of the Great Lakes.

The schooner *Chieftain* dwarfs more than a hundred of its builders at Davidson's Yard in Bay City, Michigan, in 1902. Dossin Great Lakes Museum.

CHAPTER 4

Songs of Everyday Life

AMUSEMENT SONGS, ALSO called forecastle songs, forebitters, or come-ye-alls, are story songs. While rhythm was paramount in work chanteys, sailors sang amusement songs to entertain themselves, boast of their skill, and poke fun at authority. Naturally, amusement songs lent themselves to renovation and change. Many amusement songs evolved from others, having been brought inland from the oceans and localized, or fabricated top to bottom to fit a popular melody or the audience at hand. Quite a few of the amusement songs that sailors sang concerned the steam-driven vessels that shared the water and stole some of the trade. While they might have shared the water, though, steamships did not share the singing tradition of the windjammers.

It's Me for the Inland Lakes

Superior living conditions and wages, as well as the easier discipline on Lakes vessels, lured many "shellbacks" from the Atlantic Ocean to the freshwater seas. This song was recalled in 1933 by Captain Walkingthaw of Port Colborne, Ontario. He said that he had learned this song from other Lakes sailors, but could not remember when or where.

It's Me for the Inland Lakes

Murdock, Score No. 18

If ever I follow the ships again
    To gather my spuds and cakes,
I'll not be working a deep-sea hack,
    It's me for the inland Lakes.

You get a berth that's really a berth;
    An' the jaw that the skipper takes—
No end I swear—it's a wonderful life,
    It's me for the windy Lakes.

The runs are short, the vessels good,
    An' real men are the mates;
They're men and they can handle a ship,
    It's me for the rolling Lakes.

Late gales may blow an' seas run high,
    An' the lees feel of country Jakes;
But quarters are warm and the grub is great,
    It's me for the open Lakes.

Two dollars a day they often pay,
    Much better than ocean crates;
An' when the season's done, all winter you bum,
    It's me for the inland Lakes.

Up Anchor

Robert "Brokenback" Collen said, "This song is about the sailorman's life at average. The melody goes after an old oyster dredger's song which was sung in Baltimore years ago." Collen, born in Belgium of an Irish father and a Scottish mother, sailed the Lakes for years and became a key informant for this collection. This song tells what the men did when they were off watch and resting in their crowded forecastle quarters, biding their time with music, coffee, cards, stories, and fighting. Collen wrote this version in a letter dated March 12, 1933.

> We've got the rusty mud-hook up,
>   She's green with Chicago slime;
> We're sailing with a gale of wind,
>   No more of city's grime!
> We'll head for the old blue waterways,
>   And mates, we'll drink our fill
> Of winds that hail across our bow
>   And through the hatches spill.
>
> We'll drink jamake and cuss a lot,
>   An' before our trip is done
> We'll fight and pray and fight again
>   Through spray that weighs a ton.
> We'll sit around the fo'c'sle lamp,
>   Each man in his bare feet;
> We'll slap the greasy cards about
>   In play that can't be beat.
>
> We'll tell old yarns and talk of home
>   As sailormen will do;
> We'll brag of girls in other ports
>   And wonder if they're true.
> We'll split the old harmonica
>   With all the tunes we know,
> And then begin again unless
>   We have a fight below.
>
> We'll hate each other worse than rats
>   That leave a sinking ship
> Before we reach another port
>   And give this tub the slip.
> When we drop the hook the mate will say,
>   "All aft and get your pay,"
> An' we'll roll ashore an' spend our dough,
>   Then ship another day.

The Stomach Robber

Meals broke the monotony of life in logging camps, in military forts, and on sailing vessels, so shanty boys, soldiers, and sailors became keen critics of culinary skills, such as they were. Poor cooking likely caused more mutinies than poor captaining, and whether they deserved it or not, all but the best cooks found themselves the butt of their shipmates' jokes and songs.

Robert "Brokenback" Collen supplied this version of "The Stomach Robber." When asked who wrote it, he responded, "I don't know, but he must have sailed on the old *Lucy Smith,* the same as I did." In all likelihood, sailors simply filled in the name of their own vessel whenever they sang "The Stomach Robber." Collen supplied a few translations. "Lobsters a la carte from Point Pelee" were meatballs—reputedly seasoned with sand. "Birds' nests from Skillagalee" were doughnuts. "Slumgullion" was boiled leftovers, and rarely the same dish twice. "Snails from Manistee" were hard dough patties filled with meat and vegetables.

Two more definitions, the same as those used in the logging camps, help explain the song. "Salt-horse" was salted beef and "sow-belly" was salt pork, shipboard staples that required no refrigeration. If the title's meaning is not already clear, pay attention to the closing stanza.

Sunday dinner in port. Courtesy of the Historical Collections of the Great Lakes.

      While no melody was attached to this song, it fits very well with one for "A Trip on the Erie," a canalboat song that shares many of the same, telltale lyrics. Two informants are credited with "A Trip on the Erie." One, Captain Pearl R. Nye of Akron, was interviewed in 1938. Nye was a collector and songwriter in his own right, placing about two hundred canalboat songs in the Library of Congress. Several have been published in William Hullfish's *The Canaller's Songbook*. That book also credits Yankee John Galusha of Minerva, New York, as an informant for "A Trip on the Erie."

You may talk about your pleasure trips
While roaming on the Lakes,
But the old steam barge the *Lucy Smith*,
She surely takes the cake.

   Haul in your towline,
   And heave in your slack,
   Take a reef in your stomach,
   And the kinks out of your back.

The cook's a big, fat, jolly bum,
In the galley all the time,
With salt-horse and sow-belly, lads.
He sure keeps looking fine.

He hands out cakes as old and tough
As the hide on a fighting dog's neck;
And the steaks are as thick and as hard and rough,
As the planks upon the deck.

There is one thing you must not forget,
If you would live and learn:
Keep out of the galley while the cook's on deck
Or your stomach will surely turn.

The crew to the cabin will go like saints,
Their hunger and thirst to quench;
One look at the table an' they go in a trance
An' fall from off the bench.

Lobsters a la carte from Point Pelee,
Birds' nests from Skillagalee.
Slumgullion made from rattlesnakes,
An' snails from Manistee.

They eat of the swill till their faces turn blue,
But their stomachs are robbed forthwith;
An' the stuff as they chew turns into glue,
As they curse the *Lucy Smith*.

The Sailor's Alphabet

Loggers, cowboys, miners, farmhands, soldiers, and sailors all spun the simple, set pattern of the alphabet into songs about their trades. The form is so adaptable and the range of terms so broad that rarely would two singer-composers—even two within the same occupation—come up with the same verses. Here are two versions of "The Sailor's Alphabet," the first from the 1870s during the days of sail, the second from steamboat days.

Captain Manus J. Bonner of Charlevoix said on July 21, 1932, that he had learned the first version of this song "when a hand before the mast in the 1870s." The steamer-age version is from Walter B. Wright of Oberlin, Ohio, who said he heard it aboard the freighter *Joseph Sellwood* in 1929.

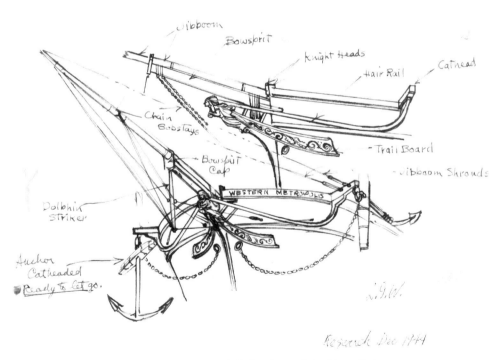

Jibboom details. Courtesy of the Historical Collections of the Great Lakes.

The Sailor's Alphabet

Murdock, Score No. 8

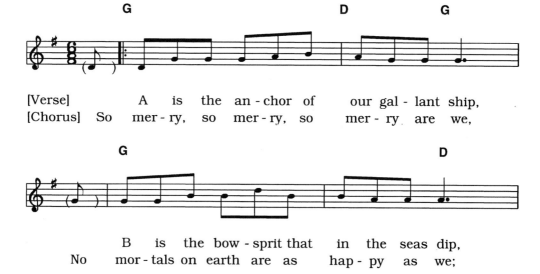

[Verse] A is the anchor of our gallant ship,
[Chorus] So merry, so merry, so merry are we,

B is the bowsprit that in the seas dip,
No mortals on earth are as happy as we;

C is the capstan so merrily goes 'round, and
Hi derry, ho derry, hi derry down, Give

D is the davits to which our boat's bound.
sailor boys rum and there's nothing goes wrong!

A is the anchor of our gallant ship,
B is the bowsprit that in the seas dip,
C is the capstan so merrily goes 'round, and
D is the davits to which our boat's bound.

So merry, so merry, so merry are we,
No mortals on earth are as happy as we;

Hi derry, ho derry, hi derry down,
Give sailor boys rum and there's nothing goes wrong!

E is the ensign at our masthead,
F is the fo'c'sle where is our bed,
G is the gun'l, against it seas splash,
H is the hawser that holds the ship fast.

I is the iron, without it we're lost,
J is the jolly boat that rows us acrost
K is the keelson as I have been told, and
L is the lany'rd that keeps a good hold.

M is the mainmast so stout and so tall,
N is the nettings that hangs our hammocks all.
O is the oars we often do row, and
P is the pennant so lightly does flow.

Q is the quarterdeck on which our good captain stood,
R is the riggin' so stout and so good.
S is the steward that weighs our beef, and
T is the tops'ls we oft have to reef.

U is the union to which our troubles pass,
V is the vang that holds steady the gaff.
W is the wheel by which we do steer, and
X, Y and Z are the rest of the gear.

For this next song, the melody is the same as the version from the 1870s, but every line and rhyme is changed. Anchor, ensign, and quarterdeck are used in both songs, as is iron, but in the earlier version iron refers to the compass, while in the latter version it means ore. See how hammocks in nettings gave way to mattresses on beds, tops'ls and capstan to winches and pumps.

A is for anchor which is sometimes called hook,
B is for bosun who is often a crook,
C is for captain, a rusty old man, and
D is for deck where the winches are ran.

E is for ensign, high up on the spar,
F is for firemen who throw the splice bar,
G is for galley where the cook does his stuff, and
H is for hatchway where one fall is enough.

I is for iron whose ore the ships carry,
J is for Jane we all love, but ne'er marry,
K is for keel deep down in the sea, and
L is for locks at Sault Ste. Marie.

M is for mattress all full of bed bugs,
N is for navy beans we eat from our mugs,
O is for oiler all greasy and gay, and
P is for pumps which he runs night and day.

Q is for quarterdeck, called the fantail,
R is for rollers that come over the rail,
S is for sailor who does his own patches, and
T is for tarpaulin that covers the hatches.

U is for union that pipe fitters know,
V is for ventilator down which the winds blow,
W is for windlass that pulls up the hook, and
X is the signature of our scholarly cook.

Y is for yells the mate often makes, and
Z is for zero in winter on the Lakes.

Scrubber Murphy

Officers of sailing vessels on salt and fresh water alike seem to believe that crewmen should be kept busy during their deck watches. Scrubbing, swabbing, scraping, painting, and mending filled sailors' lives and their songs. Iver Rolsing, a federal

A Sailing Skipper

Courtesy of the Historical Collections of the Great Lakes.

inspector of hulls at Buffalo in 1936, had been a schooner captain, and he explained that such work not only kept the vessel in good condition but kept the men out of fights and other trouble. "Scrubber Murphy" is a good-natured and exaggerated description of the busywork. Rolsing recalled a sailor known as "Blinky" Morgan who had made several trips with him and who would, under proper inducement, sing about Captain Henry "Scrubber" Murphy. The captain had earned the moniker for the persnickety persistence with which he kept his crew busy scrubbing the decks, the mast, and even his dog on the steamer *Mohawk*. So fanatical was "Scrubber" Murphy that once, when his vessel rammed the schooner *Boston*, considerably damaging both vessels, the captain's only concern was that the accident had interrupted the crew's chores. The song likely dates from about 1905, when bulk-carrying, steam-powered vessels were taking a serious cut out of the grain and ore trade that the schooners formerly had to themselves.

Mention of this song bubbled up one Saturday afternoon in the summer of 1934 from a noisy throng of local sailors in a crowded Goderich, Ontario, tavern. One in the throng, Malcolm Graham, broke into song. Soon, several other voices joined his. Graham broke off after the second stanza, however, and demanded $50,000 before he would continue or permit anyone else to do so. The next day, he reduced his price and then dictated this version of the song—for a cigar.

Scrubber Murphy

Murdock, Score No. 9

Scrubber Murphy was the captain of the steamer called *Mohawk;*
And Scrubber is the scrubber about whom all sailors talk:
From painting and from scrubbing, he's the scrubber's title got,
Given to him by the sailors of the gallant ship *Mohawk.*

It was the spring of nineteen five Old Scrubber took command,
And the orders that he first gave us was, "By your suds stand!
Into your suds dip your brooms and at her, lads, you go,
For I'm bound to have the *Mohawk* scrubbed before I go below."

The crew, all being well-drilled men and knowing what to do,
Into the suds dipped their brooms and scrubbed the bulwarks through.
"On to her deck," Old Scrubber cried, and without more ado
Those brave lads scrubbed the upper works while streams of water flew.

For ten long hours they scrubbed her down before the scrub was o'er,
Then "Rory," says he, "go scrape the mast and then we'll scrape some more."
Brave Rory for the mast did dash and never did let up
Till Scrubber cried, "Come, my lad, and scrub the brindle pup!"

"Now the scrubbing is all done," says he, "we'll start the paint";
And hearty sailors that they were, they all began to faint.
"Daniel," says he, "now go below and get the black and drab,
And with the deckhands on her side you may begin to dab."

"Rory, in the pilothouse, you go and shine the brass,
And Alec go along with him, I want you to work fast.
Ruben, on the upper deck, you go and paint the green,
And Donald, you stand by the wheel, I want you to be seen."

Then away for Chicago this noble ship set sail,
But soon across her iron deck the scrubbing hose did trail:
"Start up your pumps," Old Scrubber cried, "And let her have some spray,
For I'm bound to have her scrubbed again before we cross the bay."

When out upon Lake Michigan the weather it got thick;
Old Scrubber by the whistle stood and blew the signals quick.
"Angus," says he, "you stand by me and keep a sharp lookout,
And see that Ruben at the wheel don't turn the ship about."

At length a vessel's horn we heard a'blowin' three short blasts,
A signal that before the wind she was sailing free and fast.
The *Mohawk* crossed the schooner's bow and tore off her jibboom,
They struck, and up the lads below came running from their room.

Then came the cry, "We're sinking fast!" from the schooner's deck;
Old Scrubber turned the *Mohawk* 'round to try to save the wreck.
From ship to ship a line was paid, all hands were in great glee,
The schooner and her crew were saved and towed to Milwaukee.

And when we reached Chicago port, that city of great fame,
The orders that Old Scrubber got was "Get a load of grain."
At Halsted Street there is a bridge, I'm sorry to relate
That it was beneath this very bridge we almost met our fate.

As toward this tall and lofty bridge we slowly made the crook,
Our mast got caught and down it came and nearly killed our cook
Who in his bunk lay dreaming of what next he would dish up
To the sailors of the *Mohawk* and Old Scrubber's brindle pup.

When the wreckage was all cleared away, it was the break of morn,
We to an elevator went and got a load of corn.
Then out upon the windy lake we gaily sailed away
On our down trip for old Buffalo where all good sailors stay.

Now 'round the port of Buffalo it is common talk
How Scrubber Murphy scrubbed and scrubbed the steamer called *Mohawk*
Now come you, jolly sailor lads, our pay we will drink up,
And to Hell with Scrubber Murphy and his damned old brindle pup!

We Leaves Detroit Behind Us

This song describes life aboard a sailing vessel that had just been towed down the Detroit River. Once clear of the narrow, crowded confines of the river, vessels dropped their towlines to sail northeast the length of Lake Erie to Buffalo. Carl Joys of Milwaukee said that these fragments came from a song about a Milwaukee grain schooner. "D.C. feed" was a very fragrant mule fodder made from pressed linseed. "If one of them fellows got to windward of you, you could smell him damn near the length of the lake." The third stanza refers to the tricky winds set up around the islands in western Lake Erie, especially in late summer. This is the song as published in the *Buffalo Express* on May 21, 1903.

> We leaves Detroit behind us,
> We sets our canvas tight,
> The tug slows up and casts us off,
> Old Erie heaves in sight.
>
> She may be jes' a'ripplin',
> Or she may be blowing so
> You'd swear that whiff of D.C. feed
> Came clear from Buffalo.
>
> So we watch our tiller closer,
> We keeps our sheets all clear;
> There's no such thing as stiddy wind
> Around Lake Erie here.

The *Sephie*'s First Trip

The trim schooner *Sephie,* a fore-and-aft-rigged three-master of 260 tons burden, was launched at Goderich, Ontario, on July 1, 1869, Canada's annual Dominion Day. It sailed in the Lake Huron and Georgian Bay lumber trade through the 1917 season. Then, with nearly thirty years of service, the *Sephie* sailed down the New York State Barge Canal for ocean service during World War I. The holiday launching of this ship (which was named for the daughter of its first owner) occasioned a local celebration, as vessel launchings often did. Competition must have been keen for positions on the *Sephie*'s first crew, and it helped inspire the song from which these fragments survive. This song about the *Sephie*'s home port was well known and is attributed to John Brown of Goderich and later Cloud Bay, Ontario. Norman "Beachie" MacIvor of Goderich recalled these few stanzas in the summer of 1934, nearly seventy years after the launching they immortalized.

> I suppose that you remember when the *Sephie* she was new,
> And Johnny Buddy Antie hoped to go mate on her crew;
> He asked Mr. Martin to go mate on her first trip,
> But Old Lumber Joe said, "I don't think you're fit!"
>
> "I'll mark in her log all the sails that was bent,
> Her wake and her course and the distance she went;
> I'll take the port watch, and I'll make a fast trip."
> But then Old Lumber Joe said, "I don't think you're fit!"
> . . . .
> Buddy Antie let go the main sheet with a run,
> And she flew 'round a bend like a shot from a gun—

John Bull was aloft for to shift the fore tack,
And when he came down, we all got the sack.

Now the *Sephie*'s back home, and her maiden trip's past,
And Buddy was lucky for to ship before the mast.
And as long as the waters they roll white and blue,
Buddy Antie will never be the mate of her crew.

The *Dreadnaught*

Nothing better illustrates the European ancestry of most Great Lakes songs than "The *Dreadnaught*" and its derivatives. Lakes sailors sang of the fleet packet engaged in the transatlantic trade, and in at least two cases—for "The Schooner *John Bentely*," which follows, and the ore vessel song "The Red Iron Ore"—they remade the standard to suit local vessels and harbors. Here is "The *Dreadnaught*," as recalled in 1933 by John S. Parsons at Oswego, New York.

The *Dreadnaught*

Walton Score No. 26

She's a sau-cy trim pack-et, a pack-et of fame, She hails from New

York, and the *Dread-naught's* her name. She is bound to the west-ward where the

storm-y winds blow, Bound a-way on the *Dread-naught,* to the west-ward we

go. Bound a-way, bound a-way where the storm-y winds blow,

She's a saucy trim packet, a packet of fame,
She hails from New York, and the *Dreadnaught*'s her name.
She is bound to the westward where the stormy winds blow,
Bound away on the *Dreadnaught*, to the westward we go.
    Bound away, bound away where the stormy winds blow,
    Bound away on the *Dreadnaught*, to the westward we'll go.

The time of her sailing is now drawing nigh,
Farewell, pretty Polly, I must bid you good-bye;
And farewell to old England and the girls we hold dear,
Bound away on the *Dreadnaught*, to the westward we steer.

Now the *Dreadnaught* is hauling out of Waterloo dock,
And the boys and the girls on the pierheads do flock;
They give us three cheers while their tears freely flow,
Saying, "God bless the *Dreadnaught*, where e'er she may go."

Oh, the *Dreadnaught* is waiting in the Mersey so free,
Waiting for the *Independence* to tow her to sea;
For to round that black rock where the Mersey does flow,
Bound away on the *Dreadnaught*, to the westward we go.

Oh, the *Dreadnaught* is rolling down the wild Irish sea,
And the passengers are merry, with hearts full of glee;
While the sailors like lions walk the decks to and fro,
Bound away on the *Dreadnaught*, to the westward we go.

Now the *Dreadnaught* is sailing the Atlantic so wide,
And the dark, heavy seas roll along her black sides.
Her sails are all spread, and the red cross does show,
Bound away on the *Dreadnaught*, to the westward we go.

Now the *Dreadnaught* has arrived in New York once more;
We'll go ashore, shipmates, on the land we adore.
With our wives and our sweethearts it's merry we'll be;
We'll drink a health to the *Dreadnaught*, where e'er she may be.

Here's a health to the *Dreadnaught*, and to all her brave crew,
Here's a health to her captain and officers, too.
Talk about your flash packets, *Swallow Tail* and *Black Ball*,
But the *Dreadnaught*'s the clipper can outsail them all.

The Schooner *John Bentely*

Once it had established a new home on the inland seas, "The *Dreadnaught*" became a platform upon which sailors built other songs. Ironically, a clumsy three-masted canaller became the star of one such new song. Built in 1873 at the mouth of the Napanee River near the east end of Lake Ontario for Captain W. B. Hall of Toronto, the 525-net-ton *Bentely* had the lines of a brick, quite unlike the sleek clipper lines of the *Dreadnaught.* In the trip narrated here, the schooner clears Toronto harbor and sails eighty miles southeast across Lake Ontario to Charlotte at the mouth of the Genesee River, now the harbor of the city of Rochester, New York. The *Bentely* evidently leaks badly and requires much pumping. The crew's quarters in the forecastle are neither sanitary nor comfortable. At Charlotte the *Bentely* takes on a load of coal for the Upper Lakes and sets out for Port Dalhousie at the entrance of the old Welland Canal. Before the schooner can enter the locks, the headsails must be taken in and the jibboom unshipped and brought inboard or lashed to the foremast. Such preparations were normal for canallers. The twenty-seven-mile canal had twenty-seven locks to climb the 327-foot Niagara escarpment between Lakes Ontario and Erie. Negotiating the locks and enduring miles of towing was a tedious chore much beneath the dignity of vessels—even boxy canallers—used to running with the wind. In this song, the *Bentely* spends the entire night locking through and arrives at Gravelly Bay on Lake Erie the following morning.

  Seventy-year-old Captain Jeremiah Cavanaugh of Port Dalhousie, Ontario, recalled this song in August 1933. He said he had spent most of his life on the Lakes, that he had been a member of the *Bentely*'s crew on the trip concerned, and that he made up the song at that time "over fifty years ago." He added, "whenever men forward [crewmen as distinct from officers] would gather ashore and at once make for a saloon and have a drink or two, someone would call for a song, and then each man had to sing a song, clog [dance], tell a good story, or buy a round of drinks. I always had to sing the *Bentely.*"

 Come shipmates and listen, a story I'll tell
About a flash packet, you all know her well;
She is a flash packet, a packet of fame,
She hails from Toronto, and *Bentely*'s her name.

  Derry down, down, down, derry down.

 The dimensions of this packet now to you I'll tell,
She was built by the yard and cut off by the mile;
She's round stem and bluff forward, no deadrise at all;
And she's owned in Toronto by Alderman Hall.

 I shipped in this packet at the northern docks,
I took a streetcar from the Church Street to Brock;
And from there I steered straight for the ship
With a satchel in one hand, in the other a grip.

 But on the way down I got blazing drunk,
I lost the old satchel and busted my trunk;

I tripped and I tumbled, and down I did fall,
And I cursed the old *Bentely,* the sidewalks and all.

At last to the ship I chanced for to stray,
And the captain came forward saying, "We'll get under weigh,
We're bound for Charlotte, going there to load coal";
And down the rough lake the old *Bentely* did roll.

I was tired and weary, oh yes, I was sick
From hearing the pumps go "clackety-click."
My bones, they were sore from lying in my bunk.
And the rotten old bedclothes were nothing but junk.

Then we left old Charlotte for the Welland Canal,
And forget that last trip? Oh, no, I ne'er shall!
And then on our port bow Port Dalhousie did loom,
All hands gathered forward to top the jibboom.

We towed into the harbor, our jibboom topped high,
And all of the people they started to cry:
"Oh, where did you get it? Where did it come from?"
Or "Where in the devil does that craft belong?"

And when we got ready to go in the lock,
The Sammies all gathered like geese in a flock;
And sure Grogan was there, and he shinned up a fender
Saying, "Captain, you know me, I'm an old lock tender."

There lives in Toronto an ugly old thief,
He's called "Burk, the butcher, who sells the tough beef."
It gives us the toothache and causes much pain,
We'll murder the old villain when we go there again.

We worked at canalling that entire night
And in order to work we had to keep tight;
But now, the next morning the captain did say:
"At last we've arrived in Gravelly Bay."

The Flash Packet *Worts*

These fragments from yet a third song indicate a more positive adaptation of "The *Dreadnaught.*" These lines are from an unpublished manuscript by Dr. Charles L. Bovee of Adams, New York.

We're in a flash packet, a packet of fame,
She hails from Oswego, and the *Worts* is her name.

Captain Taylor commands her as well we all know;
Bound away to Muskegon, for lumber we go.

Soon we'll be towing through the Welland Canal;
We will sing merrily as onward we're hauled.
We'll top up our booms, boys, and then go below;
Bound away to Muskegon, for lumber we go.

You Pretty Girls of Michigan

Transplanted from salt water to fresh, "You Pretty Girls of Liverpool" easily adapted to the Great Lakes. It expresses sailors' contempt for farmers and other landlubbers who had much easier work—and shorter separations from women. Pat Banner of St. Clair, Michigan, and Captain A. E. Baker of Dunkirk, New York, recalled these lyrics in 1933. On April 4, 1935, John Brown of Cloud Bay, Ontario, said that this song's predecessor was "You Pretty Girls of Liverpool." That song has proved to be elusive, but the widely sung "Banks of Newfoundland" begins "You bully boys of Liverpool," and its melody fits quite well.

You Pretty Girls of Michigan

Murdock, Score No. 17

You pretty girls of Michigan, give ear to what I write, Of sailing on the stormy Lakes, in which we take delight; In sailing on the stormy Lakes, which we poor seamen do, While Irishmen and the landlubbers are staying at home with you.

You pretty girls of Michigan, give ear to what I write,
Of sailing on the stormy Lakes, in which we take delight;
In sailing on the stormy Lakes, which we poor seamen do,
While Irishmen and the landlubbers are staying at home with you.

They're always with some pretty girls a'telling them fine tales
Of the hardships and the hard day's work they've had in their cornfields;
And when it's eight o'clock at night it's into bed they crawl,
While we, like jovial hearts of oak, stand many a bitter squall.

You pretty girls of Michigan if you did only know
The hardships and dangers we seamen undergo,
You would have more regard for us than oft you've had before;
You'd shun to meet those landlubbers that lounge about the shore.

For oft at twelve o'clock at night when the wind begins to blow:
"Heave out, heave out, now lively lads, roll out from down below!"
It's now on deck stands every man, his life and ship to guard;
"Aloft! Aloft!" the captain cries, "send down the tops'l yard!"

And when the seas are mountain high and toss our vessel 'round,
And all about does danger lurk, the vessel may go down!
Now every man is on the deck, all ready to lend a hand
To shorten sail to weather the gale until we reach the land.

We sail the Lakes from spring to fall from Duluth to Buffalo,
While landlubbers are home with you or about their fields they go;
We sail the Lakes and money make for the girls that we adore,
And when our cash is getting low, we ship again for more!

Bonnie Highland Laddie

One of many ocean songs refitted for the inland seas was "Highland Laddie." A change here, a new place name or occupation there, and an old song found new life. This is how the Irish people of Beaver Island in northern Lake Michigan sang it, according to a field recording.

High ho and up she goes,
    Bonnie laddie, highland laddie,
High ho and up she goes,
    My bonnie highland laddie!

Was you ever in New York,
    Bonnie laddie, highland laddie?
There the sailors live and sport,
    My bonnie highland laddie!

Did you ever sail the Lakes,
    Bonnie laddie, highland laddie?
The harbors full of country Jakes,
    My bonnie highland laddie!

Did you ever work the canal,
    Bonnie laddie, highland laddie?
Horse dung sailing, worse than Hell,
    My bonnie highland laddie!

Was you ever in Grand Marais,
    Bonnie laddie, highland laddie?
Loading timbers night and day,
    My bonnie highland laddie!

Was you ever in Marquette,
    Bonnie laddie, highland laddie?
Red ore coverin' all the deck,
    My bonnie highland laddie!

Was you ever in Baltimore,
    Bonnie laddie, highland laddie?
Dark-eyed girls at every door,
    My bonnie highland laddie!

The *Three Bells*

"The *Three Bells*" was one of many Atlantic Ocean songs imported into the Great Lakes, but it deserves note for its engaging rhythm and its Great Lakes namesake, a 124-foot two-master built in 1854. The schooner ran ashore in Lake Michigan's

The *Three Bells* of Oakville and the *Erie Belle* of Port Burwell had bells above each truck, which were allowed to ring freely. Courtesy of the Historical Collections of the Great Lakes.

Good Harbor after being caught in a snow squall in November 1884. The vessel went to pieces before it could be salvaged from the bay on Michigan's northwest coast. According to notes by Loudon Wilson, bells attached to the top of each mast rang freely as it sailed.

These lyrics come from a 1933 letter by Mrs. James Rice of Grand Rapids, Michigan, writing at the direction of Mrs. Gerrit Doesburg, who asked her to set down lyrics recalled by the recently deceased Mr. Doesburg. A. E. Baker of Dunkirk, New York, also recalled parts of the song on August 30, 1933.

> They worked all day,
> They worked all way,
> As brave tars only do.
> They sought to save
> From wind and wave
> A sinking vessel's crew.
>
> "All saved" they cried,
> The shout rose high,
> Rose high o'er wind and wave.
> 'Twas a starry crew
> And captain true
> That manned the good ship *Three Bells*.

James Bird

Honored for heroism one year and executed for desertion the next, Sergeant James Bird fired the imagination of sailors around the Lakes and lived for decades in their singing.

The military ship *General Gage* with its fourteen guns, in the foreground, and the *Enterprise*. Courtesy of the Historical Collections of the Great Lakes.

Bird became a war hero on September 10, 1813, when wounded aboard Captain Oliver Hazard Perry's flagship *Lawrence* in the Battle of Lake Erie, a turning point in the War of 1812. So close was the conflict that either side might have won—Perry's American fleet or the British, under command of one-armed Robert Heriot Barclay. With the *Lawrence* nearly wrecked and its decks littered with dead and wounded men—including the injured Bird—Perry struck his colors. Seeing this, an observer on land reported a British victory. But Perry took a few men in an undamaged cutter and rowed for the American brig *Niagara,* which had not joined the battle. With a fresh command and crew, Perry reengaged the British and won decisively. The entire engagement lasted just three hours. Perry proclaimed the victory to his superiors by writing on the back of an envelope: "We have met the enemy and they are ours. Two ships, two brigs, one schooner and a sloop." Perry had just become the first person to capture a British fleet, securing his place in history. For Americans, the stunning victory washed away the shame left by General William Hull, who had surrendered Detroit to the British in 1812.

Bird had come to serve on the *Lawrence,* in part, to escape punishment for allowing the theft of some military stores that had been under his watch. After

Perry's victory Bird received similar duty, but he deserted with another soldier. A student traveling on horseback spotted the soldiers in a tavern and reported them. The men were arrested, convicted of desertion, and sentenced to die. Bird's defenders cited his gallantry on Lake Erie and asked that his sentence be commuted to life imprisonment. Bird's appeal was rejected by no less than a future president of the United States, General William Henry Harrison. In October 1814, not far from where he had been wounded aboard the *Lawrence,* Bird was executed aboard Perry's victory ship, the *Niagara.* Although this song takes Bird's side, it is accurate on the main points. The song was first written as a poem by Charles Miner of Wilkes-Barre, Pennsylvania, and published in his newspaper, *The Gleaner.*

James Bird

Hankins, Score No. 1

You sons of free-dom list-en to me, And you daugh-ters lend an ear,

You a sad and mourn-ful sto-ry As was ev-er told shall hear.

You sons of freedom listen to me,
    And you daughters lend an ear,
You a sad and mournful story
    As was ever told shall hear.

Hull, you know, his troops surrendered
    And defenseless left the West,
Then our forces quick assembled
    The invader to resist.

Among the troops that marched to Erie
    Were the Kingston Volunteers,
Captain Thomas, he commanded
    To protect our west frontier.

Tender was the scene at parting,
    Mothers wrung their hands and cried,
Maidens wept their swains in secret,
    Fathers tried their hearts to hide.

There was one among that number,
    Tall and graceful in his mien,
Firm his step, his look undaunted,
    Scarce a nobler youth was seen.

One sweet kiss he snatched from Mary,
    Kissed his mother's cheek once more,
Pressed his father's hand and left them,
    For Lake Erie's distant shore.

Soon they came where noble Perry
    Had assembled all his fleet,
There our gallant Bird enlisted
    Hoping for the foe to meet.

Where is Bird, the battle rages,
    Is he in the fight, or no?
How the battle roars tremendous,
    Dare he meet the hostile foe?

Ah, behold him—see, with Perry,
    In his flagship there he fights.
Though his messmates fall about him,
    Nothing can his soul afright.

But, behold, a ball has struck him;
    See the crimson current flow!
"Go, and leave the deck," says Perry,
    "No," says Bird, "I will not go!"

"Here on deck I take my station,
    Never will Bird his colors fly,
I'll stand by the noble captain
    Till we conquer or we die!"

He fought on though faint and bleeding,
    Till our banners high arose,
And victory had crowned our efforts,
    As we triumphed o'er our foes.

And did Bird receive a pension,
    Or was he to his friends restored?
No, nor never to his bosom
    Clasped the maid his heart adored.

Now there came most dreadful tidings
    From Lake Erie's distant shore,
Better if brave Bird had perished
    Midst the battle's awful roar.

"Dearest parents," said the letter,
    "This will bring sad news to you,
Do not mourn your first, beloved,
    Though this brings his last adieu.

"I must suffer for desertion
    From the brig *Niagara*,
Read my letter, brother, sister,
    'Tis the last you'll have from me."

Sad and dismal was the morning;
    Bird was ordered out to die:
Where's a heart not sure to pity,
    Or for him would heave a sigh?

See him march unto his coffin,
    Sure his death can do no good.
"Spare him! Hark! Oh, God, they've shot him,
    See his bosom stream with blood!"

Farewell Bird, farewell forever,
    Your friends and home you'll see no more,
For your mangled corpse lies buried
    On Lake Erie's distant shore.

Bird will ever be remembered,
    Aye unto this present day,
Oh, what can best or wrong them,
    Who engage in war or fray?

The Dredge from Presque Isle

Passage songs told nothing more than the tale of a vessel's voyage. While they offer little in terms of drama and climax, they say a lot about everyday life for working sailors. This passage song narrates the trip of a tug from Oswego, New York, to Presque Isle, Ontario, approximately seventy miles northwest across Lake Ontario. There, the tug took a harbor dredge in tow and brought it back to Oswego.

Ben Peckham provided this song in the summer of 1933. He attributed it to his father, Thomas, a blacksmith and singer-sailor who made the trip in the early 1870s. The younger Peckham said his father had called the song "The Tug *Alanson Sumner*," but that "The Dredge from Presque Isle" ("Isle" is pronounced to rhyme with "wheel") was a better title.

The night was fair, the sky was clear,
    No ripple on the sea,
When King he came into the shop
    And thus he says to me:
"We're going on a pleasure trip."
    How good that made me feel.
And then he said, "If the weather's fine,
    We're going to Presque Isle."

It was quite late in the month of August,
    And, if I remember right,
We went on board the *Sumner* tug
    At nine o'clock at night.
Bill Bishop cast off the mooring lines,
    Captain Dobie took the wheel,
And the stern being nigh, he let 'er fly
    To the place they call Presque Isle.

About the hour of five next morning,
    The light was right ahead;
Says King to Captain Dobie, "Sir,
    The *Sumner* is not dead."
"Oh no," says Captain Dobie, proud,
    As he held the *Sumner*'s wheel,
"There's no tug afloat can beat this boat
    From Oswego to Presque Isle."

Oh, now that we are landed safe,
    And made fast to the dock,
Machinists and dredgemen and others too
    Around us then did flock.
Then down to breakfast we all did go
    For mutton chops and veal;
About then, says I, "The boys live high
    On dredges at Presque Isle."

My blessing on that good old cook,
    I think her name was Ann,
She gave us each a pile of grub
    To fill a twelve-quart pan.
There was pickled feet and pork and beans,
    And also Irish veal—
You'd laugh and cry to see the pickles fly
    When we were in Presque Isle.

Now, breakfast being over and done,
    We took a look around;
Two dump scows and a bad, used dredge
    In the harbor there we found.
They were covered over with slime and moss
    From their decking to their keel;
For you must know they'd sunk them low
    In the place they call Presque Isle.

It was shortly after the break of day,
    The sky being bright and clear,
King approached Captain Dobie and said,
    "It's time to get out of here."
The dredge's line we then made fast,
    Our whistle gave a squeal,
And we headed back with the dredge in tow
    And left behind Presque Isle.

About four o'clock that afternoon,
    The wind began to blow;
Then asked Fugerhead of Austin,
    "Have we much furder to go?"
Our German friend looked pale and sick,
    For him my heart did feel.
He was not much pleased with the high seas
    When we'd left behind Presque Isle.

George Orwell and Squire Holbrook stood
    All day upon the pier.
A'watching for the tug and dredge,

But they did not appear.
At length said Orwell to Holbrook,
    "I'll bet a lemon peel,
The tug and dredge are lying now
    In the harbor at Presque Isle."

All day they watched and through the night.
    But we were on the lake,
The *Sumner* kept her towline taut.
    The dredge rolled in her wake.
Our dredgemen friends hoped for an end,

For sailing they had no feel,
And it is said some wished them dead,
    On the trip back from Presque Isle.

Now that we are landed safe,
    My song should have an end,
For just to please an old shipmate,
    These few lines I have penned.
With dump scows and with dredges all
    We nevermore shall deal,
We'll stay on shore and go no more
    For dredges at Presque Isle!

On Gravelly Bay

A common theme for the workingman is the lovestruck beauty and her meddling mother. In this song, the unlucky sailor finds himself temporarily working on a dredge making improvements in the harbor at Port Colborne, Ontario, formerly Gravelly Bay, at the Lake Erie end of the Welland Canal. He falls in love with a local girl, but evidently he is not the first—or last. Captain E. J. Buzzard of Erieau, Ontario, said that he learned the song from shipmates about 1870. Buzzard said, "I began sailing on the windjammers in 1867 at the age of fifteen and sailed for twenty seasons and then got married. My wife thought I'd make more money in the hotel business, and I guess she was right—but I had more fun sailing."

I was a handsome nice young man,
    I hailed from Cleveland town;
And for daily occupation
    I teamed for Johnnie Brown.
And all day long I'd sport and play,
    My joy I ne'er begrudged,
'Til I was sent to Gravelly Bay
    To work upon a drudge.

I had not been in Gravelly Bay
    Scarce one day, two, or three
Before a very fair young girl
    Fell into love with me
Saying, "Mike, my man, give me your hand,
    From you I'll never budge;
With you I'll stay on Gravelly Bay
    And work upon the drudge."

Her mother standing at her door
    Says, "Please, don't make such noise,
And another thing, you're far too young
    To trust among those boys.
And that young man that holds your hand,
    If I can rightly judge,
Has just the eye that'll make you sigh
    Before you leave the drudge."

"Now, mother dear, don't be severe,"
    My darling then did say,
"Never eyes so fair, or such black hair,
    Was e'er on Gravelly Bay!"
I took her to my bosom then;
    The world did me begrudge;
And for many a day she got my pay
    While working on the drudge.

But as the weeks did pass along,
    And the channel lengthened too,
A doubt oft came to my mind
    If she was really true.
	And sad to relate, it is my fate
	    Of women I'm no judge,
	For she loved not one, but all the men
	    Who worked upon the drudge!

The *Darius Cole* and *Mackinac*

This fragment comes from a song about a race between two well-known passenger steamers that ran between Port Huron and Toledo in the late 1880s and early 1900s. Built at Cleveland in 1885, the 201-foot, 528-gross-ton wooden side-wheel *Darius Cole* carried passengers and freight between Alpena, Michigan, and Toledo and intermediate ports for many years. Darius Cole, the man, had become a hero about eleven o'clock one night in 1856 when the *Forest Queen* gored his side-wheel steamer, the *Northerner*, near Port Huron and nearly sliced it in two. One hundred thirty-four passengers and crew were aboard the *Northerner* at the time of the collision. Cole hustled his passengers over to the *Forest Queen* while the vessels were entangled and then directed the launching of the *Northerner*'s lifeboats. Even though the boat sank in just six minutes, all but twelve people survived. The vessel named for Cole was renamed the *Huron* in 1906 and then the *Colonial* in 1932. Three years after that, fire destroyed the vessel on Lake Erie off Barcelona, New York, killing four.

    The other vessel in this song, the *City of Mackinac*, was a 215-foot wood-and-iron boat. Built in Wyandotte, Michigan, in 1883, the 807-gross-ton side-wheeler ran between Port Huron and Cleveland as well as ports in between. After ten years the owners had *City of Mackinac* rebuilt, renamed *State of New York*, and placed on the Cleveland-Buffalo route. In 1918 it became the *Florida*, an excursion steamer out of Chicago, and finally, in 1936, it was partially dismantled and permanently moored in Chicago harbor as the clubhouse of the Columbia Yacht Club.

    In their early days, the two elaborately appointed side-wheelers were renowned in the Detroit area for their competition. On the late-season race narrated here, the vessels evidently encountered one another near the mouth of the St. Clair River and a race was on. They took different channels into Lake St. Clair, then raced across the shallow lake until they met an upbound tow. The *Mackinac*, being on the outer edge of the dredged channel and in danger of grounding in the mud, had to slow down and lost the race.

    The first stanza and last two came from ex-schoonerman J. Sylvester "Ves" Ray of Port Huron in the summer of 1933. The others came from Norman "Beachie" MacIvor of Goderich, Ontario, that same summer. Ray said that the rest of the song, which he could not recall, described the continuation of the race to Detroit.

On the eighteenth of December,
The weather it was fair,
The *Darius Cole* and *Mackinac*
Were crossing Lake St. Clair.

The *Darius Cole* had often said
She could beat the old *Mack*'s time—
"Now, boys, here comes the *Mackinac*,
We'll leave her far behind!"

Through the Old Channel she took her course
An advantage for to find,
But when she got around the Cut,
The *Mack* was just behind.

The *Mackinac* then opened up
With all speed she could contrive,
And came 'longside the *Darius Cole*
Much to the *Cole*'s surprise.

Then through the water these straining craft,
Side by side they flew;
Great sport it was for all on board,
Both passengers and crew.

They met a tow a'comin' up,
The *Mack* outside must take;
The *Darius Cole* kept on her course
And gains began to make.

On the Schooner *Africa*

In Great Lakes taverns and saloons where it was customary for sailors to entertain their mates, a sailor with a good repertoire could be rewarded with a night of drinking and never have to show the color of his money. One such bard appears to have been Buffalo's Captain William E. "Billy" Clark, a sailor on the *Africa*. According to these scraps of a song, Clark and his mates went uptown to a saloon while their vessel awaited its turn at the Marquette, Michigan, iron ore docks. A shot rang out in the raucous bar, and Clark was wounded badly enough to need a berth in the hospital. As if that weren't enough, another man quit rather than make the return trip to Cleveland. With a fresh cargo waiting, the captain, a man named Dolan, had to make some hasty replacements. The song describes how he moved the cook to sailing duties and hired a woman to take his place.

    J. Sylvester Ray of Port Huron, Michigan, recalled these fragments in the summer of 1933. He said that he had been a member of the *Africa*'s crew in the early 1880s.

We wallowed Lake Superior through,
    And then we reached Marquette
Where Billy Clark, our singing friend,
    By Charlie Turpin was shot.
The row was commenced by a sailor lad
    And a man they called "The Moor."
But Clark to a hospital had to go,
    And we left him there ashore.

One man, he quit, another got shot,
    And Dolan was stuck fast;
He begged and prayed of Billy the cook
    To go before the mast.
Then Billy accommodated him,
    And a broad came in full bloom
A dashing female cook from the brig
    They call the *Old Half Moon*.

The Steamer *Wyoming*

Although its melody appears to be lost, this song follows the same form as "The Schooner *Africa*" and the familiar plan of beginning with a come-ye-all call and then enumerating the crew's characteristics. The wooden *Wyoming,* 350 tons and 154 feet long, was launched at Detroit in 1870. It burned and sank just off Burnt Cabin Point on November 12, 1904, while fighting heavy seas near Michigan's Pointe aux Barques.

Captain John E. Hayes of Port Huron, the city where the trip in the song is supposed to have originated, recalled these lines.

> Come all ye jolly seamen,
>   Now, as it's getting late
> And I'll sing you my experience
>   On a bad package freight.
>
> It was on the steamer *Wyoming,*
>   And it almost proved my ruin;
> I cursed the day I sailed away
>   From the city of Port Huron
>
> The captain was the meanest man
>   That ever trod a plank;
> The first mate was a son-of-a-gun,
>   And the second mate a crank.
>
> The wheelsmen, they were jolly,
>   And the watchman full of fun;
> The deckhands, they were hoboes,
>   And the firemen, they were bums.

The *Fayette Brown*

Steeped in bitterness, prejudice, and contempt for untrained sailors and the captain who hired them, "The *Fayette Brown*" is one of the nastiest songs to survive the schooner age.

When steamboats and railroads began slicing into the schooner trade in the 1870s and 1880s, vessel owners cut costs to remain competitive. Those cuts came right out of sailors' pockets. Sailors responded by organizing a union and setting a minimum wage. Riots broke out at several Great Lakes ports as union sailors tried to prevent vessels from sailing with nonunion crews.

Several early organizing bids collapsed, but a shipping boom and a shortage of experienced sailors ensured success for the 1878 creation of the Chicago Seamen's Benevolent Union. Within the year, the Chicago union opened locals at nine more ports on the Lakes. For a couple seasons, union sailors could all but name their price.

Late in the 1879 season, however, vessel owners in Cleveland, the center of the iron ore shipping trade, united to smash the union. The owners' association set up shipping offices around Lake Erie to secure nonunion seamen. The owners named an ex-union sailor who had been a policeman and prizefighter as their chief shipping officer. He hired thugs to open the docks to nonunion sailors, and the next decade was stained by the blood of waterfront rioting.

One story says that the *Fayette Brown* was tied up at Chicago and did not sail until a crew of black, nonunion sailors was signed aboard. Frank Mahaffey of

Port Colborne, Ontario, a Lakes sailor for half a century, remembered hearing the song while working on a tug that was tied up to a schooner in the Detroit River. As the *Fayette Brown* passed downbound in tow of another tug, the crew of the idle schooner "bawled it out" at the passing schooner. Mahaffey says he saw the scene repeated whenever the *Fayette Brown* was within hailing distance.

William Head of Picton, Ontario, a Canadian sailor on the Lakes for almost half a century, recalled being in Cleveland during a sailors' strike and seeing the song printed up on large cards and distributed along the waterfront. It also made for lusty singing at union halls around the Lakes.

Although best known as a symbol, the *Fayette Brown* made an impression as a sailing vessel as well. It was a trim, smart-looking schooner with a sweeping sheer to its deck and three tall, raked masts. Built in Cleveland in 1868 for Alva Bradley of that city, the *Fayette Brown* was large for its day at 533 tons. Bradley was a major stockholder in the Jackson Mining Company, the first iron-mining company set up to extract Michigan's rich deposits of the ore. Company manager Fayette Brown gave his name to the vessel, as he did to the city of Fayette, on Michigan's Garden Peninsula where the Jackson Mining Company made its first pig iron. The *Fayette Brown* sailed for twenty-three years, until a collision on Lake Erie took it in 1891.

This arrangement, by F. W. Elliott of Fairport, Ohio, contains stanzas and lines collected from Collen; W. A. Ashley and C. H. Hubbard of Milwaukee; William Preston of Grand Haven, Michigan; Malcomb McDonald of Goderich, Ontario; William Kelley and Neil Baker of Cleveland; Edward Navin of Cobourg, Ontario; and John S. Parsons of Oswego, New York. Although it contains offensive language and statements, the song is included as testimony to the presence of inexperienced black sailors on the Lakes and evidence of the hatred they sometimes faced.

Come all brave union sailor lads
    And listen to my song,
It's about a schooner sore disgraced,
    And will not detain you long.
I'll sing to you of Captain Moffet,
    The name brings up a frown,
He's the nigger-loving son-of-a-bitch
    That sails the *Fayette Brown*!

The dirty sucker of the fleet,
    What did he do for fame?
He sailed a crew of Africans
    To immortalize his name—
From waiters, aye, and bellhops, too,
    He picked up 'round the town,
He stuffed their heads, they loused the beds
    Aboard the *Fayette Brown*!

He shipped 'em all at nigger pay,
    No sailor 'mong the crowd.
They went aboard the staunch old ship
    That always had been proud.
An' finally when they'd spread her wings,
    Her canvas all drooped down
In token of the sad disgrace
    Of the schooner *Fayette Brown*!

When on the stretches of the Lakes
    Where changing winds abound
At night or day they'll lose their way
    An' run 'er hard aground.
Or when the seas are rolling high
    An' tops'ls must come down,
No nigger up aloft will dare
    On the schooner *Fayette Brown*!

An' when the autumn has set in
    With wind and snow and foam,
It'll paint them blue, the dusky crew,
    An' make them long for home.
They'll gather 'round the fo'c'sle hatch
    An' wish that they were drown'd;
They'll curse the day they sailed away
    On the schooner *Fayette Brown*!

The seasons they are very short,
    An' sailing days are few,
It's hard and tough to get enough
    To last the winter through.
When tyrants trample on your rights,
    It's time to take them down,
Like the nigger-loving Moffet
    That sails the *Fayette Brown*!

An' now it's time to close my song,
    I do so with regret;
Eight bells have struck, the watch is called,
    An' I must go on deck.
But e'er I go, I'll have you know
    The feelings that abound
In the hearts of all true sailor-men
    Who know the *Fayette Brown*!

Success to Captain Bradley, boys,
    An' all shipowners true,
Likewise all gallant captains
    Who carry union crews;
May favoring gales fill all their sails,
    An' success their efforts crown,
But bad luck to the man who disgraced the name
    Of the schooner *Fayette Brown*!

The Seamen's Union

Henry McConnell of Picton, Ontario, recalled this fragment of a Canadian seamen's union song in the summer of 1938, but he couldn't recall the melody or the author, or even the occasion on which he learned it. The Irish influence, though, is undeniable.

We are a band of seamen,
    A jolly, jolly crew,
As ever sailed the ocean
    Or wore the jackets blue.
We plow the deep dark waters,
    Without a thought or fear,
We sing and sport in every port,
    And drive away dull care.

We are a band of seamen,
    With a password and a sigh;
The shamrock, rose, and thistle
    Around our banner twine.
The maple leaf is our embrace,
    Victoria is our queen;
Not her's the blame, our union's name
    The Orange and the Green.

Here's a health to every captain
    Who ships a union crew,
Here's a health to the girls with flowing curls
    That like the boys in blue.

The Buffalo Whore

Buffalo's Canal Street was the hands-down loudest, drinkingest, carousingest, bare-knuckle fightingest, wildest street for lakeshore amusement on perhaps the whole of the Great Lakes. Situated at the foot of Lake Erie and the head of the Erie Canal, Buffalo was the farthest point reachable by Lakes vessels too large to negotiate the old Welland Canal and host to a steady stream of saltwater sailors looking for work on fresh water. Transient seamen, mariners for the local fleet, and a large number of human parasites, including the "harbor ladies," made Buffalo positively squirm with human activity. Just-paid sailors came ashore to spend lavishly in the "free and easy" saloon-theater-boardinghouses and other establishments so eager to relieve them of their wages. When the money ran out—and men can be separated from money with remarkable efficiency—the sailors shipped back out on any vessel in need of a crew to begin the cycle anew. And they were the lucky ones. Captain Herman Oertling of Milwaukee recalled in 1938 that "Down in Buffalo along Canal Street—I tell you that was a bad place. Many a men has gone in there with his pockets full of money and was never seen again." This song and the next recall the low-down, cutthroat, dog-eat-dog character of the Lakes' most colorful town. The incident has been set in Winnipeg and other localities and occupations, and Lakes sailors may well have adapted the song from somewhere else, but it no doubt describes the experiences of scores of sailors in Buffalo's waterfront district.

 Norman "Beachie" MacIvor of Goderich, Ontario, recalled this in the summer of 1934. He said he had heard it "dozens of times" but could not recall where he had learned it.

My first trip down old Lake Erie,
With some sailors to explore;
Then I met Rosy O'Flannagan,
Best of all the Buffalo whores.

She says, "Boy, I think I know you,
Let me sit upon your knee,
How'd you like to do some lovin'?
A dollar and a half will be my fee."

Some were singing, some were dancing,
Some were drunk upon the floor;
But I was over in a corner
A'making love to the Buffalo whore.

She was slick as oil on water,
I didn't know what she was about
'Til I missed my watch and wallet,
Then I popped her on the snout.

Out came the whores and
  sons-of-bitches,
They came at me by the score;
You'd have laughed to split your britches
To see me flying out that door!

Grain schooners in Buffalo harbor. Courtesy of the Historical Collections of the Great Lakes.

The Smugglers of Buffalo

These verses, recalled by Beaver Island's John W. Green, second Buffalo's nomination as the wildest town on the Lakes.

The Smugglers of Buffalo

Walton, Score No. 30

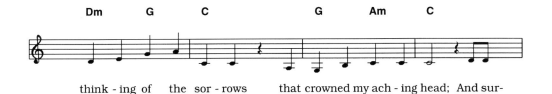
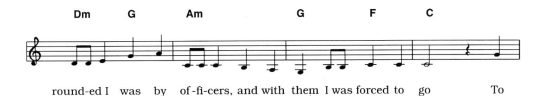

It was on the sixth of April as I lay on my bed,
A'thinking of the sorrows that crowned my aching head;
And surrounded I was by officers, and with them I was forced to go
To serve a long and dreary trick in the jails of Buffalo.

When I've done my trick and am pardoned, and once more I am free,
I'll go down to Sandusky, my true love for to see.
But, perhaps, my boys, she will give me the bounce when she does come to know
That I led a gang of smugglers to the jails of Buffalo.

Oh, the girl she came from Peterson, and the truth to you I'll tell,
She was an only daughter, and her parents loved her well.
They brought her up in fear of the Lord, but little did she know
That she was married to a smuggler that served time in Buffalo.

"And then on Superior our tubs began to rock," from "The Old Mont Line." Courtesy of the Historical Collections of the Great Lakes.

CHAPTER 5

Songs from the Iron Ore Trade

The November 10, 1975, sinking of the 729-foot *Edmund Fitzgerald* was a startling modern-day reminder that, although nature might make accommodations for human enterprise, it would not be subjugated. The *Fitzgerald*, which dropped to the bottom of Lake Superior with scarcely a cry, took twenty-nine men and a load of iron-ore taconite pellets. Whether shipped out of Lake Superior ports, as was the cargo on the "Big Fitz," or out of Lake Michigan's, heavy ore cargoes epitomized hazards on the Lakes. More than a hundred years previously, as soldiers lay dying on Civil War battlefields, sailors labored on Great Lakes vessels to rush the raw material of war—iron and copper—from mines to munitions makers. Sometimes the sailors were in graver danger than the soldiers. From 1855 to 1864, the amount of iron ore coming out of Lake Superior spiked from 1,447 to 243,127 tons. The first major shipping accident on Lake Superior, the 1862 collision that sank the schooner *Oriole* with twelve lives, involved the shipping of 501 tons of rock. (See the song about the *Oriole* in chapter 9.)

The Red Iron Ore (The *E. C. Roberts*)

This passage song was second only to "The Timber Drogher *Bigler*" (see chapter 6) for popularity on boats and in waterfront gathering places. The song tells of the mid-September trip of the schooner *E. C. Roberts* from Chicago to Escanaba, where it took on a cargo of iron ore, and the race to Cleveland that ensued with a fleet of other ore carriers.

The *Roberts*, 273 gross tons, was built in Cleveland in 1856 for Brown and Reddington of that city for the general carrying trade. It remained on the Lakes for over half a century. F. L. Robertson of St. Clair, Michigan, owned the vessel in its twilight years as a tow barge.

Captain T. J. Crockett of Port Huron shipped on the *Roberts* as the vessel's boy in the mid-1890s when it still carried ore. He said that the *Roberts* was a "handy" schooner and that the crew sang this song. Harry Anderson of St. Clair, Michigan, who had sailed on the *Roberts* the previous decade, recalled much of the song and said he had also learned it aboard the vessel.

"Death's Door" in the third stanza is the sailors' translation of the French Portes des Mortes passage between Door County Peninsula and Washington Island, the entrance to Green Bay. The French Ile aux Galets, for "island of pebbles," was similarly mangled as "Skillagalee." The Foxes and Beavers are island groups in northern Lake Michigan, and the "dummy" referred to in the third-from-last stanza was a decommissioned light in western Lake Erie. Near the end of the song, the singers might insert the name of the vessel master, whether Captain Rummage or Harvey Shannon or someone else, as a suggestion that the Old Man buy them a drink.

The song has not just two names, but two versions. The words and melody vary slightly, and both appear to have evolved from "The *Dreadnaught*" (described in chapter 4). J. Sylvester "Ves" Ray of Port Huron sang this in the summer of 1934 on his eighty-fourth birthday. He said he had learned it in the early 1870s "from a shipmate, Billy Clark of Buffalo, who composed it and dozens of others." Beaver Island's John W. Green, who also could sing the song complete, insisted that his sailor uncle, islander Peter O'Donnell, had composed it.

Railcars shuttle rock out to schooners waiting for their turn at the iron ore docks at Marquette, Michigan. Dossin Great Lakes Museum.

The Red Iron Ore

Murdock, Score No. 14

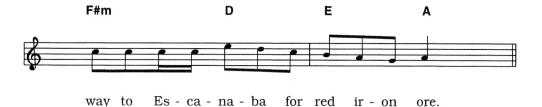

Come listen young fellows who follow the Lakes,
In iron ore vessels your living to make.
I shipped in Chicago, bid adieu to the shore,
Bound away to Escanaba for red iron ore.

In the month of September, the seventeenth day,
Two dollars and a quarter was all they would pay.
And on that same day, the north branch did take
The *E. C. Roberts* out into the lake.

The wind from the sou'west sprang up a stiff breeze,
And down through Lake Michigan the *Roberts* did sneeze,
And away through Lake Michigan the *Roberts* did roar,
And on Friday morning we passed through Death's Door.

Across the mouth of Green Bay this packet did ride
With the dark and deep water rolling over her side.
We rounded Sand Point, and our anchors let go,
We furled all our canvas, and then went below.

Next morning we hove in alongside the *Exile,*
And the *Roberts* made fast to an iron ore pile.
They let down their chutes, and like thunder did roar
As they emptied their pockets of red iron ore.

The tug *Escanaba,* she towed out the *Minch,*
The *Roberts* they thought they had left in a pinch.
And as they towed by us, they bid us good-bye,
Saying, "We'll see you in Cleveland next Fourth of July!"

We sailed out alone, through the passage sailed we,
Passed the Foxes, the Beavers, and Skillagalee.
We soon passed the *Minch* for to show her the way,
And she ne'er hove in sight 'til off Thunder Bay.

This packet rolled on across Saginaw Bay,
And over her bow there splashed the white spray.
And bound for the river the *Roberts* did go,
Where the tug *Kate Williams,* she took us in tow.

And down on old Erie, oh, Lord, how it blew!
And all around the dummy a large fleet came to.
The night, dark and stormy, Old Nick it would scare,
We hove up next morning, and for Cleveland did steer.

Now we're in Cleveland, made fast stem and stern,
And over the bottle we'll spin a good yarn.
I think Captain Rummage had ought to stand treat
For getting to Cleveland ahead of the fleet.

My song now is ended, and I hope you won't scoff;
Our dunnage is packed and all hands are paid off.
Here's a health to the *Roberts,* she's staunch, strong and true.
Not forgotten are the boys who comprise her brave crew.

Bound Away on the *Twilight*

Sail in the opposite direction—from east to west—and you have "Bound Away on the *Twilight*," a song clearly written on the "Red Iron Ore" tune. A bark built to the maximum dimensions allowed by the Welland Canal locks, the canaller *Twilight* was owned by Dunn and Cummings of Oswego, New York, in the late 1860s and 1870s. Oswego's Sam Moran, mentioned in the last verse, captained the vessel in the iron ore trade. This song was obtained in the summer of 1933 from John S. Parsons of Oswego, who learned it "many years ago from local sailors."

She's an iron ore vessel, a vessel of fame,
She sails from Oswego and the *Twilight*'s her name.
She trades to Superior where the stormy winds blow,
Bound away on the *Twilight* for ore we go.

Now the *Twilight* has left the old Cleveland pier
And the boys and the girls, they give us a cheer
Saying, "There's the bark *Twilight*, her canvas all set,
May she have pleasant weather from here to Marquette."

Her course west-by-north with the wind in her tail,
We head for the rivers and crack on the sail.
And that afternoon e'er we raised the bar light
A tug took our line and we towed through the night.

We got a good slant up Lake Huron's shore,
And we shaped her a course to the place called Detour.
Off Saginaw Bay with a fair wind we sailed
Past Thunder Bay Island and the False Presque Isle.

We made the north shore, dropped our hook in the pass,
And then to the *Walker* our line was made fast.
We passed the encampment, Sugar Island our lee,
And then towed into the locks at Sault Ste. Marie.

The tug dropped our line well out in the bay
And then on Superior we made our own way.
With our ice-rail awash and our storm canvas set,
The *Twilight* next morning hove into Marquette.

We then made our way to an iron ore dock
Where they lowered their chutes and down thundered the rock,
For six hundred tons of red iron ore,
'Twas all we could carry and fifty tons more.

Then down in her hold, we all had to go,
With shovels and spades to trim her just so.
We cursed the red ore and the town of Marquette
And some of the boys are a'cursing them yet.

Now we're out on the lake and my two hands are sore
From pushing a wheelbarrow, and I'll do it no more.

I'm humpbacked from shoveling, so listen to my roar
When we get to Cleveland, I'll shake the red ore.

Now the *Twilight* is booming down Superior again
The wind from the south with showers of rain.
We skirted Grand Island and then Grand Marais
And next day dropped our hook in deep Whitefish Bay.

Then again the tug *Walker*, she came alongside
We heaved up our anchor and away we did slide.
The *Walker* and *Twilight* through the locks did go down
With the *W. S. Lyons* of Black River town.

We plowed down Lake Huron with the wind from the west
The *Twilight* was smoking and doing her best
We raced the whole fleet across Saginaw Bay
Until our main-topsail was carried away.

Then, one day on Lake Erie we saw a pleasant sight
Right over our bow was the old Cleveland light.
Now the *Twilight*'s made fast and our trip's at an end
And we're off to the Merchant our coin for to spend.
And when it's all gone and we're sick of the land,
We'll be looking again for Captain Moran.

A Trip on the *George C. Finney*

Another evolution of "The Red Iron Ore" led to "A Trip on the *George C. Finney*," a song that wasn't about an ore boat at all, but a three-masted, schooner-rigged canaller engaged in the general freight trade. In the 1860s and 1870s, the 300-gross-ton *Finney* shipped large quantities of general freight out of its home port of Oswego, New York, to Upper Lakes ports, receiving prairie-state grain in return. These fragments evidently describe a vessel involved in that trade, as well as the preparations necessary to squeeze through the locks of the Welland Canal, called "the ditch" in this song. The *Finney* sank with all hands and a full cargo of wheat in Lake Erie in a mid-November storm in 1891. John S. Parsons dictated these stanzas at Oswego, New York, in mid-August 1933.

Come all you bold sailors who follow the Lakes,
And in a canaller your living do make.
I'll sing you a song of the winds and the seas,
Of a trip up the Lakes, and I hope it will please.

Oh, the *Finney* is lying now at the salt dock,
And the boys and the girls on their deck they do flock;
They give us a cheer when away we must go—
Bound away to Chicago the *Finney* must go.

We arrive at Dalhousie, and our work is begun,
We heave up our jibboom and our anchors take in;
We unship our catheads, our bowsprit also,
We've boarded our boat, through the ditch we must tow.

We towed all that night, and all the next day,
Until we reached Allenburg where a tug there did lay.
The tug *Minnie Battle,* she took us in tow,
    And out in Lake Erie she then let us go.
. . . .
Now the *Finney* is booming up the Lake Huron shore,
We shaped her a course as we'd oft done before;
Through Saginaw Bay with a fair wind we sailed,
Past Thunder Bay Island and the False Presque Isle.
. . . .
Now the *Finney*'s in Chicago, made fast stem and stern,
We'll go to Pete Kemmer's and spin a long yarn.
Here's a health to Jack Preston, who gave us a treat
For arriving in Chicago ahead of the fleet.

The Old Mont Line

As steam replaced sail, shippers rushed to convert fleets to this more dependable, economical form of propulsion. The fastest and cheapest conversion was to strip away most of a schooner's rigging—it slowed loading and unloading anyway—and to hitch one or more hulls behind a steam tug. Sometimes a little sail was left to catch some assistance from the wind. In this way, one tug could tow several stripped-down schooners at a time, like so many geese on a string.

    One of the most familiar strings was the Old Mont Line: the *Montmorency, Montcalm, Montpelier, Monticello,* and *Republic.* In their youth, they had been schooners on Lake Ontario. In their later years they were barges towed by the tug *Niagara.* In the employ of M. F. Merrick of Detroit, the Old Mont Line brought copper and iron south from Michigan's Upper Peninsula and coal north from Lake Erie.

    The song shows strong contempt for the smoke-belching steam tug and for changing times that had stripped the white-winged schooners of their rigging and their dignity. Captain F. W. Elliott of Fairport, Ohio, said in an interview on September 5, 1933, that he wrote the song with some crewmen one tedious day. "While draggin' along up Lake Huron and everybody grumbling, someone suggested that we ought to get up a song, and all agreed, but no one could think up an opening line." Still bored, and stuck for a line, Elliott said, he gazed astern at the string of barges behind him. The first few lines just popped into his head, on a tune similar to that of the familiar "Timber Drogher *Bigler*" (see chapter 6).

The Old Mont Line

Murdock, Score No. 10

Come gath-er 'round me, lads, and I'll sing you a lit-tle song Of a

barge trip up the Lakes, and I'll not de-tain you long. Oh,

may-be you don't be-lieve me, lads, and may-be you think I lie, But

ship in this star-va-tion tow and you'll see the same as I.

Come gather 'round me lads, and I'll sing you a little song
Of a barge trip up the Lakes, and I'll not detain you long.

    Oh, maybe you don't believe me, lads, and maybe you think I lie,
    But ship in this starvation tow and you'll see the same as I.

There's one Mont, two Monts, four Monts in a row,
And you come to the old *Republic,* the end of the rotten tow.

We dragged up both the rivers, 'twas all the tug could take,
And then we passed Port Huron and were out upon the lake.

And when upon Lake Huron, the wind came steady and strong,
We spread our wings into the wind, and the *Niagara* forged along.

We crawled up the St. Mary's and finally reached the lock,
And then upon Superior, our tubs began to rock.

And when we got to Houghton, near nine o'clock one night,
The men put up a hell of a kick and damn near had a fight.

'Twas all about our shoveling dirt, we wanted some extra pay,
The Old Man said, "You can go to Hell! I'll pay you off today."

We spent our dough at all the bars, and then in port there came
Another vessel from below, and we shipped right out again.

Loss of the *City of Green Bay*

The schooner *City of Green Bay* broke up at Evergreen Point, near South Haven, Lake Michigan, on October 3, 1887, with a load of iron ore. Six of the seven aboard died. This is abridged from the version found in a scrapbook owned by Captain Charles C. Allers of Beaver Island.

Since you ask Caruso for it.
    Friends and brothers lend an ear
To a poet's humble version
    Of a sad occurrence here.

Of the loss of life and vessel,
    Stranded on our lovely beach,
A proud schooner went to pieces
    When almost within our reach.

Her cargo was that dreaded ore
    That oft in its transportation
Has kept full many ships before
    From their ports of destination.

Sailing down from Escanaba,
    In a gale, hove to, she springs a leak!
Now they needs must run before it
    And on the beach their safety seek!

They hoist the sail and let her drive;
    No doubt that there was a prayer
To Him who sees the soul's distress
    On the brink of dark despair!

With the signal of distress aloft;
    From man to man the alarming cry,
As to the water's brink they rush,
    "Help! Oh, help! Or sailors die!"

"Man the lifeboats! See! She strikes
    Hard on the treacherous bar!"
O'er her, giant seas are breaking,
    Stripped of canvas, every spar!

Scores and hundreds gather quickly,
    Almost breathless on the shore
Where the seas are rolling madly,
    And dash and break with sullen roar.

"See, the men are in the rigging!
    Why is not the surfboat here?"
Hearts on shore are palpitating,
    Faces blanch with mortal fear!

Rescue fails! See, there falls
    Masts and rigging in the sea!
God have mercy on those sailors
    Sinking to eternity!

Steamers and sailboats competed for cargo at the Sarnia, Ontario, lumber docks. The *Sephie* figures in two songs: "The *Sephie*'s First Trip" and "We Leaves Detroit Behind Us." Dossin Great Lakes Museum.

Chapter 6

Songs of the Lumber Trade

The lumbering industry in the Upper Lakes region hit its height in the 1870s and 1880s, when enormous quantities of shingles, tanning bark, and lumber rode in sailing vessels from mills at the mouths of the tributary rivers to market. Much of it moved on timber droghers. Bluff-bowed, boxy, and specially equipped to transport squared logs, Great Lakes timber droghers were inelegant vessels. Most were two-masted canallers with nearly vertical hulls built to the maximum dimensions that could pass through the old Welland Canal locks linking Lakes Erie and Ontario. To squeeze such vessels through the locks the crew might have to lift up specially hinged davits, bring in spars, and crank up the drop keel.

For loading, timber droghers generally had four stern ports, two on either side of the stern post, one above the other. The top ports opened flush with the deck; the lower pair opened into the hold. Some droghers had bow ports as well. For loading, sailors dropped the ports open, lowered ramps into the water, and hauled the logs aboard with a line fastened to the capstan in the bow. Other ramps or "brows" led from the ports into the hold, where the mate directed sailors as they stowed timbers. Once they had loaded the vessel, the crew shut the ports and caulked them watertight for the voyage. To pack as much lumber aboard the vessels as possible, workers often trimmed sawlogs into "waneys," with the butt ends squared and the smaller ends often left in the original round of the tree with the bark stripped off.

Most products of the forests bordering Lake Michigan went to Chicago and then westward by train for the homes and farms of the treeless prairies. Lumber camps along the other four Great Lakes sent great quantities of timbers by drogher, in stripped-down schooners that had been converted to barges, or in huge rafts to Tonawanda, New York, for transshipment down the Erie Canal, or to Garden and Carlton Islands at the foot of Lake Ontario for rafting down the St. Lawrence River.

The Timber Drogher *Bigler*

James M. Jones built the schooner *John Bigler*, 344 gross tons, at Detroit in 1866 for J. Currier, primarily to carry waneys from the Upper Lakes to the head of the

St. Lawrence River. From there, logs were rafted downriver to Quebec and salt water. The *Bigler*'s career ended when it foundered off Marquette, Michigan, in 1884.

William Head of Picton, Ontario, sailed aboard the *Bigler* for several seasons and said that at 126 feet long by 26 feet by 10 feet, the *Bigler* fit snugly through the old Welland locks and had "the lines of a shoe box." He added that the *Bigler* had an extra long jibboom and carried more than the usual amount of canvas for a two-master, but its blunt bow made it slow, clumsy, and "a man-killer to steer. With a good wind, she'd roll up half the lake before her and make a great commotion, but little speed." While Head was in its crew, the *Bigler* generally carried coal up the Lakes and squared timbers down from Lake Superior to Tonawanda at the head of the Erie Canal. "Some sticks of pine loaded at Marquette and Grand Marais were so big—four- or five- or six-foot-square butts and twenty feet long and not a knot in them—that we couldn't get them through the ports and had to hoist them on deck, over the side."

In the trip this song narrates, the *Bigler* has temporarily entered the late-season grain trade. The Lakes followed the seasons—open in the warm months, shut in the cold—and cargoes changed with the seasons as well. Timber was plentiful at the beginning of the season, having been felled throughout the winter, skidded on snow to the riverbanks, and floated down the rivers on the spring melt. Late in the summer, new grain was ready for market. Wages for the short grain season ran high, and so did the spirits of the men who had to move it. The song is a good-natured account of the clumsy drogher plodding along from Milwaukee to Buffalo in the company of the swift grain clippers.

The *Bigler*. Courtesy of the Historical Collections of the Great Lakes.

The Timber Drougher *Bigler*

Walton, Score No. 28

Come all you jolly sailors and listen to my song, It's but a few short verses and will not detain you long. In Milwaukee in October I chanced to get a site In the timber drougher *Bigler* a-hailing from Detroit.

Chorus:
Watch her! Catch her! Jump up on her juber-ju,
Give 'er the sheet and let 'er howl, we're the boys to put 'er through.

Come all you jolly sailors and listen to my song,
It's but a few short verses and will not detain you long.
In Milwaukee in October I chanced to get a site
In the timber drogher *Bigler* a'hailing from Detroit.

    Watch her! Catch her! Jump up on her juberju,
    Give 'er the sheet and let 'er howl, we're the boys to put 'er through,
    You should've seen 'er howling, the wind a'blowin' free,
    On our passage down to Buffalo from Milwaukee.

It was on a Sunday morning, about the hour of ten,
The *Robert Emmet* towed us out into Lake Michigan.
We set sail where she left us, in the middle of the fleet,
The wind was from the south'rd, an' we had to give er sheet.

The wind chopped 'round to sou'-sou'-west, an' blew both fresh and strong,
And plowing through Lake Michigan the *Bigler* she rolled on.
And far before her foaming bow the silver spray did fling,
With every inch of canvas set, her course was "wing and wing."

The wind it hauled ahead, my boys, as we reached the Manitous;
Two dollars and a half a day just suited the *Bigler*'s crew.
From here unto the Beavers, we steered her full 'n' by;
An' we laid 'er to the wind as close as she would lie.

We made Skillagalee and Wobble Shanks, the entrance to the Straits,
And might have passed the fleet, had they hove to and wait,
But we drove 'em all before us the prettiest you ever saw
Clear out into Lake Huron through the Straits of Mackinac.

We made the light at False Presque Isle, and then we boomed away;
Courses and tops'ls straining for the isle of Thunder Bay.

The wind it hauled 'round, we laid on 'er starb'rd tack,
With a good lookout ahead, m' boys, for the light of Point Aback.

We made the light and kept in sight of Michigan's east shore,
A'booming for the river as we'd often done before.
But where's the schooner fleet we raced all through the night?
Can that be sails ahead, just glimmering in sight?

We plowed on down Lake Huron, the wind was steady and fast,
Port Sanilac's off to starb'rd, the river's ahead at last.
And when off Gratiot Light our anchor we let go,
Till the *Sweepstakes* hove in sight, and took the *Bigler* in tow.

The *Sweepstakes* towed eight schooners, an' all of us fore 'n' aft,
She towed us down the St. Clair and stuck us on the Flats.
She parted the *Hunter*'s towline in trying to give relief,
An' the *Bigler* smashed head-on into the yawl of the *Maple Leaf*.

She towed us down and left us outside the river light,
Lake Erie for to wander and the blusterin' winds to fight.
The wind being fresh and fair, we paddled our own canoe,
Her nose points o'er the dummy, we're hell-bent for Buffalo.

We made the "Eau," flew by Long Point, the wind was a'blowin' free;
We howled along the Canada shore, Port Colborne on our lee.
What light is that ahead that grows as we draw near?
It's like a blazing star, it's the light on Buffalo pier.

An' now, my bully lads, we're in Buffalo port at last,
Under Rood and Smith's Elevator, the *Bigler* she's made fast.
An' in Tommy Doyle's saloon we'll let the bottle pass,
For we are jolly shipmates, and we'll drink a social glass.

An' now my song is ended, I hope it pleases you:
Let's drink a health to the *Bigler,* her officers and crew.
I hope she sails for many a fall in command of Cal McKee,
Between the ports of Buffalo and Mil-wau-kee.

 Carl Joys of Milwaukee sang this version of the popular song in the summer of 1932. At that time he was in his late seventies and had sailed the Lakes for over half a century. When asked where he had learned the song, Joys said, "Milwaukee sailors know that song when they are born." Several other retired sailors recalled the complete song with remarkable similarity. Earl Clifton Beck and other folklore collectors found the song in the Michigan logging camps as well.
 Authorship most frequently is credited to "Billy Clark of Buffalo." However, John W. Green insisted that his uncle and fellow Beaver Islander, Peter O'Donnell, composed it and many other songs as well.

William Murray of White Lake, Michigan, sang a variant line of the chorus as "Jump up on her jib-bu-boom." Captain C. D. Secord of Cleveland gave the second line, "Look out for her old jib-boom." Captain Charles Morrison of St. Joseph, Michigan, substituted "the schooner *Buffalo*" for *Bigler* when he sang. Captain Martin Johnson of Traverse City, Michigan, recalled the following chorus and stanza from a song about an ore carrier:

Watch her! Catch her! Jump up on her ju-ber-ju,
Give her the sheet and let her go, we're the boys can put her through.
You ought to hear her howling, her course was down the shore;
She's bound down to Cleveland with nine hundred tons of ore.

Now we are in Cleveland, tied up 'longside the pier,
An' the boys are down on Main Street, a'drinkin' lager beer.

Without a doubt, this was the most popular song among schoonermen, and most seemed to know at least parts of it. The song is peppered with jargon and slang, so a few explanations are in order. A "site," as used in the first verse, means a job crewing on a vessel. The order "Give 'er the sheet" means to allow the sheets—the lines that control the booms—to run out. This permits the sails to swing out nearly to right angles with the keel to take full advantage of a following wind. "Courses" are the large, heavy sails immediately above the deck. They are said to be "wing 'n' wing" when the foresail is extended at near right angles to the keel over one side of the vessel and the mainsail is extended out over the opposite side. A sailing vessel is being steered "full and by" when it is tacking into the wind and the vessel's direction is as close to that of the wind as possible with its sails still full and pulling. The wind is said to be "fresh and free" when it is relatively strong and blowing from aft. The "dummy" was a decommissioned light in western Lake Erie.

"Mackinac" is always pronounced to rhyme with "saw." Only foreigners and Chicago yachtsmen pronounced it to rhyme with "lack." Point Aback is sailor lingo for Pointe aux Barques, another French name, and it is at the northern tip of the thumb on Michigan's mitten-shaped Lower Peninsula. The St. Clair Flats, often called just "The Flats," are the shallow, silt-filled delta of the river which, before extensive dredging, frequently mired vessels. Finally, the "Eau" is sailor shorthand for Rondeau, Ontario.

The song's biggest secret is in the first line of its chorus. "Watch her! Catch her!" is clear enough. Those are warnings from the officer on duty to the wheelsman and the crew to alert and not allow the vessel to get into difficulties when coming about, or changing tack. The mystery is "juberju." Its context seems to indicate it is part of the vessel, yet no part of a sailing vessel is generally known by that name. Loudon Wilson suggested that this may be a corruption of another French word, "gibre," the extension of the stem or knee piece of a vessel to which the bowsprit is attached. On some vessels, bow rails ran all the way to the gibre, giving sailors a foothold. From there, or from foot ropes, they maneuvered the standing jib and other headsails to help catch more wind to bring a sluggish vessel about as it changed tack. Another theory holds that the expression was a hyperbolic description of the wheelsman's efforts to hold the blunt-bowed *Bigler*'s course. This reasoning says that the phrase was borrowed from a dance song of the day:

> Juba dance and Juba sing
> Juba cut dat pigeon wing, Juba! Juba!

The widely sung "The *Bigler*" gave rise to additions, modifications, and whole new incarnations. Ex-schoonerman Carl Joys of Milwaukee said singers sometimes inserted this stanza next to the last:

> When we received our pay from Skipper Cal McKee,
> With our dunnage we jumped ashore, but not to go on a spree.
> For "Dave and Mose" we steered, as well you may suppose,
> And Davy rigged us up with a bang-up suit of clothes.

Dave and Mose Garson of Rochester, New York, operated a small clothing store near the Buffalo waterfront and catered especially to sailors.

The Stone Scow

The master of a large steamship sailing out of Cleveland (who asked to have his name withheld) sang this song about a stone-hauling scow to the tune of "The *Bigler*":

> I was two weeks at Cleveland
> When I chanced to get a site,
> And I shipped aboard a damned old scow
> A'hailing from Detrite.
>
> > Watch her! Catch her!
> > Jump up on her ju-bu-ju,
> > Give her the sheet and let her go,
> > We're the boys to push her through.
>
> We towed out of Cleveland
> And we had to give her sheet;
> The wind was from the sou'west,
> And against it we had to beat.
>
> But when we got to Avon Point
> The wind it hauled nor'west,
> And to beat it to Black River,
> We had to do our best.
>
> The captain was on the quarterdeck
> Just to see her foam;
> We were bound to Kelly's Island
> To get a load of stone.
>
> But when we got to Black River
> You ought to seen her reach!
> Instead of going through the piers
> We slapped her on the beach.

The Mules That Walked Our Fo'c'sle Deck

Before machine power, timber droghers often sailed with a team of horses or mules on the bow deck for hauling the heavy, water-soaked timbers aboard or working the capstan to weigh anchor, hoist the larger sails, or tow the vessel through canals. When engines replaced livestock they were called, appropriately, "donkey engines."

James Dix of Kingston, Ontario, singer of this song, said he shipped as a "boy" on local droghers in the late 1860s, became a vessel master in 1873 at the age of twenty-four, and continued sailing as long as the work lasted. Dix said that drogher life was a "man killer" and that few sailors would stay with a vessel for more than one trip. They, and other sailors, referred to droghers as "horse-manure boats," and the men aboard as "horse-manure sailors." Only they didn't say "manure." Dix said that the horses and mules became "good sailors," and when at sea they would shift tail-to-wind whenever an order was given to tack ship, and responded to the orders "quill up," "heave away," or "belay" as well. Dix said that "a sailor from Buffalo named Clark" who made a trip with him in the 1880s composed the song. Other parts were collected from S. C. Jacobson, ex-schoonerman and lightkeeper at Waukegan, Illinois; Alfred Thomas of Toronto; Al Hare of Port Credit, Ontario; and William Head of Picton, Ontario.

The mules that walked our fo'c'sle deck,
    They were two mules of fame;
They sailed the Lakes for many a year,
    Napoleon and Bones their names.

Our cabin boy was the caps'n mate,
    The mules the caps'n crew;
Their ears were long, their heels were light,
    But sailoring they knew.

They'd weigh the anchor, kedge the ship,
    And hoist the flowing sail;
But like all sailormen ashore,
    They sometimes there would fail.

Old Bones was long and lank and slow,
    His ears flopped when he walked;
Napoleon was not near his size,
    And he kept his long ears cocked.

They came aboard at Calvin's yard,
    We anchored them in the bow;
And set our course for the Upper Lakes
    With all speed the wind allowed.

As we went rolling up the lake
    Into a nor'west breeze,
Napoleon stood with his legs apart,
    Old Bones was at his ease.

And every time the mate would shout:
    "Stand by to come about!"
They'd shift their tails to the weather rail
    Without ever lookin' out.

Then one day upon our starboard tack,
    Port Dalhousie did loom,
We all stood by upon the deck
    And topped the long jibboom.

Our mules we led o'er the landward rail
    To tow us through the locks,
But they decided they'd rather sail,
    And stood there like a rock.

The mule-boy beat old Bones and swore,
    But nothing could prevail;
A canaller jumped up on the bank
    And twisted Napoleon's tail.

Napoleon "ee-onked" and dropped his head,
    He seemed to be in pain—
The canaller straightway lost his grip,
    And landed in the drain.

They wound him with his halter rope,
    Old Bones just stood and snored;
Napoleon smiled and seemed to purr
    When we brought them back aboard.

We towed up through the twenty locks,
    The Old Man had to pay;
Then with jibboom set and sails aloft,
    We again were under way.

We rolled along to Pelee Point,
    Where a tug took us in tow;
We were the last in a line of craft
    Up the rivers for to go.

Four schooners towing in a line,
    We were a pleasant sight;
But sailors must have no time off
    They might get drunk or fight.

We scrubbed and scraped and swabbed the deck;
    Our mules they were no help—
When all was cleared they'd hump their backs,
    And then relieve themselves.

The fo'c'sle deck by the post was loose
    An' far from sanitary,
Napoleon had his chosen spot,
    And he was quite contrary.

All day we towed, then Gratiot Light,
    We were out upon the lake;
We got a slant up Huron shore,
    And headed for the Straits.

When we made the Cheboygan port
    Where a cargo did await,
We cleared our hold of the upbound freight
    Squared timbers for to take.

We dropped our fore and after hooks,
    And opened our stern ports wide;
The raftsmen brought the timbers up
    And floated them 'longside.

Napoleon then looked 'round the scene,
    The first time on our trip;
He saw the timbers floating 'round,
    And said, "Let's load the ship!"

The loading waneys squeaked and squawked.
    And made some doleful sounds;
Our mules just thought it was love talk
    As they walked the caps'n 'round.

They walked the caps'n 'round and 'round,
    In calm, and sun 'n' storm;
They walked the deck ten thousand miles,
    Where a splintered path they'd worn.

We filled the hold, we piled the deck,
    Then hauled out in the lake;
Old Bones, you are a shipmate true,
    But Napoleon should be mate!

The *Jennie P. King*

The *Jennie P. King* is said to have carried the name of a well-known friend to sailors. She operated a number of comfort stations in various Lower Lake ports in the 1870s. The vessel could be identified not only by its nameboards but also by the carved figurehead, a woman's leg extended under the bowsprit. The model was said to have been Jennie herself.

    The line "To ride the halyards down" refers to sailors' practice of going aloft to the crosstrees and swinging out on the halyard so that their weight would assist sailors on deck in hoisting the heavy sails. The motley crew aboard seems to have

The lumber hooker *Gilbert Knapp*. Courtesy of the Historical Collections of the Great Lakes.

been characteristic of the slow-going, clumsy timber carriers. Larger, trimmer grain and ore carriers had the pick of the experienced seamen; droghers picked second. The song's reference to beating the schooner *Dispatch* no doubt prompted a laugh, as the only vessel a drogher could outsail was another, even clumsier drogher. The complete song, if it followed the pattern of other trip songs, probably narrated the vessel's journey all the way to its destination, which appears to have been Buffalo.

Norman "Beachie" MacIvor recited the first two stanzas aboard his harbor sightseeing boat in the summer of 1933, but he had no notion of when he had learned them. A few weeks later, the second stanza, virtually as MacIvor had given it, and the chorus and last four lines came from lightkeeper Walter "Doc" Thomas and his old shipmate "Billy" Churchill at Bronte, Ontario, as they prompted and corrected each other in Thomas's waterfront bachelor shack. Later in the summer, William Head of Picton, Ontario, who had sailed the Lakes for twenty years and fished them thirty more, supplied the remainder.

Now sit you down beside me,
    And I'll sing you a little song,
And if I do not please you,
    I'll not detain you long.
I shipped in Tonawanda
    Some timber for to bring,
From Toledo at a dollar a day
    On the barque the *Jennie P. King.*

    Hurray, boys, hurray
    Come, let us join and sing;
        We'll drink a health to old Ned Irving
    And the crew of the *Jennie P. King.*

The crew jumped in the riggin'
    And up aloft did run
To ride the halyards down,
    To see them it was fun.
Each man worked with a will,
    And soon we spread our wings,
And beat the schooner *Dispatch,*
    On the barque the *Jennie P. King.*

Upon this timber drogher
    We had a curious crew:
We had Uncle Sam's sea fighters,
    And Garibaldi's too,
An Irishman from nowhere
    Who could dance and sing,
And shellbacks from the ocean
    On the barque the *Jennie P. King.*

And on this timber drogher
    Were Canadians too, I think,
And Dutch from Tonawanda
    Who like their lager drink.
We had men from other countries
    Who like to take a fling—
A jolly crew we had
    On the barque the *Jennie P. King.*

The lad who tended the horses
    He jabbered all the day,
And whether man or monkey
    No one could ever say.
Our cook came from the *Erie*
    We thought her just the thing,
She fed the crew, and officers too
    On the barque the *Jennie P. King.*

. . . .

Now we're well down Lake Erie,
    Point Abino we clear,
Our bowsprit points to Buffalo,
    Toledo's in our rear.

A Trip on the *Lavindy*

Advancing age sent countless Great Lakes chanteys to sailors' graves, and it almost got this one, too. In the summer of 1934, J. Sylvester "Ves" Ray of Port Huron professed authorship of this song about the schooner *Lavindy,* a small, shallow-draft, two-masted lumber hooker of 125 gross tons. Built in 1863 at Allegan, Michigan, about twenty miles up the Kalamazoo River, the boat sailed for half a century. Despite its long career, it seldom ventured from the Lake Michigan lumber trade between Chicago and Michigan mill towns at the mouths of the rivers that carried snowmelt and sawlogs to the big lake. Ray had begun sailing as a boy in the late 1860s, and he retired after many seasons as master, only after most sails had been swept from the Lakes.

    Ray said he had "fetched my own name" into the song, but that it had been more than forty years since he had given the song much thought. Consequently, all he could recall at first was the fragment with his name:

> This song it was made while we was under way
> By a curly headed sailor by the name of "Ves" Ray.

The other verses came back to Ray later, so he dictated them to his friend and ex-sailor William J. Small, also of Port Huron, who wrote them down in the summer of 1934. The song describes the *Lavindy* taking a cargo of lumber down below, probably to Tonawanda at the foot of Lake Erie, and returning light, or empty, for supplies at Port Huron. Two men quit the ship there, so Ray and a friend signed on. Their trip up Lake Huron, through the Straits of Mackinac, and southward on Lake Michigan to the entrance of Hamlin Lake, just north of Ludington, Michigan, was uneventful except for a stormbound night in the harbor at South Manitou Island.

Hamlin Lake is really the swollen lower reaches of the Big Sable River immediately back of the sand dunes known as Big Sable Point. Sleeping Bear and Old Betsie are dunes farther north along the Michigan shore.

Ray said that the *Lavindy* had some good singers who helped him make up the song on the leg from Hamlin Lake to Chicago. It went after the melody of the widely popular "The Cumberland's Crew," a Civil War ballad of the Confederate ironclad *Merrimac*'s victory over the Union *Cumberland.* After the *Lavindy* tied up in the Chicago River, the crew went to a Clark Street saloon and drank for free for having written a new song.

A Trip on the *Lavindy*

Murdock, Score No. 12

Come all you young sail-ors and land-lub-bers too, An'

lis-ten to a song that I'll sing to you; It's a-

bout the La-vin-dy, the schoon-er of fame, Like-

wise her bold cap-tain, Bil-ly Park-er by name.

Come all you young sailors and landlubbers too,
An' listen to a song that I'll sing to you;
It's about the *Lavindy*, the schooner of fame,
Likewise her bold captain, Billy Parker by name.

We set sail on a Saturday from Port Huron dock,
All hands to the halyards they quickly did flock;
"Yo-hee!" and "Hi-ho!" the mate he did bawl,
An' we soon spread our wings, gaff tops'ls an' all.

The tug dropped our line, an' we heaved it on board,

With the wind on our quarter, up Lake Huron we roared;
The wind it was fair till off Thunder Bay
When we hauled 'er up close and for Mackinac lay.

We tacked through the Straits in the dead of the night,
The sky it was cloudy but the beacons showed bright;
Tall schooners and steamboats we left on our lee,
As we rounded the Shanks and Skillagalee.

All murky and red the sun did arise,
The wind backed to sou'west, and stormy the skies;
We soon doused our tops'ls, oh Lord, how it blew!
So we dropped our big hook under South Manitou.

We hove up next morning 'mid dozens of sail,
An' as we sailed out we gave 'em a hail.
Our course was sou'west, the wind blowing fair,
An' when the sun rose we was off Sleeping Bear.

Then o'er our port bow Old Betsie did loom,
We kept well to seaward with plenty of room.
When we passed the Big Sable we gave a loud cheer,
And soon were alongside of Hamlin Lake pier.

We made fast in Hamlin at a harbor dock,
An' Pelton's whole crew around us did flock:
They cursed and they swore an' the rough boards did fly;
They soon filled our hold and the deck they piled high.

Now we're again on the big lake in a record time,
So I will conclude and finish my rhyme.
This song it was made while we was under way
By a curly headed sailor by the name of "Ves" Ray.

Now you can ease your main sheet an' keep her sou'-sou'-west.
Aye, sir, sou'-sou'-west.

On the Schooner *Hercules*

This passage song narrates a voyage in 1891 from Sarnia, Ontario, at the foot of Lake Huron northward into the lake, around the head of the Bruce Peninsula into Georgian Bay and fifty miles eastward to Parry Sound for the last lumber cargo of the season. It evidently was written by crewman Jimmie McQuarie. John "Red" McDonald—sailor, singer, and fisherman of Goderich, Ontario—said that he served on the *Hercules* in the early 1890s after it had been rebuilt and rerigged as a three-masted schooner for the Georgian Bay lumber trade. He recalled the accompanying stanzas in the summer of 1949. That same summer, Captain Joseph

Glass, in his late eighties, said that a handwritten copy had been tacked up on the schooner's cabin wall for a number of seasons.

Verses make reference to the extreme hazard of navigating the island-strewn waters of Georgian Bay and the great depth of isolated Parry Sound.

On the eighth day of November
    In the year of ninety-one,
The schooner *Hercules* set sail
    For the port of Parry Sound.

We towed from Sarnia's lumber dock
    Into the river wide;
We dropped the tug above the Point,
    The stormy lake to ride.

The wind nor'west and blowing strong,
    Awash our starboard rail;
And foaming seas broke o'er her bow,
    And pulling every sail.

We steered a course of north-by-east,
    And steered it good and true;
We logged one hundred fifty miles,
    And then we hove her to.

The wind hauled north, down came the dark
    With cold and snow and hail;
Our captain being a prudent man
    Had ordered shortened sail.

We reefed her down, quite snug all 'round,
    We were nearing the rocky land;
We laid her on her starboard tack—
    Nor'westward we did stand.

The wind slacked off at twelve that night,
    And clearer grew the sky;
We brought her round on the other tack
    As close as she would lie.

Cove Island light then came in sight,
    And Curry's house on shore;
We steered a course of east-sou'-east,
    And for Cabot's Head we bore.

From Cabot's Head we made Red Rock,
    The entrance to the Sound;
And there let go her big anchor
    To keep from goin' aground.

We rode at anchor through a blow—
    Gave her forty fathoms of chain;
Then exercised our muscles
    By heaving it home again.

The captain then did go ashore,
    With the boys of his hungry crew;
The cook, he had to tend the ship
    And eat his own cold stew.

Then back on board with bellies full
    Of coffee, pork, and cakes;
We pumped her out and cleared the deck
    Rough lumber for to take.

Our captain's name was Joseph Glass,
    Our mate was Johnnie Bain,
And our sailors in rotation
    I'll now mention by name:

There was Frankie Knight and Hector McKay,
    And Desmond Gordon, too;
And Jimmie McQuarie from Michigan
    Who now does sing to you.

And now our trip is over, boys,
    We're in Sarnia town once more;
The sailors have packed their dunnage bags
    And safely gone ashore.

May fortune rest on Captain Glass,
    And the men of his gallant crew—
We'll bid adieu to the *Hercules*
    Till the spring of ninety-two.

The Old Barge *Oliver Cromwell*

A. P. Gallino, "captain" of the vessel for the trip described in this song, was living in a shack at the foot of Quay Street on the riverbank in Port Huron on July 5, 1933. In response to a query about old songs, he suggested a meeting at "Billy Small's" that evening with the promise, "I'll word you the song." Promptly at the hour agreed, he appeared at the Quay Street office of ex-sailor, ex–Coast Guardsman William J. Small's wrecking business near the Military Street bridge. With a few preliminaries, Gallino launched into his song. Small helped him sing and talk it to the end. He thought there were more stanzas, but neither man "could mind them." Gallino said crewman Hank Stone composed most of the song to another song's tune during the trip and finished it after they got back to Port Huron. Despite the old sailing vessel's dilapidated condition, the crewmen, "real canvas sailors," saw themselves as superior to the "country louts" on smoke-belching "cinder tubs."

With good-natured exaggeration, this song narrates a fruitless voyage for the lumber barge *Oliver Cromwell*. Pulled about by the nose behind tow barges until it finally was wrecked on Sand Beach, Michigan, in October 1888, the *Cromwell* labored under the same indignities in its declining years that many vessels, nobly born, suffered in the transition from sail to steam. Built at Buffalo in 1853, the *Oliver Cromwell* bore the name of the seventeenth-century lord protector of England. In its fourth season on the Lakes, the schooner suffered a collision in the

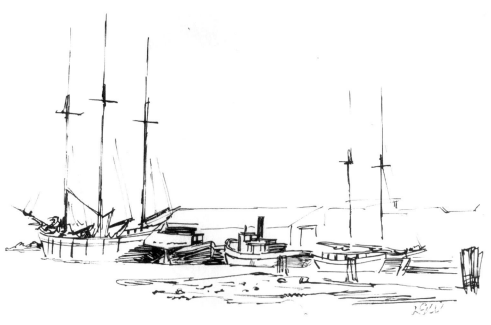

Vessels at the Ludington, Michigan, mill. Courtesy of the Historical Collections of the Great Lakes.

Straits of Mackinac and sank to the bottom. There it slept for nearly fifteen years until it was raised, rebuilt, and converted to a lumber barge.

In this song, the *Oliver Cromwell* rides at the end of a towline from Port Huron, Michigan, to Bay City on the Saginaw River. Failing to obtain a load there, the barge continued under its own sails about fifty miles further up Lake Huron to Tawas City. After further delays and much pumping to keep the leaky old barge afloat, a "puller," the tow barge *Lowell*, fetched the barge back to Port Huron.

On November first in eighty-nine from Port Huron we set sail;
The wind blew from the north'ard a sweet and pleasant gale.
The *Lowell* was our puller, a staunch and noble craft,
She was followed by the *Cromwell* with three before the mast.

    Oh, the *Cromwell*, she's a goer, you can bet your gold on that.
    She leads them all before the wind 'n' she's hell upon the tack.

With Stone at the wheel, his eyes fixed on Dunn,
Keep clear of her snoot, my boys, How the old tub can run!

Our captain's name was Gallino, our mate was Mister Dunn;
We took the lead of all the fleet, you bet that she can run.
When we arrived at Bay City, no load there could we get,
So we made fast to a boom, my boys, to keep out of the wet.

They kept us all a'working from morning until night
For fear we'd go ashore, my boys, and get a little tight.
With washing and a'scrubbing 'n' a working down the spars,
But we stood it all quite pleasantly like jolly old tars.

On the eighth day came the news, "Make ready for a start,
And shape your course for Tawas, get around, my boys, be smart.
Take in your lines both fore 'n' aft, get everything in place
For the *Cromwell*'s not afraid, the storms and wind to face."

Oh, our officers are heroes, 'n' our crew are of the best
'N' if we meet a watery grave, thank God, we'll have a rest!
It's long we lay in Tawas Bay a'rolling in the seas
'N' a'bending to the pumps, my boys, to keep the *Cromwell* free.

Then all at once, to our delight, the *Lowell*, she hove in sight
With Captain Hagan forward, it brought us much delight.
"Heave up your anchor, lively boys, your towline get in place,
We'll soon be under way again the storms and winds to face."

We crossed the Bay and cleared the Point, the snow was falling fast—
The *Cromwell* didn't fear no storms with good men before the mast.
Our puller *Lowell* we kept in sight all through that rain and snow;
We kept the towline straight, my boys, down Lake Huron for to go.

As we rolled down Michigan's wild shore across the Saginaw Bay
We put the whole lake through our pumps, then Sanilac light we raised.
Fort Gratiot's light then hove in sight as the river we drew near;
'N' we thought of friends and home again 'n' the girls that we love dear.

My song I'll now fetch to a close, 'n' the truth to you I'll tell:
It's never ship on a lumber barge, you might better be in Hell!
Two hours at the wheel, my boys, two hours at the pump,
The rest of the time a'shifting ties, which makes all hands to grunt.

If you want a job where you can shirk, ship on some cinder tub
Where the deckhands are all country louts 'n' the Old Man chews a cud;
But upon the staunch old *Cromwell*, it's only sailors send,
For we are sailors, every one, 'n' here my song will end.

A Trip on the Schooner *Kolfage*

Owner-operator Captain John McDonald, nicknamed "Minister" for the frequency with which he invoked the Lord's name, appreciated a good song even more than he appreciated heartfelt cursing. According to his sailor son, John "Red" McDonald, "The Old Man would damn near give away his schooner for a good song." In this case, the schooner was the *Kolfage*. Not much distinguished the tiny, 93-net-ton lumber hooker *Kolfage* from scores of similar boats that sailed the Great Lakes in the mid-1800s. Not much, that is, except this song. A shallow, scow-built schooner, the *Kolfage* could slip up and down rivers where deeper vessels dared not venture. Such vessels, some said, could sail on as little as a heavy dew. The *Kolfage* had seen more than twenty seasons since it came down the ways at Port Burwell, Ontario, on Lake Erie in 1869.

On this trip, the *Kolfage* stops at Chatham, Ontario, about twenty miles up the Thames River from Lake St. Clair, to load supplies for a Georgian Bay lumber camp. Ready for the tow back out into the lake, but being short of hands, McDonald signed two men, Jack MacCosh and Herb Pettigrew, for the round-trip. "They wasn't no real sailors," said the younger McDonald, "just two men the Old Man picked up to help out. They got enough of sailing on the up trip and wanted to get off. The Old Man cussed them out plenty and wouldn't give them no pay. Then he said to them, 'If you'll make me a good song, you can go.' They went away and came back the next day with this one. . . . He gave them each a dollar extra and tacked the song up in the cabin where it still was when he sold her."

The song tells how the *Kolfage* ran up Lake St. Clair before the wind, racing a steamboat into the "Cut," the dredged channel through the St. Clair Flats. With neither boat giving way to the other, the schooner struck the steamer a glancing blow, turning it aground. Before the crews came to blows, a fresh breeze blew the schooner up the river to Sarnia, where the *Kolfage* became windbound in the bay under Point Edward. The next day, after a tow into Lake Huron, the schooner had an easier race with two slow, bluff-nosed canallers mocked as "Lake Ontario clippers."

"Red" McDonald said he was a member of the crew on the trip described. He supplied these stanzas in the summer of 1934. The same summer, Robert Reid of Red Bay on the lake side of the peninsula said that a copy of the song was on a cabin wall when he purchased the vessel from McDonald. Reid recited it all the way through. When asked about the tune, he replied, "I just use any tune that fits."

> We shipped aboard the *Kolfage* at Chatham, County Kent,
> The fourth day of October, for Johnson's Harbor bent.
> Commanded by McDonald, who always fast times makes,
> Aboard the schooner *Kolfage*, Columbia of the Lakes.
>
> The tug *Vick* took our line at twelve o'clock at night,
> And down the Thames we towed 'mid moonbeams' somber light;

The schooner *John G. Kolfage* races the *Cataract* and the *Vienna.* Courtesy of the Historical Collections of the Great Lakes.

But when on Lake St. Clair, the wind came dead ahead,
We put the big hook out, and all went off to bed.

Next morning we hoisted sail in a fresh wind from the east,
The *Kolfage* plowed the lake through billows white as yeast.
We headed for the Cut with all her sails unfurled,
An' with bending masts we smashed the record of the world.

A steamer hove alongside and we ran her neck and neck
Straight into the Cut, our speed we would not check!
We struck her starboard bow to keep us off the bank,
An' our fenders scrubbed her side as we fetched up with a yank.

Angry words flew thick, their speed they had to check,
We damn near had a fight, every man was on the deck.
We cursed them high and low; they threatened to come aboard,
But the wind hauled to the south, and up the river we roared.

When Sarnia we reached late afternoon that day,
The wind again contrary, we anchored in the bay.
We towed out on the morning about a mile or so
With the *Cataract* and *Vienna* from Lake Ontario.

All three then stripped for action, a race it was to be,
The Lake Ontario clippers claimed the supremacy—
With all our canvas set, we ran north like a steer,
And when that night came on, they were far off in our rear.

Next day we reached Southampton and anchored off the shore
Just inside of the harbor while outside the seas did roar.
And there the schooner *Fulton* inside the harbor we found
In a waterlogged condition and also hard aground.

At dawn we heaved our anchor and hoisted sail once more
For northward up the lake, just off the rocky shore.
We sailed along the Cape before a sou'west breeze,
And ran into a bay among lumber piles and trees.

We took in all our canvas and tied up to the dock,
And twenty men came down along the ridge of rock.
We then got out our dinner, for we were feeling lank,
And then got introduced to some twenty-four-foot plank!

But before we started the plank, oat bags we had to tote,
And twenty barrels of flour from the bosom of the boat.
We hoisted up the flour till our fingers began to swell,
But we'd gladly hoist the flour if the planks had been in Hell!

Now the vessel is all loaded, and we are on the shore,
And vow that planks and lumber we'll handle nevermore!
The *Kolfage* rounds the bend and disappears from view—
It's good-bye to Cap McDonald, here's our best regards to you.

The Crew of the *Clara Youell*

A group of lakesmen made this song up about themselves while sailing aboard the medium-sized canaller *Clara Youell* in the early 1890s. The schooner, of approximately 300 gross tons, was built in 1872 at Port Burwell, Ontario, on Lake Erie, and named for the daughter of a prominent merchant in that port. Engaged in the lumber trade, the *Youell* sailed out of Canadian ports on Lake Huron for several seasons.

According to Norman "Beachie" MacIvor, who recalled these verses in the summer of 1934, "The men had a good time making it up" while shipping a cargo of lumber out of Goderich. There was a stanza for each member of the crew,

MacIvor said, but he could not recall them all. The song bears testimony to the fact that women sailed the Lakes, too, usually as cooks.

It is unlikely that this song was known by many sailors, but it exemplifies the practice of making up lyrics about the singers themselves and the people around them.

> It's of a stately vessel, a vessel of great fame,
> And if you want to know her, the *Clara Youell*'s her name,
> She's a sweet little vessel, of material she's so fine,
> She's the pride of Goderich harbor, and she's in the lumber line.
>
>> Hurrah, boys! Hurrah!
>> For her officers and crew,
>> We'll hoist the flag to her masthead,
>> The red, white, and the blue.
>
> She's sailed by a gentleman, one who can justly claim,
> The respect of all his sailors, Walter Colwell is his name.
> He comes down to the dock, we all think he is prime,
> He says, "My boys, the times are good, now we're in the lumber line."
>
> And Jimmy here's our mate, a sailor of renown;
> He knows about all of the Lakes, and the girls in every town.
> He's a hard-hearted driver, and he always feels inclined
> To drill us poor sailors when in the lumber line.
>
> Our stewardess is Mary, a cook beyond compare,
> She's the pride of the galley, by her we all swear.
> She's the best of all stewards, her meals you'll always find
> Are the best that are a'goin' when in the lumber line.

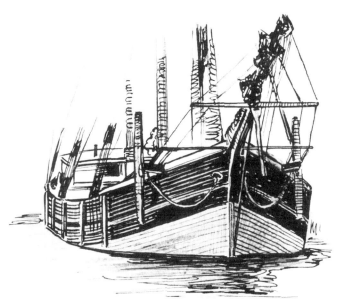

Lumber Hooker at Boyne City 1890
Note the two sets of spreaders.

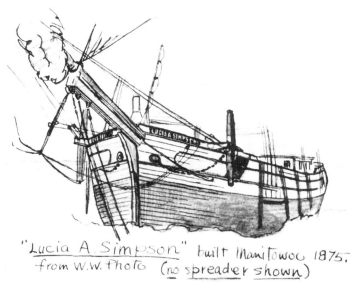

"Lucia A. Simpson" built Manitowoc 1875.
from W.W. photo (no spreader shown)

Schooner bowsprit, spreader, and martingale details. Courtesy of the Historical Collections of the Great Lakes.

The Jam on Gerry's Rocks
(The Foreman John Monroe or Young Monroe)

This is a logging song, not a sailing chantey, though sailors sang it from Buffalo to Chicago, just as loggers sang "Lake Huron's Rockbound Shore" while they labored in the pine. How is it that sailors and loggers adopted each other's songs? In many cases, the sailor and the logger were one in the same. Sailing was a warm-weather pursuit, ending when ice shut the locks and the Lakes. Logging was largely a wintertime pursuit. Until the advent of narrow-gauge railroads, logging operations needed ice and snow to skid felled trees to the riverbank, where they were stacked in huge piles to await the spring thaw, when swollen rivers would float the logs to sawmills. Many men cobbled together a pattern of year-round employment by leaping from their place on a floating log to a spot on a pitching deck.

    Such a woods-and-water laborer was a Walton family cousin. This version is similar to one that appears in Earl Clifton Beck's *Songs of the Michigan Lumberjacks*. Beck mentions Walton in the notes to another song, that of Lake Huron's rocky shore. This entry brings us full circle from woods to water and back again.

Come all you true-born shanty boys,
    Wherever you may be,
I'd have you pay attention
    And listen unto me;
It's of a true-born shanty boy,
    So manful, true, and brave,
In breaking a jam on Gerry's rocks
    He met with a watery grave.

It was on a Sunday morning
    As you will quickly hear;
The logs were piled up mountain high,
    They could not keep them clear,
Our boss, he cried, "Turn out, my boys,
    With hearts devoid of fear,
And we'll break the jam on Gerry's rocks
    And for Eagerstown we'll steer."

Oh, some of us were willing,
    And some of us hung back,
To work upon a Sunday
    They did not think it right
'Til six of our Canadian lads
    Did volunteer to go
To break the jam on Gerry's rocks
    With their foreman John Monroe.

They had not rolled off many logs
    When the boss to them did say,
"I'd have you boys be on your guard
    For the jam will soon give way."
He'd scarcely time to speak the words
    When the jam did break and go,
And carried off those six poor youths
    And their foreman John Monroe.

And when the rest of the shanty boys,
    Those tidings came to hear,
They searched the waters all around,
    They searched them far and near;
They searched the waters all around
    To their sad grief and woe,
And on the beach found mangled
    The form of John Monroe.

They pulled him from the water's edge,
    Smoothed down his raven hair;
There was one fair form among them
    Whose cries did rend the air.
There was one fair form among them
    A maid from Saginaw town
And her dreary cries did rend the skies
    For her true love was drowned.

Young Clara was a noble girl,
    Likewise a raftsman's friend,
And with her widowed mother dear
    Lived by the river's bend.
The wages of her own true love
    The boss to her did pay
And a collection she received
    From the shanty boys next day.

Young Clara did not long survive
    To her sad grief and woe,
In less than six months after
    Death came and laid her low.
In a little nook by the river bend
    There lie two lovers low
Young Clara of Denville Town
    And her shanty boy Monroe.

A canalboat catches a hoofed breeze for the passage through Ohio's Miami Canal. Dossin Great Lakes Museum.

CHAPTER 7

Scow and Canalboat Songs

LOCAL CIRCUMSTANCES SOMETIMES created small families of song. Two examples are scow songs and canalboat songs. Scow songs grew up around the small, flat-bottomed boats used to shuttle wood, stone, sand, and building materials about the Detroit and St. Clair Rivers and on Lake St. Clair in the last half of the nineteenth century. Built without keels but with centerboards that the crew could lift or crank up on pivots, scows had very shallow drafts, a mast or two, and perhaps an engine. The shallow draft made them ideal for ferrying cordwood from points along the shore to wood docks for tugs, steamers, and householders in Detroit and nearby communities.

Many Lake St. Clair wood scows were French family boats. They were ideal for ascending far up the Sydesharn, Big Heart, and Little Bear Rivers for cordwood. These little boats also carried stone and gravel for many of the foundations of Detroit and Windsor buildings, bringing much of it from the shore of Lake Huron near Sarnia. After being loaded with wood in the upper Sydesharn, a scow would float down to the junction of the Challen Ecarte on the eastern side of St. Anne's Island in Lake St. Clair and farther down to Midrech Bay, where it would hoist sail. If the lake was too rough, the scows would scuttle for shelter on the Thames or Belle River. The adventure of running from Little Bear Creek down to Lake St. Clair is told in dialect poems.

Crews of two to four operated most scows, and the captain's wife often served as cook. As the dialect in these songs indicates, these families were, more often than not, habitants. Scow songs are most distinctive for their dialect and sense of humor.

The Wood Scow *Julie Plante*

This song is usually set in Lake St. Clair, but variations place it in northern Green Bay off Menominee and Lac St. Pierre in the St. Lawrence near Montreal. Even Detroit-area versions contain references to Lachine Canal near Montreal. Nationalistic debate surrounding the song's locale and authorship arose in the 1920s and again in the 1940s. Proponents of Canadian lineage waved copies of

William Henry Drummond's 1897 volume of poetry, *The Habitant and Other French-Canadian Poems*, as the original version. Detroiters responded with recollections of singings and stage performances dating back more than fifty years. They said that Drummond had merely picked up a song in public circulation and passed it off as his own composition. As with many folk songs, the true origin seems to be untraceable, and any argument for the one, authentic version runs contrary to the fact that folk songs were passed along and kept alive by word of mouth, rather than by printed page.

Many sailors could recall bits and scraps of this one, and complete or nearly complete versions came from S. C. Jacobson of Waukegan, Illinois; William Murray of Montague, Michigan; James Putnam of Port Huron; Ralph Chene of Detroit; Harvey Bonnah of Cleveland; F. W. Elliott of Fairport, Ohio; and Peter Beaupre of Kingston. All located the incident "jus' off Grosse Pointe" in Lake St. Clair. Peter Cardinal, ex–Coast Guardsman of Muskegon, and Daniel Garrett, lightkeeper at Manistique, Michigan, used "Lac St. Pierre" and stated that they had obtained the song from Drummond's 1897 volume. This version is as Captain Putnam of Port Huron recalled the song in the summer of 1938. He recalled learning it "forty or fifty years ago," but he was not at all sure where.

Propeller vessels, with their straight sides, were natural canallers. Courtesy of the Historical Collections of the Great Lakes.

The Wood Scow *Julie Plante*

Murdock, Score No. 20

On wan dark night on de Lac St. Clair, de win' she blow, blow, blow, An' de

crew of de wood scow *Jul - ie Plante* got scar' an' run be - low. For de

win' she blow like hur - ri - cane, by - 'n - by she blow some more, An' de

scow bus' up jus' off Grosse Pointe, ten ac - re from de shore.

On wan dark night on de Lac St. Clair, de win' she blow, blow, blow,
An' de crew of de wood scow *Julie Plante* got scar' an' run below.
For de win' she blow like hurricane, by-'n-by she blow some more,
An' de scow bus' up jus' off Grosse Pointe, ten acre from de shore.

De captain walk on de fron' deck, he walk on de hin' deck, too—
He call de crew from up de hol', an' he call de cook also.
De cook, she's name was Rosie, she kom from Montreal,
Was chambermaid on lumber barge on de beeg Lachine Canal.

De win' she blow from nor'-eas'-wes', de sout' win' she blow too,
W'en Rosie cry, "Oh, Capitaine, Capitaine, w'at I shall do?"
De captain den t'row out de hank, but still de scow she dreef;
De crew he can't pass on de shore becos' he los' hees skeef.

De night was dark like wan black cat, de wave run high an' fas',
W'en de captain take hees poor Rosie an' lash her to de mas'.

SCOW AND CANALBOAT SONGS

An' den he take de life preserve an' jomp off in de lake
Say'n, "Au revoir, ma Rosie dear, I go drown for your sake."

Nex' mornin' veree earlee, 'bout half pas' two-t'ree-four,
De captain, scow, an' poor Rosie was corpses on de shore.
For de win' she blow like hurricane, an' den she blow some more,
An' de scow bus' up jus' off Grosse Pointe, ten acre from de shore.

Now, all good wood-scow sailormen, take warnin' by dat storm,
An' go maree some nice French girl, an' leev on wan beeg farm—
De win' may blow like hurricane, an' s'pose she blow some more—
You can't get drown on Lac St. Clair so long you stay on shore.

Legend of the *Rosie Belle Teeneau*

Pity poor Jean Baptiste DuChene. It wasn't enough for him to be blown to kingdom come by "barls of gun-pauder." It happened to him in two songs. It wasn't enough that he never had enough "tring for de hank"—or anchor line. People also made sport of the way the poor guy dressed. Whether captain or mate, "Batteece" was the tragicomic hero of the scow song. He has his fullest introduction in "The *Rosie Belle Teeneau*," as published in 1917 in William Edward Baubie's *French-Canadian Verse*.

De *Rosie Belle Teeneau* was wan vere fine batteau,
Was steam barge hon de reever, good many year ago.
She always looked so neat, wid de beeg moskeeto fleet,
An ah'll tole you, mah boy, she was hard boat to beat.

Down de reever if you geev her a good chance to go
Frome Isle au Peche above, to Point Pelee below,
An if de wind she blow hon her stern from behind
Shees beat all de vassalle an de boat you can faind.

Jean Batteece DuChene was the captain of dat barge;
Hees not so vere small, an he's not so vere large.
But hees tick-set and chaunkay, he go two hunnard poun,
An weigh it in de stocken, if hees got som stocken hon.

Batteece wife, and bote hees boy, an Angelique hees dauter,
Was de bes crew of de *Rosie Belle,* wen she go hon de water.
Each wan dat crew could maike de cook, or trow de hank also,
Could run de hengine down below, or maike de wissel blow.

From summer tam up to de fall, Batteece don't wear no shoe at all;
Som-tam for style he wear som pant, som-tam som overhaul.
An when he promenade de deck, wid hees uniforme all hon,
Mon Dieu, dat's grande! He look just laike de great Napoleon.

"Mah bes crew is mah familee," Batteece he always say,
When all de work was finish, hon de hind end of de day.
"Ah smoke de pipe so ezay, as Ah'm laying hon de bed;
For Ah know if we lose monay hon de Rosie, we're ahead."

Wan naight dey stop at Drouillard's dock, for taike wan barl away;
It might be feesh, it might be pork, no wan on board can say.
Was tickette hon dat barl wat say she go to Pete Marcotte
Wat keep de sailor boarding-hous at Ecorse near Wyandotte.

Dere's no plaice hon de water, every sailor man will say,
Where de wind she blow, and blow so hard, as hon de Ecorse Bay.
De naight he taike dat barl hon board, she blow and blow some more;
It look joust laike beeg tournadeau was coming down de shore.

Batteece ain't got de educate, but he notice raight-away
Hees have wan hell-of-a-tam dat naight in crossing Ecorse Bay.
"How many men we got hon board?" he ask de hengineer.
"Dere's tree below;" and Batteece say, "Send half-a-dem up here."

"Clar de deck!" Batteece he spik. "Taike down de smok-stack too,
An trow de hank as fas you can, dat's de bes' ting you can do."
"We got no tring," de mate he sing, "so de hank ain't work so well."
Den Batteece yell, "Say, who de hell is de boss of dees vassalle?"

De naight was black wen de storm attack de *Rosie Belle Teeneau;*
She hit her hard above, below, she hit her in de mid also.
De lightning flash and hit dat barl, and maike de noise much louder,
For de barl bust up de *Rosie Belle*—it's chock-full of gun-pauder.

Batteece was sitting hon dat barl, when she go off for fair.
He hav no tam for shew de rag, for he fly up in de air;
An de wind she blow hon Ecorse Bay, she blow lack 'ell som more,
An de *Rosie Belle,* she don' feel well, she's haf mile from de shore.

Madame DuChene, she go insane, and jaump down hon de water;
De only life preserve was grab by Angelique, hees dauter,
An bote de boy was dive away from de *Rosie Belle Teeneau*
Dey joust have tam for save itself before she sink below.

Jules Tourangeau, wat spear de frog, and leave down hon de marsh,
Was brong hees yawl, he hear de call, he also hear de splash;
He find de wife and bote de boy, he also find de dauter;
An soon he grab hold-o-dem, he pull it out de water.

Now if you go to Ecorse Bay, de ole-tam habitant will say
Dat if som of de 'skeetow fleet was sailing down dat way,
Dey pass a long, long way round de *Rosie Belle*'s last sleeping ground:
De sailors fear, from what they hear, dat Batteece goste she proul around.

An wen de naight was dark down dere, all de fishermen dey swear
Dat Batteece an de *Rosie Belle* was sailing hon de air;
You can see mirage, also de barge, and you also see de wreck
Wile Jean Batteece geev two-tree cheer, as he promenade de deck.

Wen dees mirage was pass away, it's quiet roun de Ecorse Bay;
De naight wind moan, de bull-frog groan, in de vere same ole way;
De snap and maud-hen trai to rest in de weed long-side de shore;
Dey have no fun, for de potter's gun was maike dem fly som more.

Dey look for Batteece high an low, for two-tree year or more,
But no wan find hees boday or de clothes de captain wore,
Till wan fine day hon Ecorse Bay, Joe Lozon it was pass dat way—
Find Batteece spendaire an hees pants joust at de break of day.

Lozon he plants poor Batteece pants in de sand long-side de shore,
He put de spendaire in also, for he can't find notting more;
Hees got no stone monument, so he use a feeshing stave,
An wid som paint, and paint-brush too, hees decorate de grave.

Joe Lozon spell some word dere, for epitaffe he say;
Ah ain't can read or write messef, Ah ain't brot up dat way.
But if you geev attention, Ah'll tole you all de rest,
So please excoose may Englishe, Ah try to do my best.

Epitaffe

Here lies de last, also de hend, of Jean Batteece DuChene;
Hees got blow up hon Ecorse Bay, while sailing hon de main.
He don't expect to go so quick, to taike hees seat in Heaven,
For he made de trip hon stannard tam, from nine to haf-pas leven.

An when de good Ange Gabrielle, will make de trompette blow
Batteece he will be boarding dere, an hees familee also.
Hees troub dey was all ovaire now, hees pants he'll lose no more,
For de captain of de *Rosie Belle* has found a peaceful shore.

Moral

You sailor man what have som wife, and have to leave awhile,
Steer clear away from Ecorse Bay, at least for two-tree mile,
An keep your eye hon any barl, if you don't know heem firsrate,
An taike no chance to spoil your pants by sitting hon de freight.

Som-tam dat barl have feesh inside, and som-tam flour from de mill,
Som-tam it's Walker wiskay too, wat com from Walkerville.
De wiskay she don't hurt you much, but she don't do you much good,
De flour she is de staff of life, and feesh de finest food;

But if gun-pauder's in dat barl, be careful what you do:
Put out your pipe and cigarette, if you know wat's good for you.
For de faudere of me was tole me so, an Ah beleeve mah faudere
Dares noting can raise hell so quick as de ole-tam gun-pauder.

De Scow *Jean La Plante*

This song bears strong similarities to songs about the *Julie Plante* and the *Rosie Belle Teeneau.* Detroiter James J. Enright claimed to have written the song in the back of a geography book in 1867 after rowing past a sorry old wooden scow on which someone had tarred the name "Jean La Plante." Enright said that he had recalled seeing scows race on the Detroit River and took the name on this scow to be a slightly misnamed tribute to the *Julie Plante* of which sailors had sung often during his youth. These lyrics come from the *Detroit Free Press,* April 10, 1927.

I'll tol' of wan boat, de scow *Jean La Plante,*
She's sail by Batteece, a Frenchman so quaint.
She's sail on de lake fo' tirty-twalve year—
De crew and de captain she's man of good cheer.

She's got wan beeg jib an' sail wid two wing,
De anchor was grindstone on two piece o' string.
She's carry de wood, she's carry de sand,
An' som'tam excurshan wid plenty brass ban'.

De crew was de mate, de cook an' de dog,
Who's bark plenty loud w'en he's get in fog.
She's bark all de day den lay down fo' rest
When Betteece she's cry, "Nor', nor', by sou'west!"

Here kom dem fas' scow dey call *Flyin' Cloud*
Cry Capitaine Batteece an' she's yall planty loud:
"Put de wheel port, look out fo' yo' head,
An' tol' Joe, de cook' fo' trow out de lead!"

Joe trow de lead and yall, "Leventeen feet!"
An' Batteece she's cry out, "Let go do main sheet!
Trow de dog ovaire an' all yo' can spare,
We mus' beat dat scow boat 'cross Lac Sainte Claire!"

De win' she's blow dees way, den she's blow dat,
She's knock down de mate an' lose de cook's hat.
Den she's change queek from sou' to nor'west—
"I'm ahead," say Batteece, as she's pull down de vest.

All day Batteece she's race 'cross de lac—
She's sleep on de feet, no tam on de back.

So dark was de night she's can't smell de han',
An' de telescop' beeg can't fin' out de lan'.

De mornin' she's kom wid de sun shinin' bright,
But de *Flyin' Cloud* scow she's nowhere in sight,
For her centerboar' catch on wan beeg catfeesh line,
An' dat was de reason she's got lef' behin'!

De *Jean La Plante* sail, dru storm she's roar,
An' stop planty place 'long de lac shore.
She's tak' on beeg barrel at Monroe wan day,
An' queek for Toledo she's sail right away.

De horn blow fo' dinner, de crew she's sit down,
Wid ev'ting happy at de table all 'roun'.
An' while dey was eat of good mushrat chowder,
Dem barrel bus' de scow—she's fill wid bus' powder!

Now on de lac all scowmen she's swear,
De scow *Jean La Plante* she's sail in de air.
An' of'en at midnight above de lac breeze,
Dey hear de beeg voice of Capitaine Batteece.

She's ride de mad wave, she's stick up hees nose,
"W'at does she say?" yo'll ask, I suppose—
Wall, she's jump on de lac, she's hist up de pant,
An' give planty cheer fo' de scow *Jean La Plante*!

De Scow *Look 'n' See*

Perhaps the heaviest accent of the French river scow songs is in this song. The "Creek of the Bear" in the first stanza is Bear Creek, which empties into Lake St. Clair from the east. The "reevair" in the fifth stanza is probably the Thames, which flows into the southeast side of this lake. The light is the beacon at its mouth. Fred M. Delano, a Detroit yachtsman, said he had learned this song "a long time ago on the Detroit River."

A scow kom sailin' down Lac Sainte Claire,
Sheengle an' cordwood she's deck load ware.
De wind blow fresh, de wind blow free,
An' speed on she's way de *Look 'n' See*.
Hout she sail from de Creek of de Bear
Hover de water of Lac Sainte Claire.

De wind get strong till she's blow one gale,
An' de *Look 'n' See* she's reef de sail.

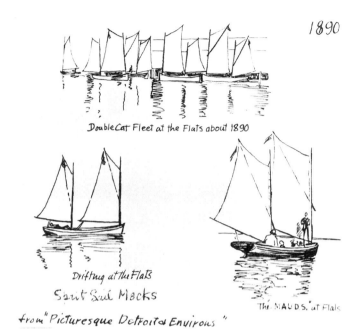

Mackinaw boats on the St. Clair Flats. Courtesy of the Historical Collections of the Great Lakes.

De water he jomp right hover de boat
An away t'ree steek of cordwood float.
From gale to hurricane blow de wind,
One bonch of sheengle float behind.

De captain she can't stan' dat no more—
De profeet all gone from dees treep sure.
An' eef all de sheengle an' cordwood go,
De sheriff she's grab an' sell de scow!
Den no more w'iskey, an' no more bread,
An' no more cabin to kover hees head.

So she yell to de mate way hover de gale,
"Batteece, stan' by to le' go de sail!
Haul in de sheet w'ile I luff de boat,
Leeve go de peek halyard! Now de t'roat!"
De sheet's haul in, de halyard's gone,
An' under de jeeb dey scoot along.

Dey reach de reevair, dey pass de light,
An' dere stopping place soon kom in sight.
Den again to de mate de captain call,
"Batteece, get ready de jeeb down haul:
T'row off de halyard, an' leeve him slack,
Eef we go by, we nevaire get back.

"Now leeve go lively, an' haul down queek!"
De mate she's pull, but de downhaul steek—
Den de captain she's hop all roun' an' roun',
"Mon Dieu, Batteece, why don' you haul down?"
"Can't do eet, captain," de mate reply,
"Eef you t'ink you can, you best kom try."

"Peetch in de hank so queek as yo' can,"
De captain yell as she forward ran;
"Peetch de hankerre 'fore you make t'ings snug,
Better do dat dan hire one tug."
"But captain, de hank's got no string on!"
"Nevaire min', peetch her in, may stop her some."

De Scow *Nettie Fly*

Detroit's Ralph Chene in 1934 claimed partial authorship of this song, saying that he was one of a group of men who wrote it in the late 1880s while working on a small scow carrying sand from the St. Clair River to Detroit. "Them were the days; we made good money and had a lot of fun doing it." Chene added that the song was well known about the river, and that he had sung it many times since the old scow disappeared.

Oh, sailors, come gather and list to my ditty,
To picture aright this hero I'll try—
He seldom was sober, and more is the pity,
He's Captain Poulan of the scow *Nettie Fly*.

He sailed from Chene Street, the wind blew a gale,
An' down Detroit River the *Nettie Fly* flew;
Says Captain Poulan, "She can carry her sail,"
Took a pull at his bottle and sized up his crew.

But all he could see was his mate, the brave fellow,
Who stood by the mainm'st with bottle in hand;
His legs they were shaky, his face it was mellow
As he thought of the boodle he'd make on the sand.

The captain looked sad, but with stern resolution
Seized hold of his bottle and took a long pull—
"By the stars and the stripes of our beloved Constitution,
If the captain ain't drunk and the mate is half full."

She was headin' sou'west with the wind on her quarter,
An' her sharp eagle eye oft peered through the gloom.
He then hauled her up seven points and a quarter,
An' shot into the Rouge not a moment too soon.

A heavy squall struck, and her lee rail went under;
An' out went her mains'l, into ribbons it flew.
While out flashed the light'nin', and loud rolled the thunder,
The captain took a drink, and the mate took one, too.

She righted at last through their manly endeavors,
An' they took in their fores'l, and stood for the bank;
They swore they would stick to each other forever,
An' pulled out their bottles and together they drank.

Says the captain to Jack, "You had better go forward
An' take in your stays'l and let go your hank,
For I've skinned my nose, my shins, and my forehead,
An' my legs are all tangled with this centerboard crank!"

In three days, they loaded an' were homeward bound;
They sailed up the river with a favorin' breeze—
They came up the river just like a scared hound,
An' the owner made money and was very much pleased.

The captain explained how they nearly went under,
How the scow and their lives they thought they would lose;
An' the last time I saw them they were in a saloon,
An' the last that I heard they were still on the booze!

The Good Scow *Alice Strong*

Experienced open-lake sailors generally held short-haul scows in contempt, and this song neatly expresses the professional seaman's contempt for landsmen—farmers especially—posing as lakers. Little is known of the scow *Alice Strong* other than what is in this fragment. A small scow by this name and outfitted with a steam-powered pile driver was built at Berlin, Michigan, and operated until 1893. A scow "running down from Cleveland" probably would be traveling easterly with building stone from Kelly's Island. It would be in the crowded traffic lanes where skilled seamanship would be necessary, but the "farmer" in charge seems to have lacked that skill. That should come as no surprise. John S. Parsons contributed this song at Oswego, New York, in 1933.

While running down for Cleveland
    On the good scow *Alice Strong,*
The captain's eyes grew weary and
    He forthwith did command
The mate to come upon the deck
    And there to take his stand.

The mate was but a farmer
    Who'd seen service with a plow;
But as he came upon the deck
    He took a mental vow,
Straight as the furrows in the field
    He would steer that scow!

Now round the corner grocery
    Where the rustics spit and chew,
He tells the startling story

How on a dark and stormy night
    He ran plumb into a steamboat,
    And sunk her out of sight!

Yim Yonson (The Scow *Sam Patch*)

Large numbers of Scandinavians immigrated to Lake Michigan and the prairie states to the west in the 1880s. Finding similarities between their homeland and their new surroundings, they quite naturally took jobs as loggers and sailors. Rather than the French accent of scow songs from the Detroit River and Lake St. Clair, "Yim Yonson" puts a heavy Scandinavian flavor on the familiar tale of a landsman-turned-sailor in over his head. This greenhorn song is set in Lake Michigan's Green Bay and sung to the same air as "The Wood Scow *Julie Plante*." It was sometimes referred to by the name of the scow, which was the same as that of the man who, on October 7, 1829, dove into the Niagara River and survived. Buoyed by the success, Patch dove into the Niagara Falls on October 17. Not one to rest on his laurels, he dove into the Genesee Falls at Rochester, New York, on November 13, 1829. That dive killed him.

    This version was obtained in the summer of 1932 from S. C. Jacobson, lightkeeper and former sailor of Waukegan, Illinois. He said he had learned it about thirty years earlier while sailing Lake Michigan lumber schooners. Other mariners knew the song or fragments of it, and said they came from "Yim Yonson's Philosophy" and "De Scow *Sam Patch*."

Yim Yonson ship from lumberyard
    Upon de scow *Sam Patch;*
He didn't know his starboard bow
    From oft de forward hatch.
He make big bluff before he sail
    That he ben sailor man,
But when de trouble struck de scow,
    Yim had to show his han'.

De scow ben in de cordwood trade.
    She sail from Sister Bay,
An' Yim he would be handyman
    Till off Twin Points one day
When yust like finger snap
    A squall on de wood scow flew
An' made her stan' on her beam's end
    An' call up all de crew.

De captain swore like crazy man,
    An' at Yim Yonson yell:
"Yump up an' rif dat tops'l queek
    Or it ben gone to Hell!"
But Yim, he say, "I will not stir
    From dis cahutan stanchion;
Der ben ten tousand tops'ls, yes,
    But only one Yim Yonson!"

An' dat's how Yim, he lose his yob,
    An' no more go to sea—
At sailin' he ben greenhorn, sure,
    An' always want to be.
Ven he was kicked from off de ship,
    He heard de captain swore;
But said, "I'd rather lan' dis vay
    Dan float along de shore."

The E-ri-o Canal

The Erie Canal inspired more music per mile than any other link in the Great Lakes waterway. Small wonder. Traversing the canal was excruciatingly slow, and monotonous in the extreme. Sailors had nothing to do but duck bridges as they were pulled along by mules or oxen, known as the "horned breeze." With their imaginations whetted by boredom and the scorn that can naturally arise between different breeds of men, the sailor-composer reached his crowning achievement for creativity and sarcasm while bumping along the canal. Butch Sullivan had been a canaller—one of the men who drove the boats through the canal—and said that sailors, canallers, and locktenders nurtured an abiding hatred for each other and often brawled in Buffalo bars. Although Sullivan couldn't recall any of the songs in particular, he said that sailors sometimes joked about his navigating skills and sang about the great storms, bad shoals, and even pirates he and his fellow canallers faced in the big ditch. "That was one sure way to start a fight," Sullivan declared.

Such rivalries were not peculiar to the Erie Canal. Edward "Ned" Navin of Cobourg, Ontario, was still a slender, active man in his seventies when interviewed about his twenty seasons on the Lakes. Navin boasted of traversing the old Welland Canal hundreds of times and said, "It was not difficult to get up a scrap there. Some of those canal hands were as tough as they come, and they'd drop their work and fight anybody, especially any sailor who criticized them, or anything, or anybody." Either this canalboat song or the next would have been enough to provoke an active night for the saloonkeepers and constabulary of Buffalo. E. W. Armstrong sang and

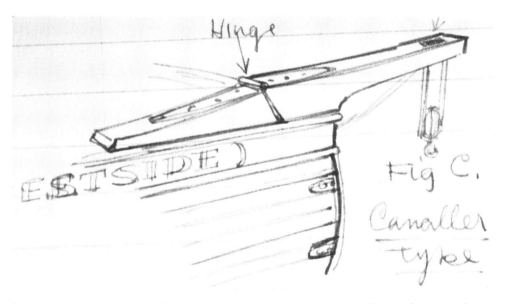

Stern davits were hinged to allow vessels to squeeze through canals and locks. Courtesy of the Historical Collections of the Great Lakes.

recited this song at Port Hope, Ontario, on August 4, 1933. Edward "Ned" Navin also sang a version of it the following day.

I just came down from Buffalo,
    On the good ship called the *Danger,*
A long, long trip on the Erie, boys,
    An' I feel just like a stranger.
Terrible winds and heavy weather—
    Forget it, I never shall
For I'm every inch a sailor boy
    On the E-ri-o Canal.

    Haul in your bo'lin', boys;
    Stand by, you sorrel mule;
    Low bridge! Duck your head,
    Don't stand there like a fool,
    For the Erie she's a'risin',
    An' our gin is gettin' low,
    An' I don't think I've had a drink
    Since we left old Buffalo.

At two days out we struck a fog;
    No land could we espy,
An' a pirate boat bore down on us
    With a goddamn wicked eye.
We hollered to the captain, boys,
    To hoist a flag of truce,
But it was the boat *Three Sisters* out
    Four days from Syracuse.

The next day out we struck a rock
    Of Lackawanna coal,
It gave the boat an awful shock,
    An' stove in quite a hole.
We hollered to the driver
    On the towpath pattin' dirt,
An' he jumped aboard an' stopped the leak
    With his lousy undershirt.

In two weeks' time we reached the Hudson
    There was Sal an' me an' Hank—
We greased ourselves in tallow fat,
    An' slid ashore on a plank.
Now Sal is in the pest house,
    An' the rest of the crew's in jail,
An I'm the only survivin' bum
    That's left to tell the tale.

The Canaller's Lament

This song offers crude testimony to the cosmopolitan composition of crews on the Great Lakes and their calmer tributaries. Although the ethnic insults are offensive, they attest to the presence of these nationalities on the Great Lakes in the late 1800s. It is a sad reality of the schooner days that were it not for slurs, some groups of people would not be represented among these songs at all. The informant for this song was Robert "Brokenback" Collen.

I shipped aboard a fat old tub,
Two mules were on the tow,
She hauled the length of the Erie Canal,
She was bound for Buffalo.

    It's aligan, baligan, lay me down die!
    Lay me down, itchy back, Mister McKay!
    Lay me down, itchy back, Mister McHulligan!

"Jimmy Galupe, haul away!" "Never again!"

The name she bore was *Prickly Heat,*
The captain's name was "Scratch";
He bawled and cursed and ranted 'round,
The world held not his match.

His voice was like an old foghorn,
His eyes like one gone mad,

He never tied up for a raging storm,
I tell you, he was bad!

Lou Flanigan was the first mate,
From the County Down he came,
He was a bloody Irishman,
He was born in Castlemain.

With a bag upon his broad shoulder,
And a mule whip in his hand,
He traveled the raging Erie Canal
Like a true-born Irishman.

In the crew were sons of other lands,
Roundheads and Scots of a feather,
Who wandered the world for a drink
 and a bed
In fair and stormy weather.

A Chink we had from Albany,
And two old alley rats,
And all the tramps and all the bums
From Schenectady's bare flats.

Luke McLuke was the only cook,
And he was a good one, too;
He hashed up punk and slimy junk,
And added some old bargoo.

His face was the color of the galley floor,
He had big and sprawly hands,
With forty horsepower he talked by the
 hour
With a voice of a cateran.

"Let go of the lines, the mules are
 hitched
To take the boat in tow;
We're off on the raging Erie Canal
With bells for Buffalo!"

And now I am in Buffalo
Walking by the canal,
And to go again in a canaller
Is a thing I never shall!

I'll ship in one of the Lehigh boats
That carries both steam and sail,
For there you get the real corned beef,
And none of your yellow male.

This song was sung by New Orleans Jim,
By Boston Tom, and Jack Gorman,
By Scrapper Red, and Denver Ed,
And Utah Slim, the Mormon.

The pyramid structure on the cigar-shaped whaleback *Clifton* appears ready to receive the crane that some say swung loose in a storm and caused it to roll over. Dossin Great Lakes Museum.

Huron boat with topsail. Courtesy of the Historical Collections of the Great Lakes.

CHAPTER 8

Songs of Beaver Island

Isolated, icebound for months at a time, and rocky with a thin soil, northern Lake Michigan's Beaver Island is a scrappy place for crops—but an Eden of song. The island, dubbed Ile de Castor by sixteenth- and seventeenth-century French fur traders, is approximately sixteen miles long and varies from two to six miles in width, its long axis lying in a north-south direction. Situated about twenty miles off the northwest part of Michigan's Lower Peninsula, the island boasts some sand dunes along the west side, a half-dozen small inland lakes, and an excellent and spacious harbor on its northeast shore. To the north and west are about a dozen other islands ranging in area from five square miles to an acre or less. They comprise the Beaver group of islands. Known locally as Big Beaver, this island is the only one in the group with continuing year-round occupation.

    Immigrants who scratched out a new home on the island saw in its soil, waters, and climate something of the place they had left behind. The people had names like Bonner, Gallagher, Kelly, and Kilty; Dunlevy, McCarthy, Martin, and Green. They came from Ireland, though not directly. In 1856, James Jesse Strang, self-proclaimed king of the Mormons, who had controlled the island, was assassinated. Irish fishermen from the north end of Beaver Island and the Michigan mainland drove his adherents across the lake to Milwaukee and ports south to Chicago. The Irish then moved in with their religion, their traditional occupations of seafaring and farming, and their traditions of folklore and song. Singing flourished, given the islanders' common heritage, their love of song, and their isolation from other people. As a refueling point and a safe harbor, Beaver Island also was a dropping-off point for other songs brought by sailors. Four months of the year, when ice locked the island away, the isolation was so complete that the only communication with the world might be by dogsled. In this environment, Irish ballads, sea chanteys, and songs of the lumber woods became a vital source of amusement and community. The balladeer was king, and island events became grist for the songwriter's mill. Many of the songs throughout this collection survived because of conditions on Beaver Island. But this chapter is about the songs Beaver Islanders composed about themselves.

    The importance of these island singers demands at least brief mention of a few individuals. A person hunting songs in the 1930s would hear repeatedly, "I learned that one from old Captain Roddy, and how he would sing it!" Andrew Roddy weighed about 250 pounds and was a big, muscular man with a big, bass voice. He acted out his songs and had a seemingly endless supply. He had owned and sailed several lumber hookers on Lake Michigan during the late 1800s. Several men who began their sailing careers with him told of how he would leave them aboard to watch the lumber being loaded while he spent the time in Chicago's sailor saloons or "free-and-easy shows," where there was much singing. During his trick at the wheel on their way back down the lake—he always took the captain's watch himself—Roddy would start humming and singing bits of the songs he had heard, and "soon he'd be singin' 'em all." His son Frank (or Francie, as he was called on the island) sang many old songs himself and said his father "never had to buy no drinks himself." Francie added that his father "never had no schoolin' at all, but he could sing any goddamn song that ever was." Other islanders agreed.

Tall, stately, white-haired, tenor-voiced, and genial Dominick Gallagher, a retired lighthouse keeper who recorded a score or more songs, paid high tribute to his Ireland-born father, who, he said, sang old songs at parties all over the island almost to the day he died. "With a few drinks he'd sing all night." Pat Bonner, an unassuming, diminutive sailor, farmer, and fiddler, supplied the music for island dances for several decades on his "Stradivarius fiddle"—a faded label on the inside said so—and composed one of the songs here. And how can one describe John W. Green: sailor, lumberjack, farmer, and singer par excellence. His father, several uncles, and grandfather were all good singers. In his mid-seventies, even after his singing voice was gone, Green dictated several score songs and fragments. In answer to an offhand question about how many songs he knew, he replied, "probably about a hundred." A list of songs and titles compiled by his daughter indicated that he may have known twice as many. In answer to another question, he stated somewhat apologetically that he sometimes had to hear a song twice or even three times before he could sing it himself.

Lost on Lake Michigan (The Gallagher Boys)

Late in October 1873, four men set sail from Beaver Island in the twenty-four-foot sailboat *Lookout* to get winter supplies. Brothers Johnny and Owen Gallagher and their friend Tommy Boyle sailed off with the brothers' father, Seamus Gallagher. After sailing out of Beaver Harbor, they made the forty-mile passage to the entrance to Grand Traverse Bay and the thirty-mile trip southward to Traverse City, where they loaded provisions, including supplies for Johnny's upcoming wedding to an island girl named Nancy. A late-season storm began to whip up as they loaded, and by the time they were ready to set sail for home the wind was blowing the tops off the waves. Captain Andrew Roddy, who was in Traverse City with his own boat, prevailed upon the elder Gallagher not to venture out into the gale. The younger men sailed off without him and evidently made it almost all the way home. Although the *Lookout* washed up on the island, it came in empty. The islanders held a wake for their four lost friends, only to have one of the dead men come sailing home with Roddy, unaware that he had lost his sons. The tragedy was immortalized in two songs, this one and "The Gallant Tommy Boyle," both written by Dan Malloy.

John Malloy, then eighty, dictated this, except for the tenth stanza, without hesitation, in 1932.

Come all brother sailors, I hope you'll draw nigh,
For to hear of your shipmates, it will cause you to cry;
It's of noble Johnny Gallagher, who sailed to and fro,
He was lost on Lake Michigan where the stormy winds blow!

"Oh Johnny, my dear son, in the dead of the night
I awoke from a dream which gave me a fright,
And to Traverse City I forbid you to go
To cross o'er Lake Michigan where the stormy winds blow!"

"Oh Mother, dear Mother, those dreams are not true,
I will shortly return and prove it to you;
And the Lord will protect us, let it blow high or low
When we cross o'er Lake Michigan where the stormy winds blow."

"Oh Nancy, lovely Nancy, don't stop me, my dear,
I'll surely return, come dry up your tears.
At home in our cottage full bumpers will flow
When I've crossed o'er Lake Michigan where the stormy winds blow!"

It was in October of seventy-three,
They left Beaver Harbor out to a calm sea;
And to Traverse City, their destination to go,
They crossed o'er Lake Michigan where the stormy winds blow!

They left Traverse City at nine the next day,
And down to Elk Rapids they then bore away;
They took in their stores and to sea they did go,
They were crossing Lake Michigan where the stormy winds blow!

At ten that same night a light they did spy:
"That's Beaver Island, we are drawing nigh!"
They carried all sail and the *Lookout* did go,
They were crossing Lake Michigan where the stormy winds blow!

Says Johnny, "My boys, there's land on our lee,
That's Beaver Island, but there's a high sea!"
With the wind from the nor'east, oh boys, it does blow!
There's a squall on Lake Michigan where the stormy winds blow!

Johnny looked at his craft and then to his crew
Each man's at his station, they're brave hearts and true;
"Stand by your fore halyards, let your main halyards go."
There's a squall on Lake Michigan where the stormy winds blow!

Now the *Lookout* is running before a hard gale,
Her rudder unships and overboard went her sail!
The billows are foaming like fountains of snow,
She sinks in Lake Michigan where the stormy winds blow!

The Gallant Tommy Boyle

In this song, Dan Malloy focuses on the 1873 passing of Tommy Boyle, one of the unlucky three in the foundering of the *Lookout*. The song refers to his older brother Jack and an earlier incident in which Tommy had saved his uncle Hughie and two other fishermen when their boat capsized as they were driving net stakes. Pat McDonough recalled this song, except for the second stanza, which came from Mike O'Donnel in 1940.

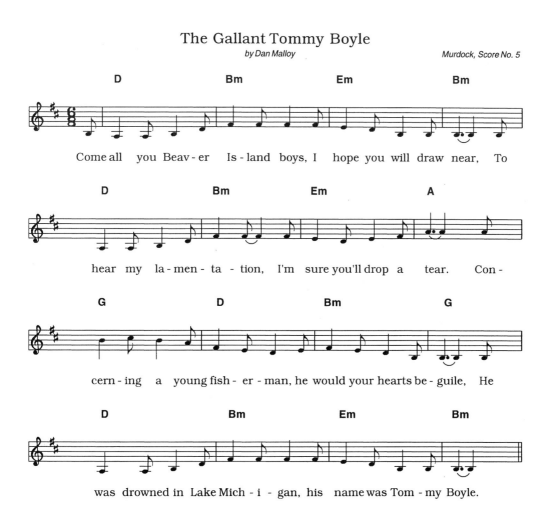

Come all you Beaver Island boys, I hope you will draw near,
To hear my lamentation, I'm sure you'll drop a tear.
Concerning a young fisherman, he would your hearts beguile,
He was drowned in Lake Michigan, his name was Tommy Boyle.

When his father heard the news, distracted he did run,
Crying, "Neighbors dear, what shall I do? I've lost my darling son!
Like a pilgrim I will wander, and I'll travel many a mile,
And all my lifetime I will mourn for my own son Tommy Boyle."

The Reverend Father Gallagher, great praise to him is due,
He reconciled his father, and he preached the Gospel true.
He prayed for his salvation, that the angels on him smile,
I hope he's at rest in Paradise now, that gallant Tommy Boyle.

He was proper, tall, and comely, his age was twenty-three;
He was as fine a young man as you could wish to see.
He was proper, tall, and kind to all, and on his face a smile,
And I hope he's well rewarded now, that gallant Tommy Boyle.

He was a gallant boatman, and fishing he did know;
And when they were imperiled, to release them he did go.
He saved a crew and his uncle too, and Heaven did on him smile—
And I hope he's well rewarded now, that gallant Tommy Boyle.

Now to conclude and finish, "Dear Jack," you'll understand:
"I'm going to meet my mother dear, she's in that blessed land.
She was always kind and true to me, and I think it but little toil
To sing her praise, God rest her soul, my brother, Tommy Boyle."

The Ill-Fated *Vernon*

Considering the small crews and their local composition, the loss of one boat could devastate an entire generation of a tiny port town. The sinking of the new passenger and freight propeller *Vernon* was just such a disaster, taking the lives of six young Beaver Island men. The *Vernon,* 694 gross tons, foundered in a bad storm off Twin River Point in northwestern Lake Michigan on October 25, 1887. Only one sailor, Alex Stone, survived. The vessel had been launched in Chicago only the year before and was considered entirely seaworthy. The steamer *Superior,* herself in serious trouble in the high seas, passed within sight of the floating wreckage and saw life rafts with men and women clinging to them, but it was unable to help. Captain C. R. Baker of Cleveland reported that he, too, passed along in a schooner shortly after the *Vernon* went down. He saw some men clinging to wreckage in the water, "but we were stripped down to double-reefed courses and headin' into a terrific wind and sea and could do nothing to help them." This song, attributed to Frank McCauley, commemorates the vessel and the six island boys who lost their lives. It is utterly unsympathetic to those who saw the wreckage but continued on in the stormy night.

    John W. Green dictated this song in the summer of 1932. He said that he had heard it shortly after the *Vernon* was lost. In 1938, Mary McCauley showed a manuscript version of the song with the same number and sequence of stanzas, but with different lyrics in many lines.

> All you true-feeling Christians, I hope you will draw near
> And learn my doleful story, I'm sure you'll drop a tear,
> Concerning our dear comrades who lately left our shore;
> They left us to lament, who'll never see them more.
>
> On October twenty-fifth the *Vernon* steamed away,
> On board our six dear friends with spirits light and gay.
> And little did they think as they bid their friends good-bye
> That their fate would be so soon in watery graves to lie.
>
> It was on a Friday evening they headed up the lake,
> And no one thought that the *Vernon* would be lost before daybreak.
> Their peaceful sleep was broken by cries that filled the air—
> The steamer she was sinking, grim death at them did stare!
>
> It was off Two Rivers Station the *Vernon* did go down
> With five and twenty passengers, for Chicago she was bound.
> Some of them manned the lifeboats, more the rafts did take,
> In hopes some passing vessel would save them from the lake.
>
> The morning dawned in terror for that cold and drowning crew,
> Adrift in the icy water, praying to be rescued.
> The snow was driving down as some numbed by the cold
> Sank in the roaring lake, their sufferings untold.
>
> What sudden hope is this that brightens up each eye!
> It is the joyful sight of a steamer drawing nigh.
> Oh God! What anguished hearts as she sped swiftly on!
> What doom awaited them before the setting sun!
>
> Here I ponder their fate, it fills my heart with grief
> To see them cold and dying, they could get no relief.
> Their strength is failing fast, in the angry lake they die
> Far from their family and friends as they bid this world good-bye!
>
> Oh, who was this unknown wretch that saw his fellow man
> Fighting for life in the water and would not lend a hand
> To save them from this cruel fate? No pity did he feel
> This base and cruel man whose heart was hard as steel!

The *Pere Marquette 18*

The twin-screw steel car ferry *Pere Marquette 18*, 2,909 gross tons, foundered for unknown reasons in the predawn hours of September 9, 1910, twenty miles off

Sheboygan, Wisconsin. Before the ship went down, the crew ran two strings of railroad cars overboard in an attempt to save it. The vessel went down stern first in the middle of Lake Michigan. A sister ship, the *No. 17,* responded to a radio distress call soon enough to save most of the sixty-plus aboard, but more than two dozen, including Captain Peter Kilty of Beaver Island, perished. Captain Manus J. Bonner, Kilty's brother-in-law, recited this song in Charlevoix, Michigan, in July 1932. Bonner said that he had learned it from hearing sailors sing it and that Frank McCauley of Beaver Island wrote the song shortly after the tragedy.

Out through the piers at Ludington one dark September day,
The *Pere Marquette 18* steamed proudly on her way.
Her captain, Peter Kilty, looked on his ship with pride,
As powerfully she drove o'er the tempestuous tide.

And none upon the noble ship, as she moved on and on,
Had dreamed that any harm could come to them ere dawn,
That before the sun would set, grim death their fate would seal,
And the dark and rolling waters claim that massive frame of steel.

Her captain stands upon the bridge, the mate draws quickly near,
He shouts, "We're sinking, Sir! We cannot keep her clear!"
No terror's in the captain's eye as he goes quickly down
Where anxious voices he hears, "The leak cannot be found!"

"The steamer is sinking! She's sinking!" is the word on every lip,
And awed and ghastly faces look on the foundering ship.
Though dangers fast surround him, he yields not to despair,
The captain stands among his men, no fear or panic there.

In calm, determined tones he speaks to his anxious crew,
"Fear not; man all the pumps; this ship will weather through!"
"Is there a chance for life?" a score of eyes implore,
"With God's good help," he answers, "We'll reach Wisconsin's shore."

Alas his hopes are shattered, for with a mighty roar
The waters rushed in aft, and through her vitals tore.
God help those struggling seamen! Depict it if you can,
The tragedy enacted there upon Lake Michigan!

It was but a short time later the *P. M. 17,*
With white foam at her bow, arrived upon the scene
Where floating wreckage told of that fated crew,
Of the twenty-eight brave sailors who bid this life adieu.

Farewell then Captain Kilty, your loss we'll long deplore,
May your soul evade the lake, and reach a tranquil shore

Where storms will assail you not, and calmer lees abound,
Where gentler seas are running, and only joys are found.

Farewell to those brave sailors, who now lie in the deep,
May peaceful days be theirs, and a long and tranquil sleep.
And may their wives and orphans an early solace earn
For the lost on the *Pere Marquette* who never will return.

The *Clifton* Tragedy

Four Beaver Island men died when the *Clifton* disappeared in northern Lake Huron with all hands on September 22, 1924. The boat and the four men live on, though, in songs written by islanders—four songs, by coincidence. The freighter, one of the distinctive "whalebacks" built so that waves would wash right up and over its rounded sides, had loaded crushed stone at Sturgeon Bay, Wisconsin, for Detroit. With twenty-eight officers and crew, the *Clifton* cleared the Straits of Mackinac and made it at least as far as Forty-Mile Point in Lake Huron, where the wrecking tug *Favorite* sighted it battling a fifty-six-mile-an-hour southwest gale. The 308-foot *Clifton* disappeared with all hands. It is believed that the cargo shifted in the heavy seas or that an unloading crane added the previous winter tore loose and swung out over one side, causing the vessel to list and roll over. Two days after the disappearance, the Canadian freighter *Glencairn* found broken hatch covers and part of the *Clifton*'s pilothouse thirty miles northeast of Goderich, Ontario. One of the islanders lost in the sinking was Captain Emmett Gallagher. His brother, Peter, wrote this song. This version is from a collection of songs held by Helen Collar.

A gray-haired mother knelt in prayer
Before the holy light
And the image of the Christ was there
To cheer her through the night.

She prayed to Him to save her boy
He, who on the Lake of Galilee
Had changed a raging tempest
To a calm and peaceful sea.

Now across the bay of treacherous
 Saginaw
The seas roll mountain high
The hurricane now sweeps her deck
With lightning in the sky.

The thunder roared; a deluge poured;
The sky is black; 'tis night.
The *Clifton* struggles gamely on
Though she fights a losing fight.

The captain's face is pale and set,
His voice is hoarse and stern
As he turns to the helmsman,
His hand on the ship's chadburn.

"Part a Point! Steady!
We'll hold her in the wind."
The helmsman answering turns her
To the order given him.

But He who ruled the waters
Held the fate of the stricken ship
Thought fit, perhaps, to take them
On that long, eternal trip.

"Christ have mercy on our souls, boys!"
Spoke the captain to his men,
And each sailor hoarsely murmured,
Clear, though lowly, the "Amen."

With her cargo fastly shifting
She is broadside to the sea
Now no human power can save her
"Christ, we trust alone to Thee."

"Pray, oh Mother Mary, for us!
Thou to whom thy Son didst say

That each favor thou wouldst ask Him
He would grant. Oh, Mother, pray!"

"Thou of whom the theme was written
Mother Mary, Star of the Sea
Be our guiding star, and Mother
Intercede, we pray to thee."

The Seaman's Lament

This song is attributed to islander Frank McCauley. It was obtained in the summer of 1932 from a scrapbook of Captain Charles C. Allers of Beaver Island.

My seafaring comrades, attend to my lay,
For death, that grim reaper, has taken away
The fair Emmett Gallagher, so loyal and brave,
And in Lake Huron's waters has found him a grave.

On the steamer *Clifton,* a captain was he.
He was genial and cheerful, kindhearted and free;
May his soul with bright angels to Heaven ascend,
For the poor and the needy, they found him a friend.

September the twentieth, nineteen twenty-four,
He took on his cargo and steamed from the shore;
Then to the eastward his course he did steer,
Little dreamt our bold hero that death was so near.

Now twilight it deepens, and far in the west
The sunbeams have faded; all nature's at rest.
But see those dark cloudlets, and swift is their flight,
And bright lurid flashes illumine the night.

Then Emmett, his crew to the deck he did call,
Saying, "Boys, be prepared for the worst, one and all!
My comrades get ready your lives to defend,
For yonder dark cloud does some evil portend."

Now the tempest is raging with strength in its might,
And loud rolls the thunder, and dark is the night;
And the mad billows leap like wild beasts from their lair,
And in their wild rush not a life will they spare!

And as they roll on over that structure of steel,
The steamer does tremble from foretop to keel;
For those mighty forces that swiftly roll on
Have torn out their vitals—all hope now is gone!

Now the steamer is sinking! O pity their plight!
O'er that wild waste of water no help is in sight.
There's none to console them, and it grieves me to say
To Huron's dark waters its toll they must pay.

God help their poor parents who shortly will mourn,
When they learn that their dear ones will never return.
And kind loving sisters in silence will weep
For the loss of their brothers consigned to the deep.

Farewell then, my comrades, no more shall we meet,
Your sweet smiling faces no more shall we greet;
No more your lithe footsteps our pathways shall tread,
Until Huron's dark waters shall give up its dead.

The *Clifton*'s Crew

This song is attributed to Pat Bonner, who reportedly wrote it a month after the wreck. From all accounts, he was a better fiddler than he was a poet.

The *Clifton's* Crew

by Pat Bonner
Murdock, Score No. 3

We have heard of many happenings since last year first began,
With crimes and troubles caused by war and earthquakes in Japan.
But sorrow had not filled our hearts 'til the news it come around,
The steamer *Clifton* she was lost and all her crew were drowned.

'Twas on one dark September day the last was ever known
Of the missing freighter *Clifton* that was loaded deep with stone.
With her derrick standing forward and her hatches battened down,
She was last seen passing down the Straits, for Detroit she was bound.

'Twas when down on Lake Huron she had steamed way out of sight
For to seek her destination and to battle with the night.
We thought not of our comrades, there beneath those stormy skies,
Lake Huron's waters for to end their young and happy lives.

As the night drew on with darkening clouds, the wind would shift and change
With a heavy sea from the southwest and a downpour of heavy rain.
The thunder in its anger crashed as the lightning lit the deep,
Where darkness in its fury dwells and desolation sweeps.

As time went on the rolling seas her cargo shifted then,
And soon all hopes had vanished there among those thirty men.
The crew had all got orders from their captain and their mate
To wear their life belts through the night on that foundering ship of fate.

It is hard to say, we know not when that fatal hour came.
But the waters of Lake Huron soon claimed many a mother's son.
And home today where orphans' tears has mourned a father, too,
Who had lost his life that stormy night among the *Clifton*'s crew.

We had hoped at first it was not true; we wished them safe from harm,
Or had seeked some peaceful shelter from the fury of the storm.
But it's where Lake Huron widens there's no sheltering port in view,
It is where the *Clifton* she had sunk with her cargo and her crew.

Some may have thought of home and friends, some thought of God alone,
And of their wives and children that are awaiting them at home.
'Twas but a few days later that some wreckage washed ashore,
And told the tale of the missing ship and our friends we'd see no more.

Her captain, Emmett Gallagher, a man so brave and young,
And his parents' home that now must know the tidings of their son.
It is now the pangs of sorrow that will pierce a mother's heart,
As she learns the time has come so soon her boy from her must part.

'Twas but a few short weeks before when Emmett he had said,
"There's a place out in Lake Huron that will not give up its dead.
'Tis called a sailors' graveyard." These words he was known to say,
As he stood out on the *Clifton*'s deck, he showed them where it lay.

We had there three more friends of ours, who are in his company
Brought up on Beaver Island and had followed up the sea.
'Twas Anthony McDonough, Joe Shied, and Peter Burns;
We had hoped to meet them back again and wished their glad return.

Young Anthony, a mate aboard, he sailed the ocean blue.
He had come back to the Great Lakes and had joined the *Clifton*'s crew
To be among companions of his early boyhood days.
He was doomed like many more on board to fill a sailor's grave.

Among our four companions on the *Clifton* that were drowned,
Joe Shied he was the only one of them was ever found.

Their lifeless forms in silence now are drifting far and wide,
'Til they waste away from day to day and wear with time and tide.

Their fathers, they will not forget that day so sad and long,
When their thoughts were of the *Clifton* and their dear boys that are gone.
Also their sisters they will weep and mourn their brothers dear,
Whose smiles they'll nevermore behold their saddened hearts to cheer.

Our homes had not beheld the like in many years before,
Not since the steamer *Vernon* sank out off Wisconsin's shore
As some may hold the memory still, but some were then not born
Who perished on the *Clifton* through the darkness and the storm.

There are three of them, 'tis sad to say, no mother home have they;
They are gone before their children and are long since laid away.
They say there is a mother who has seen through many storms
And has prayed for those who called her in danger and in harm.

She is our Blessed Mother, as the holy people say,
Is called the Queen of Heaven, and had sorrows in her day.
She has list' to many a midnight prayer from many a sailor boy,
And with God has blessed these hidden graves, they now in peace may lay.

'Tis well for us to think upon the words that God has said;
We are told from out the Scriptures we should not forget the dead.
You may kneel at your bedside when the quiet shadows fall,
Then in your prayer remember those who were once among us all.

And ask that He may gather with the angels in their flight,
And forget the steamer *Clifton* and that dark September night.

The *Clifton*

This fourth, fragmentary version of a *Clifton* song is of unknown authorship. It comes from a recording in Box 8 of the Walton Collection. The singer's name is not known.

Steaming out of the Straits of Mackinac
She blew her last salute.
Five whistles told her company's name,
Four blasts then told her owner,
As she cleared for Detroit City,
With her cargo all of stone,
"Steer southeast by east" was ordered,
"Southeast by east" came the reply.
. . . .
Then the *Clifton* squared away

The wind blew on her after-quarter
'Til abreast of Saginaw Bay,
When a terrible squall burst on her,
With a change of wind and sea,
And without a moment's warning,
She is forty miles from lee!

And her able crew of sailors,
All so young, so brave, so gay,
Little dreamed that ere the morning,

They would find a watery grave!
Leave no farewell words behind them,
Balm to hearts that soon must break,
In the springtime of their manhood,
Ah! How cruel the hand of fate.

Broken now the ties that bind them,

To this life they once held dear,
In a fairer land to find them,
In a holier atmosphere.
Never more to hear their footsteps,
Never more to clasp their hands,
'Til we are with them numbered,
In a fairer, brighter land.

The *U.S. Lightship 98*

Not all Great Lakes lights stand sentinel on shorelines, islands, and rocks. Some of the most dangerous hazards to navigation lay hidden, just beneath the waves, waiting to gore the vessels that pass over them. When it was too expensive or too difficult to build on top of shoals, the U.S. Lighthouse Board stationed lightships nearby to warn sailors away from the rocks, shoals, and other high spots in the lake bottom.

On good days, lightship tenders found life to be stupefyingly dull. On stormy days, the tiny, anchored beacons bucked and rocked sickeningly—as long as the anchors held. During a cyclonic storm on November 9 and 10, 1913, the lightship at the foot of Lake Huron dragged its heavy anchor nearly to shore. In the same storm, the *Number 82* off Buffalo broke loose and foundered with its six-man crew.

Lightship No. 57 at Gray's Reef. Courtesy of the Historical Collections of the Great Lakes.

This song is a fair-weather description of *U.S. Lightship 98*. Built at Muskegon, Michigan, in 1915 and stationed off Buffalo for two years, the "98" next stood guard near submerged rocks where traffic converged at the entrance to Little Bay de Noc and the way to the iron ore loading docks at Escanaba, Michigan. The song is attributed to Beaver Islander Frank McCauley, who worked as a cook on the Light Vessel, or *L.V. 98*. This song was in a scrapbook kept by Dan Garrett, keeper of the light at Escanaba, Michigan. Garrett had been a cook on the "98" at Lansing Shoal, also in northern Lake Michigan, forty miles west of Mackinaw City.

They may boast of their dreadnaughts and cruisers likewise,
Sub chasers and airplanes that soar in the skies;
But there is another whose fame I'll relate,
It's Uncle Sam's little watchdog, the *L.V. 98*.

In the lanes of our shipping a boulder does lie,
Which nature has formed as the ages rolled by;
And beneath the lake's surface in silence does lay,
Like a beast in the jungle in wait for its prey.

Her watch room is white and her hull is bright red,
And a background of black o'er her main deck is spread.
Her tall, stately tower is looked on with pride,
For it warns all mariners these rocks to avoid.

Her deep-throated siren, how loud it does roar
When the fogs and the mists envelop our shore;
Her miniature beacon, it shines out so bright,
As it sends forth its rays and illumines the night.

Two skilled engineers to her engines attend,
And to keep them in order, their energies bend.
The cook and the seamen, the captain and mate,
Comprise the whole crew of the *L.V. 98*.

Sometimes we are lonely and feel indisposed,
For we are estranged from our friends and our foes;
But there's one earthly blessing I'm sure we enjoy—
That no bill collector ever can us annoy.

In the watches of night not a sound can we hear,
But the gulls and caw-weens that bring us some cheer,
With their wrangling and clamor they bring some respite,
As they sound their weird notes in the stillness of night.

Now my seafaring comrades, wherever you roam,
Remember this watchdog has guided you home;
When you're safely landed do not hesitate
To take off your hats to the *L.V. 98*.

The Fisherman Yankee Brown

Paul Bunyan, legendary logger of the North, is well known in folklore, but his feats seem to have been equaled by the lesser-known Yankee Brown, a fisherman who made his camp on Beaver Island at the turn of the century. At the time, whitefish and lake trout abounded around the many shoals in that part of Lake Michigan. According to local reports, as many as twenty groups established fish houses and drying reels about the ample and well-protected harbor at St. James. No laws regulated the seasons or the size of the meshes in the nets, and daring fishermen in single-masted fishing boats extended their operations over the area and even into northern Lake Huron. Many a Beaver Island boy had his first sailing experience as a helper on one of these small vessels. This song relates some of Yankee Brown's heroics. It has lost several stanzas, one of which told of Yankee sailing into the harbor so fast before a storm that he went halfway across the island before he could get his anchor out and stop. Yankee Brown was actually islander Wesley Brown, who had come from New York by way of St. Ignace. The song follows in melody, and sometimes words, the logging song "The Shanty Boys in the Pine." Brothers Pat and Dan Bonner recalled these lines at Pat's Beaver Island home in July 1938. They credited this song and many others to prolific Beaver Island composer Frank McCauley.

The Fisherman Yankee Brown
by Frank McCauley

Murdock, Score No. 1

My boys, if you will listen now, I'll sing you a little song,
It's about a man you know well whose tales are always strong.
He is a well-known fisherman who lives here in our town,
He's a very noted lawyer, and his name is Yankee Brown.

Oh, sing titty high, high titty um,
With a whack ful-lor-il-lie.

He was born way down in York State in a family of sixteen,
And his boyhood deeds would fill a book, the greatest ever seen.
He farmed and lumbered half the state, but found it too confined,
So he came to Beaver Island in the year of seventy-nine.

When here he took up fishing and he followed up his trade,
And several times he's told me that his fortune he had made.
He says he's acres by the thousand and pond nets by the score,
And twenty thousand dollars in a bank in Baltimore.

His boat he calls the *Mattie,* and the truth to you I'll tell,
Several times he has rebuilt her and he can sail her well.
For once when beating down the lake he had to come about,
He heeled her in the seas so far she scooped up thirty trout.

He swore when he was fishing once down on Hog Island Sound,
That alone he caught a whitefish that weighed a hundred pounds.
At first we didn't believe him, then he began to swear,
He said he'd bring his young son out and prove the story there.

Oh, when he went to Charlevoix, to preach the Gospel there,
He swore that he was Antichrist, and for them to prepare!
His feats they are most numerous, and the truth now I must tell:
The old Nick never will be at rest till he gets the Yankee in Hell!

Flying their flag upside down as a distress signal, sailors on the schooner *J. H. Rutter* cling to the rigging in a November 1, 1878, gale. The *Rutter* was heavily damaged, but the forty-four-man crew was rescued. Ivan H. Walton Collection, Bentley Historical Library, University of Michigan.

CHAPTER 9

Disaster Songs

The largest surviving group of amusement chanteys, and the ones that most seem to have caught people's attention on land, are the disaster songs. There is probably no equal area of commercial waterways that, if drained, would reveal as many lost vessels as the Great Lakes. The severe weather, particularly in autumn, the large number of vessels, the daring of men spurred on by high wages, and the lack of navigational aids all tended to swell the list of disasters. It is to be expected that many of these losses would be commemorated in song. Themes of mortal peril, bravery, and tragedy fire the imagination and romanticize life on the Lakes. While people who have never sailed might have trouble relating to shipboard tasks such as reefing a sail or kedging a vessel, everyone can relate to the danger of sailing on deep water in a storm. After steam power made sailing and work chanteys obsolete, sailors continued to make up songs about dangers faced and vessels lost. Unfortunately, there has been no shortage of subject material.

Lake Huron's Rockbound Shore (The Ill-Fated *Persian*)

The schooner *Persian*, a canaller hailing from Oswego, New York, cleared Chicago late in the season of 1869 with a cargo of grain for its home port. The *Persian* passed through the Straits of Mackinac and into Lake Huron shortly before a violent storm descended. Nothing more ever was heard of the vessel or its eight-man crew. John Long, who owned and sailed the vessel, and all the other men aboard hailed from Oswego. After the disaster, there was a persistent rumor that a schooner named *Allen* had collided with and sunk another schooner, possibly the *Persian*, in the mouth of Saginaw Bay on the night the storm hit.

Shortly after word of the disappearance reached the *Persian*'s home port, Patrick Fennel, an Oswego poet and a close friend of Daniel Sullivan, the vessel's mate, wrote a poem under the name Shandy Maguire. Lakesmen picked up the poem, set it to music, forgot the author's name, and carried it far and wide. Fifty years after the loss of the *Persian*, folklorist Franz Rickaby found men singing it in northern Michigan logging camps and published it in his *Ballads and Songs of the*

Shanty-Boy (Harvard University Press, 1926). A decade later, folklorist Earl Clifton Beck found a considerably different version in Michigan logging camps.

The *Buffalo Express* published a version on March 9, 1887, with several lines changed, two verses missing, and no credit to author Patrick Fennel. The full version appeared later that year in Fennel's *Lyrics and Songs,* published at Oswego.

The *Belle Sheridan.* Courtesy of the Historical Collections of the Great Lakes.

Lake Huron's Rockbound Shore

Oh, sad and dismal is the tale that I'll now relate to you,
That of the schooner *Persian*, her officers and crew;
They sank beneath the deep blue seas in life to rise no more,
Where wind and desolation sweep on Huron's rockbound shore.

They left Chicago on their lee, their songs they did resound—
While they, so full of joy and glee; for homeward they were bound,
Not thinking that the sword of death would smite them on their way;
While they, so full of joy and glee, upon Lake Huron lay.

In mystery their fate is sealed—they did collide, some say,
But that is all can be revealed until the Judgment Day—
Until the angels take their stand and wade the waters blue,
And then bring forth this loud command, "The schooner *Persian*'s crew!"

They were a crew of Oswego lads; sailors born and bred:
'Tis His request that they should rest in such a stormy bed.

They were a crew of gallant lads, their loss we do deplore;
While on the beach their bones will bleach off Huron's stormy shore.

Dan Sullivan was the mate's name, a man both true and brave
As ever yet by fate compelled to fill a sailor's grave;
He sank beneath the deep blue sea, in life to rise no more,
Where the wind and desolation sweep Lake Huron's rockbound shore.

Farewell, Dan, your friends will mourn your fate upon the main;
Oh, long will they look for your return back to Oswego town again.
They will miss the love-glance of your eye, and your hand they'll clasp no more;
In watery depths you now do lie, far, far from friends and shore.

The sailors' names I do not know, excepting one or two,
They sank beneath the deep blue sea—they were a luckless crew;
Not one of them escaped the wreck to tell the story o'er;
In watery depths they now do lie, far, far from friends and shore.

No gentle mother was there to press their brows, their aches and pains;
No loving wife was there to kiss their cold lips o'er again;
No loved one there, no sister nigh, they met their fate alone;
Down in they deep they all do sleep far from their friends and home.

Around Presque Isle the seabirds scream their mournful notes along,
In memory of the *Persian*'s crew, a melancholy song.
And years grow on, and days roll on, and their faces you'll see no more.
In watery depths they now do sleep, far, far from friends and shore!

Loss of the *Maggie Hunter*

A song with similar verses and the same melody as "Lake Huron's Rockbound Shore" commemorated the loss of the *Maggie Hunter*, a workhorse in the general carrying trade. The boxy canaller had long been a familiar sight on Lake Ontario when, late one autumn evening in the early 1880s, it lumbered out of the harbor at Oswego, New York, with a cargo of coal for Toronto, a mere 140 miles across the lake. The run was routine enough, but a gathering northwest storm made Captain Frank Nixon and his crew more watchful than usual. Nixon, skilled and experienced, was not afraid to take a calculated gamble, and he had shrugged off the warnings of other captains who were coming into Oswego as the *Maggie Hunter* was being towed out into the lake. Intent on making this short haul and mindful that there would not be many more with winter closing in, Nixon continued out into the lake—and on to a watery grave. No one knows what happened out on the lake that night, and the bodies that washed ashore bore few clues. Versions of the song put the crew at different sizes, but all have fewer than ten and agree that the cook was a woman.

    This version is spliced together from accounts by several people, including William Head of Picton, Ontario, who in 1933 rearranged and modified fragments obtained from "Doc" Thomas of Bronte, Ontario, Al Hare of Port Credit, Ontario, and Nelson Hudgins of Picton, Ontario. Several more stanzas come from Edith Fowke's work in 1947 with C. H. J. Snider, who contributed verses recalled by Sara Eliza Rorke of Picton, whose husband and brother had sailed Ontario schooners. Fowke collected two other verses from John Charlton of Hillier, Ontario.

> Sad and dismal is the tale to you I will relate,
> It's of the *Maggie Hunter*, her crew and their sad fate.
> They sank beneath the waters deep, on earth to rise no more,
> In one of those dreadful gales that sweep Lake Ontario's shore.
>
> They left Oswego on their lee, and the whitecaps high did roll,
> They were bound for the Queen City with three hundred tons of coal.
> There was no jollier crew sailed on the Lakes and seas
> As the canvas they did make on her and set it to the breeze.
>
> When they got outside the Oswego piers, the wind was blowing a gale,
> And by the order of their captain, it's supposed they shortened sail.
> Above all the captains on the Lakes, Frank Nixon was their chief,
> And he sailed for Toronto City with his canvas closely reefed.
>
> They sang their songs so merrily as she dashed the silvery spray,
> But little were they thinking they soon would pass away.
> Little did that gallant crew think they were doomed to die,
> But at dawn of day the next morning on the bottom cold they lie.
>
> The whitecaps dashed before her bows, like thunder they did roar;
> As if singing a sad requiem, she would plow the Lakes no more.
> Two Norman brothers were before the mast, their duty for to do,
> Along with four other men composed the *Hunter*'s crew.
>
> George Sharpe, who was their mate, from Port Credit, too, did hail,
> He was as good a mariner as ever hoisted sail.
> In vain they'll look for his return, he's bid this world adieu,
> He's one of the ill-fated six of the *Maggie Hunter*'s crew.
>
> As dusk came down and darkness next, it was a fearful night,
> The ill-fated *Maggie Hunter* she's now far out of sight.
> She's now far out of sight, my boys, now will be seen no more,
> Down in the deep now all do sleep, far from their friends onshore.
>
> Six months afterward the cook was found floating near the shore,
> The many friends that loved her will never greet her more,
> A hatch, a boom, a broken spar, the drowned woman's pale, dead face,
> Of that stout craft and gallant crew, remained the only trace.

Between Oswego town and Fair Haven, it was supposed she lay,
But that is all to be revealed upon the Judgment Day.
When the angels they shall take their stand in all the heavens bright
And tell of the *Maggie Hunter*, lost on that dreadful night.

So come all of ye that follow the land and a living there do make,
It's little do you know, my boys, of the dangers of these Lakes.
Whenever there a storm arise, think of the night it blew,
And the *Maggie Hunter*, she went down with all her gallant crew.

The Schooner *Thomas Hume*

Although vessels that "sailed away" with all hands left no survivors, plenty of material remained for speculative stories and songs. Some boats became ghost ships that haunt the Lakes eternally, in futile search of snug harbor. Others found immortality as the storied victims of cataclysm and supernatural destruction. The 209-gross-ton *Thomas Hume* found a troubling sort of immortality after it went down in Lake Michigan with all on board in 1891. Built at Manitowoc, Wisconsin, as the *H. C. Albrecht*, the two-masted hooker was acquired by lumber baron Thomas Hume of Muskegon, Michigan, at the close of the 1887 shipping season. He had the vessel rebuilt, slapped his name on it, and put it into the lumber trade between his port city and Chicago. When the *Hume* disappeared so dramatically four years later, a song quite naturally sprang up to explain its demise. The lyrics tell the familiar story of a boat gambled and lost in the quest for the top dollar brought by runs made shortly before the stormy close of the season. The *Hume*, however, did not set sail at the end of the season, as the song says, but at the beginning. It left Chicago on May 21, 1891. And when it left, it wasn't loaded with wheat, as the song holds; it was virtually empty. As the song passed from singer to singer, its hold was filled and its date with destiny moved clear to the end of the shipping season. So now, a song sung to answer questions about an unexplained sinking leaves us with questions of its own.

William Nicholas of the Steamboat Inspection Office in Chicago recalled this version in the summer of 1933. He said he had learned it "about forty years ago" as a young man sailing the Lakes.

The Schooner *Thomas Hume*

Walton, Score No. 29

The schoo-ner *Hume* is staunch and strong, She's weath-ered man-y a blow, Her hold is full of prair-ie wheat, She's bound for Buf-fa-lo.

The schooner *Hume* is staunch and strong,
    She's weathered many a blow,
Her hold is full of prairie wheat,
    She's bound for Buffalo.

Lake Michigan is long and wide,
    Lake Michigan is deep,
And gallant sailors man her ships,
    Their friends for some do weep.

The Old Man walks the after deck,
    He eyes the evening sky;
"All hands aboard—Cast off!" says he,
    "Cast off!" the mate replies.

She tows out of the river mouth,
    Aloft her flowing sail;
She clears Chicago's harbor light
    Before a sou'west gale.

The *Hume* fears no late-season storm,
    All gallant lads her crew;
It's double rates and double pay,
    Her canvas all is new.

The cabin boy looked long to land,
    The Old Man out to sea;
The mate casts anxious looks aloft,
    "All hands stand by," says he.

They're sailing on the northern star
    Well off the western shore,
November seas break on her deck
    And 'long her bulwarks roar.

The wind hauls north and bares its teeth,
    An' mountainous grow the seas;
They wash across her slanting decks
    An' on her riggin' freeze.

The night comes on all thick and dark,
    She disappears from view—
And that's the last was ever seen
    Of that gallant ship and crew!

November nights are anxious nights
    For the sailor's friends ashore—
November days are mournful days
    When his vessel is seen no more!

The Loss of the *Gilcher*

An innovative steel hull made the 301-foot *Western Reserve* the marvel of Great Lakes shipping in 1892. Just two years old, the 2,392-gross-ton freighter already had steamed to several record-setting hauls. No one demonstrated more confidence in the *Western Reserve* than Captain Peter G. Minch, who boarded the vessel at Cleveland on Sunday, August 28, with his wife, two of their children, a sister-in-law, and a niece. This run to Lake Superior was to be a happy mix of business and familial pleasure. When the Lake Superior winds kicked up on the thirtieth, the officers, in consideration of the women and children aboard, anchored within the sheltering arms of Whitefish Bay. Once again confident that they could run the lake safely, they weighed anchor and steamed to the north and west. About 9 P.M. the ship sagged oddly. A tremendous crack split the deck just ahead of the boiler house and ran down both sides of the hull.

The twenty-seven crewmen and passengers piled into the two lifeboats, one of wood and one of metal, and quickly pulled away from the crippled vessel. In ten minutes the *Western Reserve* had slipped beneath the waves and was settling for the lake bottom, six hundred feet below.

As the freighter went under, the metal yawl capsized, pitching eight crewmen and the captain's son into the waves. The people in the wooden lifeboat rushed to the rescue but could save only the boy and the ship's steward. Crowded and cold, the survivors huddled and prayed for salvation. Another freighter passed very close to them, but without signals or flares, they could not attract the attention of anyone on board. The yawl drifted sixty miles to within a mile of the Michigan shore, where, at 7 A.M., it dove, bow first, under the breakers. The wheelsman, a strong swimmer, grabbed a life preserver and made it to shore. Everyone else, including Minch and his family, drowned in the lake. Could anything deal a more crushing blow to confidence in the new steel-hulled freighters?

Yes, and it happened less than two months later.

The *W. H. Gilcher*, a near-identical twin to the *Western Reserve*, was nearing the close of its first season on the Lakes as it steamed through northern Lake Michigan. A crew of twenty-five shepherded a load of hard coal from Buffalo for Milwaukee. The 2,414-gross-ton *Gilcher* never made port. One report said that someone found a bottled message written as the *Gilcher* had been attempting to ride out a storm off the Manitou Islands at 9 P.M. on October 28, 1892. Unlike the *Western Reserve*, the *Gilcher* left no survivors. The song alludes to theories that brittleness and structural weakness of the new steel hulls caused the twin tragedies.

John E. Hayes of Port Huron recited these lines in the summer of 1933.

On October twenty-eight
    Oh, how the wind did scream!
The last time that the *Gilcher*
    And crew were ever seen.
Of death these jolly lads
    Never once did dream,
As routed for Milwaukee
    They through the Lakes did steam.

It was sad news came back:
    She never reached her port,
And stormy Michigan
    Claimed all of them on board.
The cause of her sad loss
    Is unknown up to date;
Did she collide or founder?
    None can e'er relate.

Stick to your timber boats
    As long as you can
For they lay-to rough nights
    Out on Lake Michigan.
It was a fearful night,
    The *Gilcher* should turned-to,
But she held to her course
    'Til off the Manitous.

Says a sailor's hurried note
    That later came to light,
They were breasting mount'n'us seas
    At nine o'clock that night.

Not one of them was saved
    And someone is to blame,
For that same fate before
    Her sister ship o'ercame.

She disappeared from view,
    The *Gilcher* is no more!
She's joined her sister ship
    Lost scarce a year before.
Lost in Lake Michigan
    They did not reach the shore,
The gallant ship and crew
    Will sail the Lakes no more!

Lost on the *Lady Elgin*

Named for the wife of Canada's governor general, the *Lady Elgin,* a 252-foot-long side-wheel passenger steamer with a beam of nearly thirty-five feet, was built at Buffalo in 1851. After some years of service based in Buffalo, the owners sold the vessel. It became a popular passenger and excursion steamer hailing out of Chicago. The *Lady Elgin,* at 1,037 gross tons, was a natural choice for the Milwaukee Union

The *Lady Elgin.* Courtesy of the Historical Collections of the Great Lakes.

Guards, a local militia, which bought a block of tickets for the boat's regular run through Lake Michigan to catch a September 7, 1860, appearance in Chicago by Democratic presidential candidate Stephen A. Douglas. After a full day, the tired travelers steamed out of the Chicago River shortly before midnight under threatening skies. Passengers and crew numbered 393, and the vessel carried a large cargo of freight and cattle. Two hours later, despite the hour and the weather, some excursionists were still dancing and enjoying the band on the festively lighted deck when off Winnetka, Illinois, the *Lady Elgin* ran into heavy seas, rain, and wind.

Suddenly, the Chicago-bound schooner *Augusta,* packed solid with lumber and running along the shore before a nor'easter, emerged from the black night and gored the *Lady Elgin* amidships. The *Augusta,* suffering damage only to its headgear, shook itself free of the mortally wounded *Lady Elgin* and continued off into the darkness. The *Lady Elgin* was gone in about twenty minutes.

News of the late-night disaster reached shore about 6:30 A.M. with one of the lifeboats. For hours afterward, people watched helplessly from shore as passengers and crew washed toward them, clinging to pieces of wreckage, only to drown within sight of refuge as the rollers crashed and boiled on the sandbars.

The enormity of the disaster, the worst on the Great Lakes up until that time, prompted a number of poems and songs. One of the first was produced by Chicago printer Henry C. Work, who wrote it for the next day's edition. His tribute became a national best-seller, even during the Civil War. The song seemed to have a special appeal among lakesmen, who sang it in forecastles and taverns for decades after the disaster. The song is credited with giving name to the town of Elgin, Oregon, established September 28, 1885, by William Hamilton, who had heard a niece and nephew singing "The Loss of the *Lady Elgin.*"

In a chilling four-year anniversary of the sinking, the new bark *Mojave* disappeared without a trace from a clear Lake Michigan. The crew was composed almost entirely of men from the *Augusta,* including Captain Darius Nelson Malott.

With a death toll ranging from 279 to 350, the loss of the *Lady Elgin* remained the worst disaster on the Lakes for fifty-three years. In 1913 another excursion steamer, the *Eastland,* rolled over at the dock and killed 835, a Great Lakes record unlikely to be surpassed. The *Eastland*'s victims died in the Chicago River, where the *Lady Elgin* had begun its final voyage.

Lost on the *Lady Elgin*
by Henry C. Work, circa 1860

DISASTER SONGS

Up from the poor man's cottage, out of the mansion door,
Sweeping across the harbor, and echoing along the shore,
Fanned by morning breezes, drawn by the ev'ning gale,
Cometh the voice of mourning, a sad and solemn wail.

    Lost on the *Lady Elgin,*
    Sinking to rise no more,
    Numbered with that three hundred,
    Who failed to reach the shore.

Staunch was the noble steamer, precious the freight she bore,
Gaily she swept the harbor but a few short hours before.
Gaily she loosed her cable, joyously rang her bell,
Little did they think ere morning it would toll so sad a knell.

Hark, 'tis the voice of children weeping for parents gone;
Children that slept at evening, orphans at wake of dawn.
Sisters for brothers weeping, husbands for missing wives,
These are the ties that were sundered, in those three hundred lives.

The Shores of Michigan (The *Antelope*)

Some names, sounding fleet and exotic, were used over and over again. "Antelope" was one such name, applied in the late 1800s to schooners, propellers, a brig, a scow, a barge, and even a tug. These vessels shared more than a namesake; they shared misadventure. Most or all the *Antelope*s sank, ran aground, collided, caught fire, or met with some other disaster. One of the worst *Antelope* disasters occurred in Lake Michigan and left but one survivor, Thomas Peckham of Oswego, New York, who is credited with composing the song.

    Edward Navin of Cobourg, Ontario, contributed the second, fourth, and fifth stanzas and the first half of the sixth and last stanzas in the summer of 1933. Israel La Roche of Wolfe Island, Kingston, Ontario, added the first stanza and some variations on Navin's lines. Ben Peckham added the third stanza and some lines of the seventh, and said that his father, Thomas, had been a sailor on the *Antelope* and wrote the song. Thomas Parsons's son, John, of Oswego, New York, added the last half of the sixth stanza, rewrote the seventh, and changed lines in some other stanzas.

A rough sketch of the *Antelope*. Courtesy of the Historical Collections of the Great Lakes.

The Shores of Michigan

Murdock, Score No.14

You all may bless your happy lot, who dwell safe upon the shore,
Free from the tempests and the blasts that 'round us sailors roar.
It's little you know of the hardships, nor do you understand
The stormy nights we do endure off the shores of Michigan.

On the sixteenth of November, from Chicago we set sail;
Kind Providence did favor us with a sweet and pleasant gale.
With our canvas spread all to the wind and our hearts as light as air,
We left Chicago far behind, our colors flying fair.

Besides our captain and our mate, there were eight of us on board;
Two lads shipped in Chicago, their names I never heard;
They were two gay and lively lads, from Ireland they came;
Their friends may weep, they're in the deep, they'll ne'er see them again.

On the seventeenth in the morning, an angry storm did rise;
And fearful billows loud did roar, and dismal grew the skies.

We reefed her down, made all things snug, and then contrived a plan
To save the life of the *Antelope* off the shores of Michigan.

On the eighteenth in the morning—and what I say is true—
The ice upon our riggin' froze, and the cold winds fiercely blew!
And no one thought in a few short hours that very afternoon,
Some would be froze and some be drowned—the *Antelope* was doomed!

The cold increased, the tempest raged, the huge seas loud did roar—
With our canvas gone, both anchors out, we were drifting toward the shore!
Our captain said to his brother John, "I think I see the land,
But only one can save us now from the shores of Michigan!"

We drifted with each pounding sea, and then we struck stern on:
Our mainm'st at the deck was broke, our mizzenm'st was gone!
The huge seas raked her fore and aft, and then she swung broadside,
And three men overboard were swept into that raging tide.

Our captain tried to swim ashore, our precious lives to save,
But by his brave and manly act, he was lost beneath the waves.
And only one of that gallant crew was in life once more to stand;
And for miles and miles the *Antelope* lined the shores of Michigan!

These lines come from a song about another *Antelope* that met a similar fate on Lake Superior:

Our deck was coated with tons of ice, but not a sailor knew,
Some would be froze and some be drowned of our big freighter's crew.
The huge seas raked her fore and aft, the cold wind loud did roar,
We struck stern on and swung broadside to our doom on Superior.

Cruel Waves of Huron

The three-masted, 240-ton schooner *William Shupe* of Port Huron broke up on a shoal about five miles north of its home port and destination on May 19, 1894. Every member of the crew survived, but in a cruel twist of fate, four volunteers that went out to help the disintegrating vessel drowned. The *Shupe* had been sailing from Alpena to Port Huron when it waterlogged in rough seas off Sanilac County in the thumb of mitten-shaped lower Michigan. Buoyed by its cargo, the *Shupe* wallowed on until it was caught in the teeth of a sixty-mile-an-hour gale that carried off canvas, deck load, and cabin. With the stricken vessel drifting helplessly, the crew lashed themselves in the rigging. The men clung there for twenty-four hours until the *Shupe* finally settled to the bottom north of Port Huron and began to break up about two hundred yards from shore. A local tug, the *Thompson,* took volunteers and a yawl out to assist the schooner. A spar projecting from the wreckage speared the little boat, and it capsized. All were lost except Dan Lynn, who was hauled out of the breakers five hours later, unconscious, a mile down the shore.

In the meantime, the lifesaving crew from Sand Beach arrived by rail. After several attempts, the crew succeeded in shooting a line over the splintering schooner and took off all on board in spite of huge seas breaking over the vessel's deck. Lynn recovered from his near-drowning and received the Congressional Medal for his heroism.

This version was reconstructed by A. P. Gallino, J. Sylvester "Ves" Ray, and William J. Small, all Port Huron sailors, in Small's home one evening in the summer of 1933. They said it went to the melody of "The Two Orphans," which presented a riddle, as there doesn't seem to be a song by that name. Lee Murdock, who produced the scores in this book, thought he recalled the phrase "the two orphans" in a song he remembered as "The Milwaukee Fire." When he looked in Harry B. Peters's *Folk Songs Out of Wisconsin,* where he thought he had seen the song, Murdock did not find it. There was, however, a song called "The Newhall House Fire," about a tragic 1883 fire at a Milwaukee hotel. The words and the melody fit together fairly well. However, a few pages earlier in the book he found "The Brooklyn Theater Fire," a song about a similar 1876 tragedy. That melody fit these words much better. And the chorus concludes, "don't forget those two orphans."

Have we made a leap of logic, or has Murdock unlocked the mystery of "Cruel Waves of Huron," and done exactly as some sailor-singer did a hundred years before him?

The Lake Huron fishing vessel *Belle Jane Ann* of Kincardine. Courtesy of the Historical Collections of the Great Lakes.

Cruel Waves of Huron

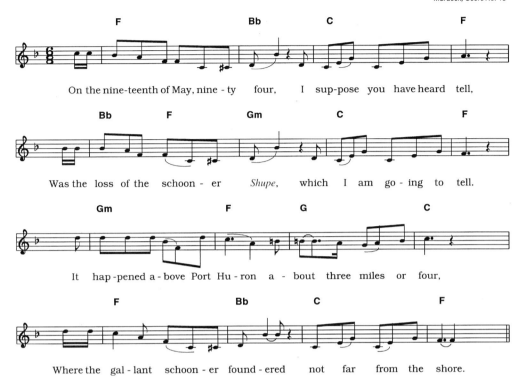

Murdock, Score No. 13

On the nineteenth of May, ninety-four, I suppose you have heard tell,
Was the loss of the schooner *Shupe*, which I am going to tell.
It happened above Port Huron about three miles or four,
Where the gallant schooner foundered not far from the shore.

The seas were rolling high, loud roared the northeast blast;
The schooner was trying for port, a distress flag on her mast.
The news had reached Port Huron of the schooner *Shupe*'s sad plight,
And Captain Cox and crew steamed forth the storm to fight.

Their tug it neared the wreck, whose canvas had carried away;
Her cabin and deck load gone, deep in the seas she lay.
Her crew in the rigging were lashed, they had given up all hope
When the *Thompson* breasting the gale upon their visions broke.

The *Thompson* neared the wreck and finally launched her yawl,
And five brave sailor lads responded to the call.
There was King and Lewis and Mills and Little and Daniel Lynn;
They pulled for the drifting *Shupe* out in the awful din.

They reached the foundering craft, her gallant crew to save,
When against a fallen spar they were crushed by a giant wave.
Oh, pray for their souls you on shore! You friends and parents and wives!
Five brave young sailor lads are fighting for their lives!

The lifesaving crew of Sand Beach came by a special train;
They cannot launch their boat, though they try again and again!
The *Shupe* drifts in on shore; a lifeline is made fast,
And her crew is saved from death in the teeth of the stinging blast.

"But where is the volunteer crew?" those on shore in frenzy ask;
No ships of oak, nor men in that raging storm can last!
Only stout Dan Lynn is saved; five hours he fought the sea;
Four other brave sailor lads sank to eternity!

The Foundering of the *Asia*

So vast and distinct is Lake Huron's Georgian Bay that it might be considered the sixth Great Lake. It's an especially dangerous body of water, lacerated with islands and rocks. Pirates are rumored to have haunted its labyrinthian channels. Around the Great Lakes and along the Georgian shore in particular, "The Foundering of the *Asia*" became a favorite. The song tells of one of the Lakes' greatest disasters, and in passing from one singer to the next it acquired a variety of verses and arrangements. Canadian-built, the 450-gross-ton propeller *Asia* cleared Collingwood, Ontario, on September 13, 1882, with shanty boys and supplies for the start of the logging season at camps near the mouth of the French River, farther up the bay. The vessel stopped at Owen Sound to take on additional passengers and freight for Manitoulin Island and Sault Ste. Marie at the entrance to Lake Superior.

As the *Asia* steamed out, its decks showed all the signs of fast and heavy loading. Boxes and barrels crowded the hurricane deck, horses stamped on the main deck, and men curled up wherever they could as the vessel headed north into a freshening breeze.

By morning, wind and seas had built to alarming proportions. Captain J. N. Savage directed the *Asia* toward the lee of Lonely Island, some miles away, but the craft foundered about noon within sight of shelter. Those who made it to the lifeboats had to survive repeated capsizings. Only two made it all the way through: seventeen-year-old Duncan A. Tinkiss and another teen, Christina Ann Morrison. They spent the afternoon, the night, and the next morning in the captain's metal lifeboat, watching luck and life run out for the handful around them. Bobbing about in a boat without oars, stowing the dead beneath the seats, the young pair finally washed ashore. An Indian helped the exhausted teens into his canoe and paddled to Parry Sound, where they related one of the Great Lakes' worst disasters.

These stanzas come from several sources, including clippings and recollections. The seventh through ninth stanzas came from Mrs. Robert Reid of Red Bay, Ontario, in 1934. She had sailed as cook on Lake Huron lumber schooners for eight seasons in the 1880s and early 1890s, and learned the song by listening to sailors singing it.

Loud roared the dreadful thunder,
    And stormy was the day,
When the *Asia* left the harbor
    To cross the Georgian Bay.

One hundred souls she had on board,
    Likewise a costly store,
But on her trip this gallant ship
    She sank to rise no more.

There were three and thirty shanty boys,
    All hearty, strong, and brave,
All bound for Byng Inlet,
    But they found a watery grave.

The men cried "Save the captain!"
    As the waters round them raged,
"Oh, no," cried he, "ne'er think of me,
    'Til all on board are saved."

The cabin boy was first to die
    So young, so brave, so true.
His parents weep, while his body sleeps
    In Georgian's watery grave.

I'll never forget MacDougall,
    Which was the purser's name,
When immortalized, the deeds he did
    Were handed down to fame.

Likewise young Willie Christy and
    His newly wedded bride
Were bound for Manitoulin,
    Where their parents did reside.

"Oh, had we only left the boat
    Last night on Owen Sound,
Oh, Willie dear, why came we here,
    To in these waters drown?"

"Mama will say, why such delay?
    But oh, she must excuse,
'Twill make her sad, likewise my dad,
    When they hear the dreadful news."

Their earthly cries would rend the skies.
    Which awful must have been,
For the storm that day on Georgian Bay,
    Was awful to be seen.

Of all the souls she had on board,
    Two only are alive:
Miss Morrison and Tinkiss,
    Are all that did survive.

Miss Morrison and Tinkiss,
    Their names I can't forget,
Were saved in a lifeboat,
    Which four times did upset.

Around each family circle,
    How sad the news to hear!
The foundering of the *Asia,*
    Still sounding in each ear.

But in the deep they're fast asleep,
    Their earthly trials are o'er.
Out on the beach, their bones do bleach,
    Along the Georgian shore.

The Dismasting of the *Cummings*

A near-wreck occasioned this song about the canaller *M. J. Cummings,* a 137-foot schooner built at Oswego in 1874 and named for a local vessel owner. A workhorse in the general cargo trade, the 330-ton *Cummings* sailed from Oswego into an Ontario gale that stripped away its sticks and sails. Believed at first to be sunk, the

Cummings and its crew survived, their good fortune immortalized in this song. But the *Cummings* sailed on borrowed time. Ten years to the month after it had survived the dismasting, the schooner sank with a cargo of coal. Although it went down in just fifteen feet of water just three-fourths of a mile outside the Milwaukee harbor, six lives were lost. Some old sailors had fuzzy recollections of a few verses from a song about the second accident, but that song, like the *Cummings*, appears to be lost forever.

    John S. Parsons recalled this song in the summer of 1933 and said he had learned it from local sailors soon after the dismasting. Parsons said he understood that it was composed by Thomas Peckham of Oswego.

> In eighteen eighty-four, upon the first of May,
> The schooner *M. J. Cummings* from Oswego sailed away.
> With her canvas spread aloft, her hull all tight and sound,
> The *Cummings* left the harbor, for Chicago she was bound.
>
> The *Cummings* left the harbor, she sailed out in the lake,
> On board a jolly crew and four hundred tons of freight.
> Her booms well out to leeward, around the seagulls soar,
> With a fair wind to Dalhousie, she skirts the southern shore.
>
> But as the next day dawned, the wind in fury blew,
> And caught the good ship *Cummings* and her Oswego crew.
> Sad news came o'er the wire; it was sad news to me—
> "The *Cummings* is dismasted and sunk beneath the sea!"
>
> On all our streets that day, sad hearts did wear a pall—
> The *Cummings* she was lost in a Lake Ontario squall!
> She was sailing off the shore a'howling up the lake
> Before a strong nor'easter when she met her tragic fate.
>
> At noon came other news, and it raised our hearts in praise—
> "The gallant crew and ship were from the waters saved!
> The *Cummings* was dismasted, she lost her spars and sails,
> But those on board may still face other Ontario gales!"
>
> Three men were in the riggin,' her canvas for to stow,
> When a racing angry squall struck her a savage blow.
> She faltered and lost her way, her tops'ls taken aback,
> Her forestays snapped, then parted with the sound of a cannon's crack.
>
> Three men were in the riggin', her tall masts staggered and fell,
> Her lee rail went deep under, and her captain loud did yell:
> "Cut the riggin' adrift; lend a hand to those boys in the treacherous waves!"
> The good ship righted herself, and her brave boys all were saved.

And now to conclude and finish this song I've tried to write—
The *Cummings* is now in Buffalo, and will stay there 'til made right.
And when she gets her outfit, and clearance for to go,
May her sails have pleasant gales till she arrives at Chicago.

The Fierce *Alpena* Blow

The side-wheel steamer *Alpena* found some small measure of immortality in the very storm that killed it. For years after its disappearance, sailors reported seeing the ghost ship sailing on stormy nights. The *Alpena* could scarcely have been on a more mundane mission when, on October 16, 1880, it vanished with sixty to eighty people aboard. The 653-gross-ton freight and passenger steamer had taken on a load at Muskegon, Michigan, and skipped twelve miles south along the Lake Michigan shore to the usual topping-off stop at Grand Haven. From there, the *Alpena* began the cross-lake excursion to Chicago. This was a daily, bread-and-butter route for the Goodrich Transportation Company of Chicago, and the *Alpena* customarily exchanged whistle blasts with its sister ship, the *Muskegon,* as they passed at mid-lake.

Passengers and crew had enjoyed the seventy-two-degree highs of an Indian summer day as the *Alpena* began preparing for its trip. About midnight, though, a wind scourged Lake Michigan with such tremendous force that sails were stripped from oaken masts and thermometers dove to freezing. Some said it was a gale; others called it a tornado. In the retelling, it was known for years as "the big windstorm." Daybreak found close to a hundred grounded, foundering, or tattered vessels littering the lake and shores. The *Alpena* was not among them. After several days of futile searching and the recovery of flotsam, including the piano from the *Alpena*'s salon, the boat was declared a loss. About 120 lives were lost in the windstorm that night, half of them with the side-wheel steamer that gave the storm its other name: "The Fierce *Alpena* Blow."

Captain Manus J. Bonner of Charlevoix, Michigan, recalled these fragments in July 1932. He said that he had learned them aboard Lake Michigan schooners as a young man in the 1880s.

The Fierce *Alpena* Blow

Murdock, Score No. 16

In eigh-teen hun-dred eigh-ty, in Oc-to-ber, the six-teenth day,

The *Al-pe-na* met her doom, and now be-neath the wa-ters lay.

She was cross-ing wide Lake Mich-i-gan, she was both staunch and true,

But she sank in the rag-ing wa-ters with her pas-sen-gers and crew.

In eighteen hundred eighty, in October, the sixteenth day,
The *Alpena* met her doom, and now beneath the waters lay.
She was crossing wide Lake Michigan, she was both staunch and true,
But she sank in the raging waters with her passengers and crew.

The steamer cleared Grand Haven in the evening's ominous light,
She was bound for Chicago when she steamed out in the night.
Captain Napier was on the bridge, on board a jolly throng,
No one had any fear, the *Alpena* was staunch and strong.

She steamed out in the night, her course was south, southwest;
Some stayed in her bright saloon, some passengers went to rest.
Then a cold wind came from the north, no stars shone in the sky,
And a hurricane descended, and the seas grew wild and high.

Awakened from their slumbers with cries that would rend your heart,
"All hands on deck to save your lives, the vessel is going apart!"

No welcome port was near them, they got no friendly aid,
And not a soul was left alive to tell the dreadful tale.

No sun came with the morning, only the tempest's roar—
The passengers grew fearful as the storm down on them bore.
Then a panic seized each heart, their loved ones for to save,
The steamer plunged and labored, death rode each mounting wave!

The steamer plunged and labored in the teeth of the northern blast
No lifeboats could be lowered, each plunge must be her last!
The big seas raked her decks, and spray by tons did strike—
The noble steamer faltered, the *Alpena* sank from sight!

It was a few days later some wreckage came ashore,
Sad news it brought to us, our friends to see no more.
Sad parents walked the beach, 'tis sad for them to know
Their dear ones, they were lost in that fierce *Alpena* blow.

Someone is to blame for this, who it is no one can say;
It could not have been Captain Napier, as honest as the day.
But may their souls all rest in peace, is our most earnest prayer,
And may it be the same with all good Christians everywhere.

The Loss of the *Gilbert Mollison*

The schooner *Gilbert Mollison*, 316 gross tons, sank with all hands during a late-October storm in 1873. The two-masted vessel had left Chicago with a cargo of corn for its home port of Oswego, New York, on the twenty-fourth and was last sighted three days later in severe weather off South Manitou Island in Lake Michigan. Some time later, the *Mollison*'s empty yawl came ashore at Good Harbor, Michigan. The *Mollison* was a "home boat" built in Oswego in 1871, owned there, and carrying a local crew, so its loss left several empty places at Oswego dinner tables that winter.

    This comes from a manuscript in the possession of Ben Peckham of Oswego, New York, in the summer of 1933. He knew nothing of either author or air.

Another proud and gallant ship,
    Another noble crew,
Have sunk beneath the angry waves,
    Beneath the lake's dark blue.
No more will her flowing snow-white sails
    By gentle winds be filled,
Nor will those lost ones more be heard,
    For they in death are stilled.

No more across the white-capped wave
    Will she go bounding free;
No more will her silvered wake be seen
    Upon the moonlit sea.
For her smooth sides of oak at last
    Have yielded to the waves
Which now are holding sure and fast
    The loved ones in their graves.

She often has in days gone by
    Bore kind hearts upon her deck,
But some of them are mouldering now
    Along with the sad wreck;
And some are in the drifting sand
    Which lines the weary shore
Where the lonely night winds sigh
    Where the dreary seabirds soar.

And now kind friends are waiting,
    And watching o'er the main
For the forms of loved ones missing
    But their watching is in vain;
For they nevermore across the waves
    Back to their friends be borne;
They are sleeping and are waiting for
    The resurrection morn.

Kind mothers, too, are waiting for
    Their sons across the sea;
But those kind sons will nevermore
    Come back again to thee.
And for those sons will mothers' eyes
    Be wet with bitter tears;
And for them, too, will mothers' hearts
    Be sad the coming years.

A young wife waits the coming of one
    That she loved so well;
How good and kind that husband was
    She now alone can tell.
And down her cheeks the tears will fall
    Like drops of summer rain
To wet the place where once he trod,
    But will never trod again!

And brother, too, is waiting still
    To welcome brother home,
To share with him that hallowed place
    Which now seems so alone!
But those loved ones, too, have found
    A home beneath the sea,
In lonely graves and rocky caves
    Where other loved ones be.

There is a time that's coming,
    The Good Book it has said,
When the dark waves will open wide
    And give up the long-lost dead.
Oh, that will be a glorious time
    When life's voyage is done,
And until that time we'll bid farewell
    To the crew of the *Mollison*.

Let the Lower Lights Be Burning

A number of ex-schoonermen recalled this revival hymn as a favorite of Captain Henry Bundy, an evangelist who piloted a succession of gospel ships named *Glad Tidings* in the 1880s and 1890s. One vessel, a steamer, is said to have borne a gold cross on its foremast and gold trim on its forecastle. When in port, Bundy held services to steer men clear of the shoals of their devil-may-care ways and on a course for the Savior's Great Lighthouse. In his memoir, P. P. Bliss relates the description of his associate, evangelist Dwight L. Moody, of the dramatic scene that inspired the hymn Bliss wrote:

> On a dark, stormy night when the waves rolled like mountains and not a star was to be seen, a boat rocking and plunging neared the Cleveland harbor. "Are you sure this is Cleveland?" asked the captain, seeing only one light from the lighthouse.
> "Quite sure, sir," replied the pilot.
> "Where are the lower lights?"

"Gone out, sir."
"Can you make the harbor?"
"We must or perish, sir!"

And with a strong hand and a brave heart the old pilot turned the wheel. But, alas, without the light to guide him, he missed the channel, and with a crash upon the rocks, the boat was shivered, and many a life lost in watery grave. Brethren, the Master will take care of the Great Lighthouse: let us keep the lower lights burning!

Bliss told the story in his *Memoir of P. P. Bliss*, edited by D. W. Whittle and published by A. S. Barnes and Company of New York in 1877.

Let the Lower Lights Be Burning
by Phillip Bliss, Circa 1871

Bright-ly beams our Fa-ther's mer-cy from His light-house ev-er-more;

But to us He gives the keep-ing of the lights a-long the shore.

Let the low-er lights be burn-ing! Send a gleam a-cross the wave!

Some poor faint-ing, strug-gling sea-man you may res-cue, you may save.

Brightly beams our Father's mercy
    From His lighthouse evermore;
But to us He gives the keeping
    Of the lights along the shore.

Let the lower lights be burning!
    Send a gleam across the wave!
Some poor fainting, struggling seaman
    You may rescue, you may save.

Dark the night of sin has settled,
    Loud the angry billows roar;
Eager eyes are watching, longing
    For the lights along the shore.

Trim your feeble lamp, my brother!
    Some poor sailor, tempest-tossed,
Trying now to make the harbor,
    In the darkness, may be lost.

The Schooner *Oriole*

Just 1,447 tons of iron ore shipped out of Lake Superior in all of 1855. On August 8, 1862, with the war under way, more than a third of that amount, 501 tons, sailed out of Marquette harbor on the 141-foot three-master *Oriole*. About 3 A.M., the aging side-wheeler *Illinois* emerged from a thick fog and struck the 403-ton *Oriole*, cutting it in two. Twelve of the thirteen people aboard the *Oriole* died, including Captain John McAddams, his wife, and his mother-in-law. The sole survivor in Lake Superior's first fatal collision was the cook.

    Ben Peckham of Oswego, New York, recalled these stanzas one day in the summer of 1933.

Attention give both young and old
    And listen unto me,
While I relate the hardships and
    The dangers of the sea:
I'll sing to you of the *Illinois*
    And of her reckless crew,
How she sank the schooner *Oriole*
    All in the waters blue.

It was in the month of August,
    In the year of sixty-two;
They were sailing on Superior,
    With hearts both light and true;
When suddenly a crash was heard!
    No hand was nigh to save,
The schooner faltered, filled, and sank!
    They sleep beneath the wave.

Besides the captain and his wife,
    They had some passengers too:
And before the mast eight seamen brave
    Belongin' to her crew.
Now twelve of them a'sleeping lie
    Where the stormy billows roll!
And only one escaped the wreck
    Of the schooner *Oriole*!

God bless these wives and widows,
    God bless these orphans, too;
God bless all these good people
    Who're mourning for this crew.
And God bless all while here on earth,
    A few more days we'll spend;
And I say again, God bless us all,
    And here my song shall end.

The Steam Tug *Olson*

When sailing vessels carried forest products, coal, grain, and iron ore, tugboats forged a vital link in the transportation system. Tugging was lucrative, and several hundred of these small, powerful vessels towed the larger craft through connecting rivers and canals and in and out of harbors. From the late 1880s on, however, as schooners lost more and more business to steam-powered bulk-carrying "freighters," competition among tugs grew keener and meaner. Tugs ran farther and farther out into the Lakes in search of tows. Buffalo tugs at times went as far west as the mouth of the Detroit River to pick up inbound sailboats. Tugs from other locations went just as far. They were built for harbor conditions, however, not for the pounding storms that sweep the Lakes, and more than a few were lost or suffered serious damage. The Buffalo tug *Olson,* according to this song, steamed out into Lake Erie one night apparently looking for inbound grain schooners. It had gone about ten miles—to Windmill Point on the Canadian shore—when it ran into a southwest storm that doused the fires under its boiler.

    Beaver Island's "Francie" Roddy, who sailed Lake Michigan for more than twenty years, recalled this song in the summer of 1932. He said he had learned it from his father, who "could sing songs all day without stopping—with a few drinks."

Come, listen to me one and all,
    A story I will tell
Of the wreck of a gallant tug one night,
    You all did know her well.

She was the steam tug *Olson,* boys,
    She belonged to Buffalo;
She steamed out of the harbor late
    In hopes to get a tow.

This tug was built both stout and strong,
    Likewise she was well manned;
With an engineer, a fireman,
    A wheelsman, and deckhand.

Our captain's name was Michael Carr,
    No better in the land;
And a young man on a pleasure trip
    Composed this little band.

We steamed as far as Windmill Point,
    No vessels came in sight;
A blow came on, the seas rolled high,
    And stormy grew the night.

We were seated in the pilothouse,
    A'listenin' to a song
When our engineer came forward fast
    Sayin' "Captain, there's something wrong!

The water's making in her hold,
    Our pumps can't keep her free!"
He left the wheel and went below
    To see what it could be.

He soon came running back on deck,
    The leak could not discern;
The water came a'pourin' in
    From somewhere in the stern!

The captain shouted, "Head 'er round,
    An' point 'er for the light!"
The clouds grew thick and threatening,
    A'roarin' came the night.

We signaled to a passing tug
    That went along the shore;
Our signals did not reach her crew
    And far from us she bore.

This sketch illustrates one of the many vessels said to have simply "sailed away." Courtesy of the Historical Collections of the Great Lakes.

Our engine stopped, we lost our way,
    We wallowed in the sea,
We drifted before the sou'west gale
    Fast on a dangerous lee.

The rain and seas drove o'er our deck,
    We tried to build a raft,
But our pilothouse had carried away,
    Likewise our cabin aft.

We were foundering in Niagara,
    And scarce could shout no more,
Two men came out in a small boat
    And took us to the Canada shore.

The Wreck of the *Julia Dean*

West of the Straits of Mackinac in northern Lake Michigan lies a group of twelve islands. The largest and best known is Beaver Island; the most dangerous is Skillagalee, or Ile aux Galets. On October 6, 1855, the 150-foot wooden brig *Julia Dean* stranded on the Skillagalee shoal and the lake hammered it into splinters. The vessel's master, Captain E. S. Wilson, blamed the misfortune on people who lived on Beaver Island. At the time, the island was home to James Jesse Strang, self-proclaimed king of a faction of Mormons who had split with Brigham Young. Strang had moved his followers to the island in the late 1840s. Mainlanders viewed the king and his adherents with great fear and suspected them of mischief in the shipping lanes, including piracy. By 1852, Strang's island community was large enough to get him elected to the Michigan legislature. As state representative for that part of Michigan, King Strang had considerable say in the appointment of the keeper for the Skillagalee light. Captain Wilson said that a false light had lured him onto the rocks, and he blamed it on the Mormons. The Strangites vigorously denied the charge in their newspaper, the *Northern Islander,* in an issue published the following year. The denial became moot because Strang was assassinated and fishermen from St. Helena Island and the surrounding area drove the Mormons from the island. The surviving fragments of this song do not say anything about the accusations of a false light.

    Mrs. Manus J. Bonner of Charlevoix, Michigan, recalled these verses in 1932. Her husband, a schooner sailor and captain for half a century, said he had heard it many times on the long reaches of Lake Michigan to and from Chicago. Major D. W. Whittle published the song in a book of verse in 1887.

Nigh forty years have passed away
The sailors on the island say,
    Since the wreck of the *Julia Dean.*
Caught near the land some miles below,
She foundered in the fiercest blow,
    The Straits have ever seen.

A howling wind, a clouded sky,
A shallow sea, waves running high,
    With island on the lee—

This briefly is the tale they tell;
The crew and captain labored well,
    But could not set her free.
. . . .
In summer days the south winds blow,
And waves and ripples come and go,
    Lapping her rugged keel:
As if in sorrow for their rage,
They seek all vainly to assuage,
    The old ship for her ill.

All summer long the wild birds sing,
As 'eath the wave they dip their wing,
    And shining plumage preen.
Above the cliff the pine trees bend,
And their sweet odors seaward send,
    Over the *Julia Dean*.

Sweet requiem this, of island green,
Meet requiem for the *Julia Dean*,
    Down by the circling shore.
Winds and waves forever heard,
Murmuring trees and song of bird,
    Blending forevermore.

The Schooner *Jenkins*

The latest navigational satellites and computerized weather detection systems can't prevent a shadow from falling over the Great Lakes each November, the year's deadliest month. As vessels push to make just one more run before the winter shutdown, storms add cold and ice to the usual recipe for trouble. It can be a delicate race. For vessel owners, quitting too early means missing a trip that could have helped spread the expenses of a season already shortened by winter. But running too long could mean losing cargo, vessel, and crew. People in Great Lakes towns depended on these late-season deliveries to put more food on their winter tables, a little variety in their pantries, and that dreamed-for doll or sled under the Christmas tree. The crews themselves were understandably impatient to finish the trip, prepare the vessel for winter, and leave for a few months of home and hearth. Many late-season tragedies occurred when severe storms swept the Lakes, overtaking heavily laden vessels. This and the next half-dozen songs relate November tragedies.

    Just two years old and about as many hours away from the winter layup in its home port of Oswego, New York, the lumber schooner *Isaac G. Jenkins*, 327 gross tons, went down with all hands in a severe blizzard on Lake Ontario on November 30, 1875. On board at the time were Captain John Brown, two mates, and four sailors, all from Oswego, and a woman cook from Buffalo. Built at Algonac, Michigan, the canaller was full of wheat from Chicago.

    This compilation is patched together from several versions. The first stanza came from Captain Israel La Roche of Wolf Island, Ontario. He recalled it and a scattering of lines from the song as he had learned it on board Lake Ontario timber schooners shortly after the loss of the *Jenkins*. The remaining stanzas are from the May 31, 1928, *Oswego Palladium-Times*. William Murray, who spent all his life at or around Murray's Inn on the channel between White Lake and Lake Michigan, learned the song as a young man listening to lumber vessel sailors singing in the inn's barroom.

Come, shipmates, listen to my story,
    I'll sing you one both sad and true,
How dark one night 'neath the stormy waters
    Sank brave John Brown and his crew.

'Twas on a bright November morning,
    They left the snow-clad shore behind;
Each noble heart on board was yearning,
    As thoughts of home rose in his mind.

They longed to see those smiling faces
    That often met them, but no more
Will those dear ones or places
    See them cross the threshold o'er.

For beneath Ontario's heaving billows,
    Those brave men now are safe to rest,
Sleeping on their rocky pillows
    Beneath the cold waves' stormy crest.

There sleeps John Brown, the good ship's master,
    And McDonald, mate of the ill-fated crew,
Who, along with the rest of the sad disaster,
    Were as kindhearted men as I ever knew.

There sleeps John Stewart, as kind a sailor
    As ever stood on a vessel's deck;
James Otis, too, as good a man
    And as brave as the rest who sank with the wreck.

Their shipmate, too, was William Bonner,
    A good, kindhearted, honest man,
You knew him well, a man of honor,
    You miss the grip of his friendly hand.

Shipmates, I know that you will miss him,
    Men like him, 'tis hard to find;
His children, loved ones, they too miss him,
    And his loving wife he left behind.

When the snows of winter fast are falling,
    And hunger stands at the widow's door,
Remember charity is your calling,
    And he who gives will have the more.

When the dark waves are wildly rolling,
    On old Ontario's rocky shore,
When the seabirds are idly soaring,
    Remember those the waves roll o'er.

Sometimes, shipmates, you may be missing,
    Sometimes o'er you the waves may roll,
And o'er your head 'neath the heaving billows
    The birds may soar, the ship's bell toll.

The Wreck of the *Belle Sheridan*

Many vessels that sailed the Lakes in the late 1800s were small, family-run affairs, owned by one man and crewed by his brothers, sons, and cousins. The two-masted, 200-gross-ton *Belle Sheridan* was just such a boat. When it sailed out of Charlotte harbor, now a part of Rochester, New York, in November 1880, five of the men aboard the twenty-eight-year-old boat were McSherrys. The Old Man was James McSherry; four of the six crewmen were his sons. Loaded with coal and bound for its home port of Toronto across Lake Ontario, the *Belle Sheridan* ran into a severe storm on November 7, 1880, and broke up on a bar off Weller's Bay. Three of the brothers died, as did owner-master James McSherry and the mates. The lone survivor was James McSherry Jr., who lashed himself to some wreckage. Despite losing his father and brothers on the Lakes, McSherry Jr. sailed them for years as master of his own vessels.

This song appeared in the *Toronto Evening Telegram* on January 7, 1933, as recalled by John S. Parsons of Oswego. He attributed it to Mike Ryan, also of Oswego.

In the year of eighteen eighty,
    On a clear November day
With coal bound for Toronto,
    They left the Charlotte Bay.

They watched old Charlotte harbor
    Till it was out of sight;
They thought of old Scott Street slip,
    Which was the boys' delight.

They sailed along for many miles,
    The crew stood on their deck;
They little knew they would be lost
    All in a fearful wreck.

The first mate was John Hamilton,
    A man who knew no fear,
He'd sailed the Lakes from time to time
    For over twenty years.

The second mate was Samuel Boyd,
    A powerful giant and true,
With the captain and his four brave sons
    Composed the schooner's crew.

They sailed upon the stormy waves,
    And tossed the silvery spray;
They watched the moon appearing
    At the closing of the day.

The moon was dull and muffled,
    The clouds were gathering nigh,
The rain then came in torrents
    And dismal was the sky.

"This storm will be a hard one,"
    The captain then did say,
"I only wish that we were back
    Once more in Charlotte Bay."

They ran before it all that night
    And anchored at break of day;
"She's hard aground," the captain cried,
    "On the bar off Weller's Bay!"

They shouted to the farmers
    Who had gathered on the shore,
And to save their lives the farmers tried
    To reach them o'er and o'er.

Hours passed and the captain died,
    He was lashed to a stay!
And then, a short time afterward,
    Young Eddie passed away.

"The oldest and youngest's gone!"
    The other brothers cried;
Then one secured a loosened plank
    And for the lifeboat tried.

He was picked up by the lifeboat,
    And carried to the shore
Where for many hours unconscious
    Lay inside a farmhouse door.

His three remaining brothers,
    With the first and second mate,
Saw their last hour approaching,
    And death their only fate.

The ship then broke in pieces,
    Three of the crew were found,
The others sleep in Weller's Bay
    Far from their native ground.

The Car Ferry *Marquette and Bessemer No. 2*

Leaden skies portended heavy weather as the car ferry *Marquette and Bessemer No. 2* began one of its routine Lake Erie crossings on December 7, 1909. The big, 2,514-gross-ton five-year-old with the reinforced steel hull was built to make these trips year-round, so an early-December storm was not about to keep the car ferry and its cargo of railcars loaded with structural steel from clearing Conneaut, Ohio. The storm, though, blew up into a blizzard and prevented the car ferry from making its destination of Port Stanley, Ontario. Storm watchers in both Conneaut and Port Stanley heard the big boat's whistle as it vainly sought safe harbor in the blinding snowstorm. It never made it. All aboard lost their lives. The lucky ones presumably drowned quickly. The following day, about fifteen miles off Conneaut, where most of the crew had lived, searchers found a yawl from the car ferry. It bore nine frozen corpses.

    In the summer of 1933, Captain William E. "Billy" Clark of Buffalo recalled these verses, which echo the opening lines of "Loss of the *Maggie Hunter*" and "The Timber Drogher *Bigler*." He remembered, but could not reconstruct, lines that told of the steamer's whistle in the storm. Duncan MacLeod, also of Buffalo, was brother to the vessel's master, Captain R. R. MacLeod, and mate, J. C. MacLeod. Duncan MacLeod said that he had heard the song a number of times about Buffalo harbor, but had no desire to commit it to memory.

Loud roared the dreadful doomday
    And stormy was the night
When the car ferry *Bessemer 2nd*
    Left the port called Conneaut.
With two and twenty sailors
    All hearty, strong, and brave,
Bound for a port called Stanley
    But they met a watery grave.

    Let us all unite together
    A father and a mother
    A sister or a sweetheart
    Will grieve their lot with pain.
    Let us wave our hands in sorrow

O'er the dark blue Erie waters
    For the loved ones we will
    Never see again!

I shall not forget MacLeod,
    That was the captain's name,
Who had crossed the lake for many's a time
    And none were made in vain
Excepting this one time
    When he went to meet his doom
For the storm that night was an awful sight
    The worst that was ever seen.

The Loss of the *Souvenir*

Enjoying unseasonably pleasant weather for a late-November evening, the schooners *Souvenir* and *Minnie Corlett* sailed out of their home port of Pentwater, Michigan, on November 1872 for Chicago across Lake Michigan. The *Souvenir* carried 800,000 shingles, its companion a full hold of lumber and a deck load of squared timber. About 11 P.M., the wind veered to the northwest and whipped up into a gale as the mercury dropped to zero. Terrific winds hurled a blinding snow at the schooners. Daylight found the *Souvenir* on a sandbar near the Claybanks south of Ludington, Michigan. A lone man was on deck, at the wheel. No one else was in sight. There was no life crew to rescue him, and the people who gathered onshore thought the seas might have made that impossible in any case. Unable to help him, they hailed him above the roar of the surf. "Tie a rope around yourself," they hollered, "and let the other end float ashore." He signaled back, "No." Those gathered onshore could only guess whether he thought the effort would be futile or he was simply too exhausted to try. Still, they held their vigil as William Girard, the Ludington lightkeeper, made for the crippled *Souvenir* in a small vessel, fighting the waves alone. Girard reached the schooner about noon. The survivor, though still alive, was by then unconscious, and soon breathed his last, in sight of land and help. He was the mate, Fred Whitcomb. His fellow crewmen were Captain Charles Craine, Steward John Perry, and seamen Charles Dagle, Peter Hallene, Richard Moore, and Thomas Thayer. The other schooner, the *Minnie Corlett*, was a scow with a flat bottom and it scraped up high and dry on the shore. The whole crew escaped, though some suffered badly frozen feet and hands.

Oceana County Pioneers (Pentwater News Steam Printers, 1890) attributes this song to A. J. Woods.

> Gone was summer with its sunshine, with its mild and favoring gales,
> And the chilling blast of autumn with its snow and sleet prevails;
> Fierce and still more fierce the west wind beats against our wave-washed shore;
> And the lake gave fearful warning none must tempt its dangers more.
>
> But the gallant hardy seamen, used to toil, to dangers bred,
> Laughing at the winds and billows, viewing storms with naught of dread.
> Heeded not the warning given, manned their gallant craft once more,
> Bade adieu to friends and kindred, and prepared to quit the shore.
>
> While as if to lure them onward, milder blew the winds that day,
> And the raging, restless billows sunk again to sportive play;
> And to those who watched and waited for their loved ones came no fear,
> When by brave men manned and guided, sailed the gallant *Souvenir*.
>
> But no man can read the secrets nature chooses to withhold;
> Winds and waters scorn man's prowess and refuse to be controlled;

And before the night was ended, ere they reached their destined port,
Winds and waves in all their fury made the fated bark their sport.

What those brave boys met and suffered through that long and fearful night,
When the mad sea came upon them in its wild, resistless night,
How they toiled, till chilled and helpless, powerless to combat the waves,
They were swept from off the vessel, and consigned to watery graves.

Whether all went down together, or were swept off one by one;
Whether in the night they perished, or held out 'til rise of sun;
God in mercy only knoweth, it is not for us to know,
Best it is we may not fathom every fearful night of woe.

All we know is that ere midday, torn, dismasted, tempest-tossed,
At the sport of winds and billows, there was thrown upon our coast,
All that evermore might greet us, of that vessel staunch and true,
Which but yesternight departed, with the *Souvenir,* from view.

Of the seven brave men who manned her, only one now trod the deck,
When upon the shore she drifted, an unsightly, shapeless wreck;
And he, too, crippled, chilled, and helpless, he could only gasp and die.
Bruised and crippled, chilled, and helpless, he could only gasp and die.

Mourn we for the loved departed, taken in their pride away;
Mourn we with the stricken kindred who are with us here today.
May we be of grace enabled, as our hearts and anguish swell,
To take home the warning given, knowing "God doth all things well."

The Old *Bay State*

The *Bay State,* an early propeller of about 372 tons burden, foundered in Lake Ontario with a loss of everyone aboard, twenty-two lives, on November 2, 1862. Buffalo-built and ten years old, the vessel was reported to be in good repair at the time of its sinking, and the cause of the disaster remains a mystery.

John S. Parsons, who said he had learned this song as a boy hanging around the local harbor, was the source for this song. Ben Peckham of Oswego, who recalled about half the song, said that his father, Thomas Peckham, had composed it.

Come all good people from far and near, and listen to my lay;
And I'll sing some verses to you that I have written this day.
Come all you jolly sailor lads and listen to my rhyme,
I will sing you the loss of the old *Bay State* that sailed in the Crawford Line.

It was quite early in November, I think the second day;
They were taking in some merchandise, in Crawford's dock she lay.
The deckhands and the deckmen, too, were hurrying to and fro,
Because they knew her time was up, and off she had to go.

It was between ten and eleven this boat got under way;
Her colors were a'streaming fair and she steamed away.
And gaily down the river that night as she steamed forth so late,
That was the last we ever saw of the propeller old *Bay State*.

Now the old *Bay State* is steaming along the southern shore,
Steering the same course that she had always steered before.
And little did those aboard that night think before the rising sun
That they had steered their final course, that their last voyage was done.

Now the old *Bay State* is lost, and all on board besides!
No more upon the foaming billows will she so proudly ride.
She had been out in many a storm, and weathered many a blow—
It's hard to think so many lives down with her had to go!

The *Carter* and the *Erie Belle*

In November 1883, the Canadian schooner *J. N. Carter*, its hold full of lumber and more piled high on deck, was caught in a freezing blizzard on the way down Lake Huron. In danger of foundering from the mounting burden of ice that froze on the vessel and deck load, the captain attempted to put in at Kincardine, Ontario. The schooner was unmanageable, though, and ran ashore just south of the harbor entrance. The crew was taken off, and after the storm subsided, salvagers brought ashore the deck load to float the vessel. As the steam tug *Erie Belle* from Windsor strained to pull the *Carter* free, the tug's boiler exploded, killing the four-man crew.

This version comes from a battered copy owned by Dave Remington of Kincardine. He, with the help of veteran schoonerman Colin Graham, supplied a number of lines and words that were too blurred in the manuscript to read. Neither man knew anything about the author. A number of former schoonermen living along Lake Huron's Canadian shore in 1934 mentioned the song and supplied fragments.

In the late month of November upon a low'ring day
The schooner called the *Carter* stood across the Georgian Bay.
Merrily to her mastheads the heavy sails were drawn,
And the *Carter* gathered headway and westward boiled along.

'Twas the last trip of the season, and soon it would be o'er,
And rapidly astern we left the fading shore.
A cold breeze from the nor'west was blowing all the day
As the lumber-laden *Carter* crossed the Georgian Bay.

We rounded at Cove Island, the entrance to the lake;
The cold wind veered to north'ard and seas began to make.
Cape Hurd we left to le'ward as off the rocky shore
We steered down Lake Huron as we'd often done before.

Then threat'ning grew the sky, and clouds loomed in the west,
And what those clouds may mean seafaring men know best:
Darker grew the sky, down came the northern gale
As southward drove the *Carter* beneath her shorten'd sail.

Southward drove the *Carter* in snow and following seas;
Ice on her spars and deck load by tons began to freeze.
With the first dim gray of morning, as southward on we bore,
We heard the roaring breakers of Kincardine's curving shore.

We hauled her hard to port, full on the harbor light,
And she wallowed in the seas before the norther's might:
She would not take her helm, she soon began to reach—
We missed the harbor piers and drifted on the beach.

We chopped the icy halyards to ease her fearful plight,
And saw help gathering on the shore in that cold morning light.
Each man climbed in the riggin' all freezing, wet, and numb;
Then saw six lads from the village in a lifeboat for us come.

They took us all to shore, but the owners, ill at ease,
Thought only to save the vessel before the lake did freeze.
Then Diamond, Gunther, and Walker a bargain quickly made
And wired for a tug, the *Carter* for to save.

The *Erie Belle* responded, and for Kincardine steamed,
But of her awful fate no one on board did dream!
The wind and seas grew calm, and the *Erie Belle* began
To work the stricken schooner free from the dang'rous land.

The *Carter*'s stern was floated, her bow was working free,
When the *Erie Belle* tauten'd her line for her final pull to sea—
There was a sudden roar and fragments filled the air—
And those aboard the *Carter* could only stand and stare!

The *Erie Belle* was blown in fragments o'er the sea
And four brave sailor lads hurl'd to eternity!
The *Carter* she was freed, the *Erie Belle* no more,
Her bones lie in the sand just off Kincardine's shore!

The Steamer *Idaho*

In another late-season tragedy, Captain William Gillis decided on the night of November 6, 1897, to take the steamer *Idaho* out into a Lake Erie gale, despite storm warnings flying from the weather office tower at Buffalo. The 1,110-ton propeller, built in Cleveland in 1863, carried $45,000 in sugar, coffee, and general merchandise. It was to be one of the last cargoes Milwaukee would see until spring. The *Idaho* fought its way past the protective arm of Long Point, Ontario, on Erie's north shore when Gillis had a change of heart and decided to turn about and run for cover. He certainly knew the risk of turning the *Idaho* broadside to the storm, but he must have figured that the odds were better than letting the thirty-four-year-old steamer suffer the continued, head-on pounding of the storm. He was wrong. As the *Idaho* laid in a trough, a giant sea swept aboard, quenching the steamer's boiler fires. Now dead in the water, the boat lolled and rolled under repeated assaults by wind and wave. The *Idaho* filled and sank in about fifty feet of water, stem first, before a single lifeboat could be launched. The second mate and a deckhand managed to climb up a spar projecting from the wreck. Eight hours later, the exhausted men were rescued in dramatic style as Captain Frank Root maneuvered his steamer *Mariposa* close enough to the spar that his crew could pry the survivors' frozen fingers free of the stick and haul them aboard. The nineteen other men aboard the *Idaho* died. One body washed up on Long Point and was buried there. Almost a year later, the body of Captain Gillis washed ashore at Port Maitland, Ontario, closer to the harbor he had sought to regain than to the place where he had given the order to return.

 The source for this song is not clear in the Walton Collection's notes.

On the sixth day of November,
 On a dark and stormy night,
Great clouds arose and darkened up the lake.
 The papers gave a warning
 Of a fierce and awful storm—
"Now the vesselmen stay in if not too late."

The captain gave his order,
 The ship was cleared to go,
It's little did he think of their sad fate.
 It was the steamer *Idaho*,
 With nineteen men or more,
Sailed out upon that wild and maddened lake!

Oh! What care greedy owners?
 Oh! What care they for the lives
Of sailors when there's money to embrace?
 They simply gave their orders
 With a frown upon their face
"You go, or there'll be others in your place!"

Oh think, dear friends, of fam'lies
 And of their saddened homes,
And little ones without a father's care.
 And think, dear friends, of parents
 When first they hear the news;
It'll bow their heads and drive them to despair!

Oh think what were the thoughts
    On board the *Idaho* that night
When pounding seas rolled fierce and mountains high!
    They thought to save their vessel,
    In vain it was to try,
And nineteen sailor lads went down to die!

When news came back next morning
    To the port of Buffalo,
Crowds rushed to the docks in deepest woe.
    They hoped the news untrue,
    But all were lost but two
Of those on the ill-fated *Idaho*.

The schooner *Moonlight*, built at Milwaukee in 1874, foundered in 1903 with a load of iron ore off Lake Superior's Michigan Island. Dossin Great Lakes Museum.

The Final Chapter

Donkey engines, steamboats, and the dismantling of vessels and crews eventually smudged out work aboard schooners. As the jobs disappeared, so did the songs that lightened the labor. Every dead-end lead and dried-up memory encountered in the search for these songs stood as a reminder that a rich and colorful way of life had blown away, as if on a breeze. But let's not finish on a mournful note. Let's close with a hearty song about the proud schooner *Moonlight* racing through a Great Lakes fleet in its prime. Hooray for a race down the Lakes!

The Crack Schooner *Moonlight*

Great Lakes vessels carried more than wheat, stone, and lumber. They also carried a considerable load of pride, and when two vessels ran side by side, that pride was on the line. They raced for bragging rights and for the reputation that could bring them cargo on the water and drinks on land. For more than a decade after its launching in 1874, the big grain-carrying schooner *Moonlight* was Milwaukee's pride at 777 gross tons, 206 feet long, and with a beam of 33.6 feet. The vessel's original owners, David Vance and Company, insisted on the best building materials available. Built to "clipper lines" with a pronounced sheer and three tall, raking masts, the *Moonlight* carried the usual schooner rig, and on its foremast when running before the wind, a large square running sail. In light winds, staysails flew from the main and mizzen gaff topmasts. The *Moonlight*, with the schooners *Julia B. Merril, Anna M. Peterson,* and *Angus Smith,* made up "Milwaukee's Crack Schooner Fleet." Harley M. Boyce captained the *Moonlight* for a number of seasons while in his late twenties and early thirties, earning a reputation as a vessel master who ran with a lot of sail and a taste for a good race. The song describes a race that begins after a string of three vessels, the *Moonlight* in the middle, is towed out into Lake Michigan after having been windbound in the Chicago harbor. With a strong wind blowing, the *Moonlight* hoists a good spread of canvas for "a race down the Lakes" to Buffalo. The crew hoists a broom up the mainmast as a challenge to the other vessels—a custom imported from the Atlantic and credited to Englishman Sir Francis Drake, who "swept the seas" of the Spanish Armada in the late sixteenth century. In the song, the *Moonlight* quickly gets to windward of the vessel immediately ahead, stealing its wind, and skirts the west shore of Lake Michigan, the first leg of the trip.

A session with a group of ex-sailors in the U.S. Marine Hospital in Chicago the afternoon of September 3, 1932, produced this synthesis. Fragments came from Captains H. M. Boyce and W. A. Ashley and mate James M. Leaman of Milwaukee and from ex-schoonerman and lightkeeper S. C. Jacobson of Waukegan, Illinois. The men added, subtracted, and rearranged until they had exhausted their recollections and satisfied their memories.

Among the collaborators was "Sheets," who reaped ridicule as a "boy" a half century earlier by bringing sheets aboard a schooner to use in his forecastle bunk, "Gasoline George," who was reported to have gotten his liquids mixed on one occasion, "Gus," "Foghorn," and a few others. Some maintained the song was a capstan chantey. Others said it was "a saloon song." Jacobson said he had heard the song many times in his first years on the Lakes, and that forgotten stanzas told of the *Moonlight* and other grain schooners racing all the way to Buffalo. Even in this fragmentary form, it is a spirited description of a group of sailing vessels starting out on an exciting trip. Inquiries in Buffalo and other Lake Erie ports brought ready recognition, but no more stanzas.

The side-wheeler *Sheboygan* and a schooner under sail pass each other. Courtesy of the Historical Collections of the Great Lakes.

The Crack Schooner *Moonlight*

Murdock, Score No. 8

Oh, we towed out on the *Moon-light*, dropped the tug in the gale, With the

old *Law* be-fore us and the *Por-ter* on our tail, See her

can-vas go-ing on to a heart-y hal-yard song, Hoo-

ray for a race down the Lakes! Hoo-ray for a race down the

Lakes (down the Lakes), Hoo-ray for a race down the Lakes. See her

can-vas go-ing on to a heart-y hal-yard song, Hoo-ray for a race down the Lakes!

Oh, we towed out the *Moonlight*, dropped the tug in the gale,
With the old *Law* before us and the *Porter* on our tail,
See her canvas going on to a hearty halyard song,
Hooray for a race down the Lakes!

> Hooray for a race down the Lakes (down the Lakes),
> Hooray for a race down the Lakes,
> See her canvas going on to a hearty halyard song,
> Hooray for a race down the Lakes!

Oh, the wind's northwest and a'blowin' all the night,
See them big seas roll with their bonnets all white—
And off our sta'bird rail are half a hundred sail
Hooray for a race down the Lakes!

To the windw'rd of the *Law* we points her long jibboom,
An' high atop her main truck goes the old cabin broom—
Oh, we'll never shorten sail 'til we bury her lee rail
Hooray for a race down the Lakes!

The rainbows playing forward and the foaming wake aft,
An' her decks all a'slant beneath her groaning masts—
See the Old Man grin as she bullies in the wind
Hooray, for a race down the Lakes!

See us walk upon the foremast, o'er our stern the dimming shore,
As we leave the *Law,* the *Damforth,* and others by the score—
See us gaining to the lead and pay the groaning masts no heed,
Hooray, for a race down the Lakes!

Oh, we'll skirt the western shore, for ahead is Milwaukee,
'N' all day and night we'll drive her 'til the Straits are on our lee—
Let the old ponds roar as they've often done before,
Hooray for a race down the Lakes!

When the *Moonlight* was just fourteen years old, its proud owners sold it to a Cleveland concern that cut it down into a barge to be towed by steamships in the coal and ore trade between Lakes Erie and Superior. On September 17, 1903, laden with ore and fighting a Lake Superior storm, the *Moonlight*'s towline was cut. The once-grand sailing vessel, bereft of its clouds of canvas and forsaken by the smoke-belching steamer that had been towing it around by the nose, foundered off Michigan Island, one of the Apostle Islands.

Courtesy of the Historical Collections of the Great Lakes.

GLOSSARY

aft: Toward the rear of the vessel.
bark or barque: Vessel with three or more masts, square-rigged except for the hindmost mast, which is rigged fore-and-aft.
barkentine or barquentine: Vessel with three or more masts, more than one of them rigged fore-and-aft, the foremast square-rigged.
beam: Widest point of the vessel's hull.
before the mast: The part of the vessel for sailors, as opposed to the area for officers in the aft.
belay: An order to make fast or cease hauling.
block: A wooden or metal case holding one or more pulleys and outfitted with a hook at one end.
boat: From small pleasure craft to thousand-footers, vessels on the Great Lakes are boats, not ships.
boatswain (bo'sun): Petty officer in charge of vessel maintenance.
boom: Spar projecting from a yardarm from which a studding sail is set; "Out booms" tells the crew to set those sails in addition to those regularly carried, giving the vessel more speed.
bow: Forward end of the vessel.
bowline (bo'lin): Line used to haul the leading edge of a sail forward; a mooring line from the front of the boat to the pier.
bowsprit: Spar extending forward and up from the bow to support foremast stays and headsails.
boy: An apprentice seaman and the lowest-ranking crewman aboard, he could be anyone from the youngest member of the crew to the oldest.
brace: To maneuver or secure a sail, as in bracing the mainsail. Ashore, a sailor said to be bracing his mainsail likely was taking a few strong pulls on a bottle. As a noun, a rope through a block at the end of a yard used to swing it horizontally.
bridge: The raised platform from which a vessel is commanded.
brig: Vessel with two square-rigged masts.
bulwarks: Sides of a ship that extend above the top deck.
canaller: Vessel built to the maximum width that could fit through a canal system, often having sheer sides and a blunt bow and stern; also workers who assisted vessels making their passage through the canal.
Cape Horners: Vessels that regularly sailed around Cape Horn.

Cape Stiff: British for Cape Horn, so named for the severe weather that prevails there.

capstan (caps'an): A vertical drum mounted on a spindle and used to wind up a line or cable. Wooden capstan bars are inserted into a ring of sockets around the top, or capstan head, and men or beasts walk around the capstan, pushing on the bars, to turn it. To prevent the capstan from rewinding, hinged, metal pawls attached to the capstan will drop into a notched pawl ring that surrounds the capstan and is mounted to the deck.

catfall: Heavy tackle used to hoist anchor.

cathead: Heavy timber extending over a vessel's bow to which the anchor is hoisted.

chafing leather: A piece of leather used to protect sails and rigging at friction points.

chantey: A song sung to coordinate pulls or similar efforts by a group of laborers; also spelled *shanty*.

cinder tub: Sailors' derogatory term for a steamboat.

clew: Lower corner on a square sail; a sail is clewed up when the clews are hauled upward and inward to the yard in preparation to furling.

clipper: Long and narrow with three masts, this vessel was built for speed and had its widest point aft of the midpoint.

cordage: The lines in a ship's rigging.

counter: After part of a vessel's hull where the lines converge toward the stern.

courses: Large, heavy sails set from the lowest yard of each mast; "Courses being free" means not clewed down; "Haul snug your flowing courses" means set for maximum pulling; "Courses wing-and-wing" means that fore and main sails are set on opposite sides of the vessel to catch as much of a following wind as possible.

the Cut: The dredged channel through the Lake St. Clair Flats.

davit: One of the crane arms supporting the vessel's small work or life boats.

dead horse: An effigy thrown overboard to celebrate the end of a sailor's first month of service, that month's wages having been paid in advance and promptly handed over to settle debts at a boardinghouse.

Death's Door: The opening to Wisconsin's Green Bay.

ditch: A canal; on the Great Lakes this usually meant the Erie Canal.

dock: The water space between piers; a vessel's loading and discharging place; not the pier itself.

dogwatches: Half watches of two hours each, from 4 to 6 P.M. and 6 to 8 P.M..

drogher: Derogatory name for a slow and clumsy vessel, often used in the Great Lakes lumber trade.

drudge: Dredge.

dummy: A navigation buoy without a bell.

dunnage: Originally meant material put beneath the ship's ballast to protect the hull from damage; later came to mean a sailor's clothing and personal belongings.

ensign: Flag showing a vessel's nationality.

figurehead: Ornamented figure carried on the bow, just below the bowsprit.
the Flats: Shallow, marshy area at the northern end of Lake St. Clair south of Lake Huron.
flickers: Crew's quarters.
fo'c'sle song: Typically, a song sung during idle times for amusement.
fore: Toward the front of the vessel.
fore-and-aft: Vessels in a row, one astern of another.
fore-and-aft rig or **schooner rig:** Sails set from spars extending from the masts toward only one side of the vessel, rather than from spars that cross the masts as in a square rig.
forebitter: Another name for a foc's'le song.
forecastle (fo'c'sle): Originally a forward raised structure above the main deck, it came to refer to a space forward and below the deck where the crew slept.
foremast: Mast nearest the bow.
full-and-by: A vessel's course when it is sailing "by," or as close to the wind as possible with all sails "full."
furl: To roll up and secure sails on a yard or boom.
gaff: Spar that spreads the top edge of a sail.
gaff tops'ls: A topsail, usually triangular, with its foot along the gaff and its luff upon the topmast.
galley: Area where food is cooked.
gangplank: Movable plank used for boarding or leaving a vessel.
greenhorn: Inexperienced seaman, especially one making his first trip.
grog: Formerly, diluted rum served to British sailors; later a general sailor term used for intoxicating liquor.
gunwhale (gunnel): The highest trim along the sides of a vessel.
halyard or **halliard:** Line used to hoist a yard or sail.
handspike: A metal, spike-shaped hand tool.
haul: To pull, usually on a line; "Hauled her wind" means to change a vessel's course so that the wind appears to "haul," or change direction.
hawser: Heavy cable used as an anchor or mooring line.
hold: Cargo storage area.
hook: Anchor.
horned breeze: Oxen that towed vessels through the Erie Canal.
hull: Main structure of the ship, essentially its bottom and sides.
hurricane deck: Upper deck.
Indiaman: Slow and heavy British ship engaged in the early India trade.
iron: Compass.
jib: Triangular sail set on a stay running from a jibboom or bowmast to the head of the foremast.
jibboom: A spar extending forward beyond the bowsprit of a ship from which a headsail or jib is set.
jolly boat: The small boat a vessel carries for exterior work; a yawl.

kedge: A small anchor, or to inch the vessel ahead by pulling on a small anchor dropped ahead of the vessel.
keel: The bottom timber of a vessel's hull.
keelson: The inside timber at the bottom of the hull.
knots: The speed of a vessel in nautical miles (6,080.27 feet) an hour; not a measure of distance.
landlubber: A landsman at sea, especially one who is clumsy or sick.
lanyard (lan'ard): A light line, usually used to lace equipment to rigging.
lead: To sound for depth by dropping and raising a lead weight on a light line.
lee: The side of a vessel or island away from where the wind is coming.
lightship: An anchored, lighted vessel that marks hidden shoals and hazards.
log: Record in a vessel's logbook.
luff: Leading edge of a fore-and-aft sail, or to head into the wind.
lumber hooker: An old, awkward vessel engaged in the lumber trade.
L.V.: Abbreviation for "light vessel," an anchored vessel that carried a light warning vessels of shoals and submerged obstructions.
mainmast: Tallest mast on a ship, generally the second from the bow whenever there is more than one.
main yard: The lowest spar crossing the mainmast, it is the largest yard on a ship and carries the mainsail.
mast: Vertical spars that hold sails and yards.
masthead: Top part of a mast.
mate: Chief mate of a vessel.
mizzenmast: Third mast from the bow.
mosquito fleet: A collection of small craft.
oakum: Loosely twisted hemp or jute impregnated with tar and used to caulk between deck and hull planks.
Old Man: Vessel master.
on beam's end: When a vessel is tipped over on its side.
packet: Vessel making regularly scheduled trips carrying passengers, mail, and express freight.
pawl post: A strong, vertical post on which the capstan rotates. Pawls are short iron bars on pins that are set to prevent the capstan or windlass from rewinding.
pennant: A triangular flag tapering to a point or swallowtail, used for identification or signaling.
poop: The after deck from which the officer in charge directs the trim of a vessel's sails and its course.
pigboat: A unique style of boat built with a rounded top to ride low in the water and let the waves roll over its deck; whaleback.
port: The left side of the ship when the observer is facing forward.
propeller: A screw-driven steamboat.
puller: Tow barge.
purser: The officer who handles the vessel's papers, accounts, and ship's store.
quarterdeck: The after part of the deck from which officers issue commands.

reef: To reduce a sail's area by making the reef points fast to a boom or yard, thus eliminating part of the sail from the wind.
rigger: One whose job it is to set up a vessel's rigging while in port.
royals: Fourth tier of sails up from the deck of a ship; those just above the topgallant sails.
schooner: A vessel of two or more masts rigged with large gaff-headed sails.
scow: A flat-bottomed boat used to transport bulky material such as sand, stone, and gravel.
scrubber: A captain who keeps his crew busy cleaning, scraping, painting, and scrubbing the vessel.
scupper: The gutter along the edge of the deck, or the holes in the bulwarks that let water drain.
Shanks: Waugoshance Point in northeast Lake Michigan.
shanty: Work song; see **chantey.**
sheer: Upward curve of a vessel's deck between amidships and the ends.
sheet: Line used to control the position of a sail. A sheet is boarded, or the sail is sheeted home, when it is hauled around nearly parallel with the keel to enable a vessel to sail close to the wind. "Give her sheet" means let the sheet pay out so that the sails will be at right angles to a following wind.
shellback: Ocean sailor.
shroud: A rope, usually used in a pair, that gives a mast lateral support and keeps it upright.
site: A job; a trip on a vessel.
Skillagalee: Corruption of Ile aux Galets, French for "island of pebbles," in northern Lake Michigan.
skysails: The fifth and highest tier of sails usually carried on a square-rigged vessel; the main skysail is the one on the mainmast.
sloop: Vessel with one mast rigged fore and aft, and a jib.
slop chest: Shipboard compartment for clothing that was to be sold to the crew, usually in charge of the boatswain.
spanker: Fore-and-aft sail set from the after mast of a square-rigged vessel; the spar from which it is set is the spanker boom.
spar: Any pole, including mast, yard, or boom.
splice the main brace: To receive an extra ration of rum, which was as rare as a repair to the main rope; to get drunk.
square rig: An arrangement in which yards cross the masts horizontally so sails extend equidistant on either side of the masts.
stanchion: Vertical supports in railings or between decks.
starboard: The right side of the vessel as the observer is facing forward.
starboard tack: A vessel's course or distance made when the wind is coming over the starboard bow.
stay: Standing rigging that supports a mast.
stern: The aft end of the vessel.

steward: Crew member who oversees the supplying, storage, and provision of food and drink.

string: A line of vessels being towed behind a steam tug.

studding sails (stu'n's'ls): Light, square sails set from booms extending from the yardarms.

surfboat: Rescue boat used by lifesaving workers in heavy seas.

tack: Line holding down the lower weather corners of courses; "With her starboard tacks aboard" means that the starboard tacks have been hauled forward and to windward so that the vessel is now close hauled with the wind coming over the port bow; also means to change course by bringing the hull around and shifting the sails.

tar: Slang for sailor, likely derived from the tar used as a preservative on many wooden vessels.

tonnage: Dead weight tonnage is the carrying capacity of a vessel; gross tonnage is its internal capacity measured in units of 100 cubic feet; net tonnage is internal capacity in units of 100 cubic feet less space lost to the boilers, engines, lockers, quarters, and other areas not available for carrying fright.

topgallant sails (t'gan's'ls): Third tier of square sails; those just above the topsails and below the royals.

topsails (tops'ls): Second tier of sails, just above the courses and just below the topgallant sails. In the later years of the sailing era these were divided, for ease of handling, into lower and upper topsails.

trim: To distribute the cargo in a ship so that it would float on an even keel.

trimmers: Workers who did not sail with the ship, but who went into the hold to distribute the cargo evenly.

truck: Small, circular piece of wood capping the top of a mast.

up or down Lake Michigan: For sailors in the 1800s, Chicago was regarded as being at the head of the lake, so vessels traveled up to Chicago and down to Mackinac; this put Milwaukee above Green Bay and meant that vessels sailed down to Cleveland from Chicago.

vang: Tackle running from the end of the gaff boom to the deck.

waney: Logs on which the butt ends were squared to more easily fit aboard lumber vessels.

warp: To haul or move a vessel to a new position by using a line made fast to a kedge anchor, buoy, or wharf.

watch: One of two halves of a vessel's crew designated by the terms "port" and "starboard," they are on duty on alternate four-hour periods, except for the two-hour dogwatches between 4 and 8 P.M.; "off watch" means off duty.

way enough: An order to cease rowing when a boat has sufficient momentum to reach its destination.

weather rail: The windward side of a vessel, that from which the wind is blowing.

weigh: To heave up, as an anchor.

whaleback: A unique style of boat built with a rounded top to ride low in the water and let the waves roll over its deck; pigboat.

wheelsman: Crewman who steers the ship.
white squall: A storm in which rain, snow, and surf make everything look white, obscuring vision.
windjammer: A sailing vessel or sailor, considered a derogatory term when used by steamer men.
windlass: A winding mechanism that operates like a capstan, but is mounted horizontally and has two winding drums.
winds: A wind if "fair" when it is from an angle of less than ninety degrees from directly astern; "free" when well astern and "following" when full astern.
windward (wind'ard): Toward the direction from which the wind is blowing, but outside the vessel.
Wobble Shanks: A corruption of Waugoshance Point in northeast Lake Michigan.
yardarm: Either of the projecting ends of a yard on a square-rigged sail.
yawl: The small boat a vessel carries for exterior work; a jolly boat.

NOTES ON SOURCES AND INFORMANTS

The primary source for this book is the Ivan H. Walton Collection in the Michigan Historical Collections at the University of Michigan's Bentley Historical Library. The eighteen boxes that comprise the Walton Collection contain the correspondence, articles, recordings, class notes, travel diaries, musical scores, transcripts, clippings, lyrics, background, notes, lists, and jots that make it the richest collection of Great Lakes chanteys in existence. Only Walton knew for certain why he chose one version of a chantey over another, or the precise ways in which he melded two or three recollections into one arrangement. As improvised as that may sound, it is in keeping with the tradition in which these songs thrived. Although some of the men who sang these songs bloodied knuckles in disagreements over their proper arrangement, we shouldn't. While some songs, such as disaster songs, had fairly consistent arrangements, others varied. Any chanteyman who passed up an opportunity to insult the Old Man or the cook simply to remain true to some irrelevant standard would have been seen as displaying a woefully underdeveloped power of imagination.

Sources listed here are according to Walton. Years, rather than precise dates, are provided because Walton sometimes spent more than a day in one place, and songs might be drawn out and reassembled over a period of days. Anyone wishing to delve into the collection personally should begin with the finding guide at the library. The best parts of the collection are the recorded music (cassette copies are available at the library), the field notes (Box 2), and song lyrics (Box 3). Untold treasures may await the patient researcher who can decipher the chicken-scratch handwriting with which Walton filled hundreds upon hundreds of index cards.

Walton attempted to determine the composers of the songs he heard, but the nature of the folk tradition obscured most origins. The songs changed and shifted like the winds that accompanied the work. Over the years, several variants or strains of one song might develop, and separate camps of men would swear that they knew which was right, and who had composed it. In many cases, they appear to have misattributed authorship to the man who brought it to their region, not to its true author.

Walton's collecting succeeded on the strength of a few rich informants. Fortunately, they were scattered around the Great Lakes and brought him distinct selections. The collection is, by no means, the complete repertoire of Great Lakes songs. Walton was in a race against time and sometimes lost, or arrived in time to catch just a scrap of a song.

Ben Peckham was a major informant living in Oswego, New York, and credited his father, Thomas, with many of the songs he recalled. Thomas Peckham sailed the Lakes in the 1860s and 1870s and died about 1882. He was said to have been the sole survivor of the wreck of the *Antelope* and the writer of the song commemorating that event. Ben, who said his father "could write a song any time for a free drink," also credited him with "The Dredge from Presque Isle," "The Old *Bay State*," and perhaps "The Schooner *Oriole*." The younger Peckham also supplied a manuscript of "The Loss of the *Gilbert Mollison*." Another Oswego ex-sailor, John S. Parsons, credited Thomas Peckham with "The Dismasting of the *Cummings*." Parsons himself was a treasure chest of song and a source for nearly a dozen of the songs in the collection.

Captain William E. "Billy" Clark of Buffalo was a principal informant on nearly a dozen other songs, and he may have written some himself. William Head of Picton, Ontario, attributed "The *Jennie P. King*" to "a sailor named Billy Clark who would make up songs while on a trip and sing them in harbor saloons for free drinks." Informants also credited Clark with two of the Lakes' most popular voyage songs, "The Red Iron Ore" and "The Timber Drogher *Bigler*." However, Beaver Island's John W. Green staunchly maintained that his Irish uncle and fellow islander, Peter O'Donnell, had written both of those songs. It's likely that neither Clark nor O'Donnell wrote either song, but heard them elsewhere and brought them to their communities.

Robert "Brokenback" Collen of Chicago contributed to at least eight of the songs here, most of them traditional chanteys. Brothers Harry and George Parmalee of Waukegan, Illinois, made several contributions, also of old standards. J. Sylvester "Ves" Ray of Port Huron, Michigan, remembered the words to "Heave Her Up and Bust Her," "The *Darius Cole* and the *Mackinac*," "The Schooner *Africa*," and "A Trip on the *Lavindy*."

SOURCES FOR WALTON'S STORY

The story of Ivan Walton's search comes from his own correspondence and travel diaries, the memorial service written by his son in 1968, a paper that university colleague George M. McEwen delivered to the Michigan Folklore Society on March 29, 1969, a February 15, 1947, profile in Michigan alumni magazine, and a June 4, 1990, interview with Walton's son, Lynn, and daughter-in-law, Sue.

SOURCES FOR WILSON'S STORY

Loudon G. Wilson's story comes from four pages of autobiographical material he wrote in 1970, an article by Robert W. Graham in the January/February 1994 issue of *Michigan History Magazine*, and the biographical sketch that introduces Wilson's collection at the Historical Collections of the Great Lakes at Bowling Green, Ohio. Additional insight came from Loudon's son Craig, who reviewed portions of the manuscript.

Work Chanteys

Much of the organization and writing in the chapters on work chanteys comes from an unpublished Walton manuscript, "Sailors on Lakes and Sea." A few songs that he included—"Stormalong," "The Black Ball Line," "The Dead Horse Chantey," and "Paddy Doyle"—have been omitted here because they came from previously published works and contained neither Great Lakes origins nor lyrics.

Beaver Island Songs

Parts of the introduction to chapter 8 come directly from Walton's "Folk Singing on Beaver Island," which appeared in 1952 in *Midwest Folklore.* Walton did not have this chapter in his outline, but so much of his collecting happened on this musical time capsule that it warrants inclusion as a chapter.

BIBLIOGRAPHY

Baubie, William Edward. *French-Canadian Verse.* Chicago: Lakeside Press, 1917.
Beavis, Bill, and McCloskey, Richard G. *Salty Dog Talk: The Nautical Origins of Everyday Expressions.* London: William Collins, 1983.
Beck, E. C. *Songs of the Michigan Lumberjacks.* Ann Arbor: University of Michigan Press, 1941.
Bone, David W. *Capstan Bars.* Edinburgh: Porpoise Press, 1931.
Bowen, Dana Thomas. *Memories of the Lakes.* Cleveland: Freshwater Press, 1940.
Boyer, Dwight. *Strange Adventures of the Great Lakes.* New York: Dodd, Mead, 1974.
Colcord, Joanna Carver. *Roll and Go: Songs of American Sailormen.* New York: Bobbs-Merrill, 1924.
———. *Sea Language Comes Ashore.* Cambridge, Mass.: Cornell Maritime Press, 1945.
Dana, R. H., Jr. *The Seaman's Friend: Containing a Treatise on Practical Seamanship, with Plates; A Dictionary of Sea Terms; Customs and Usages of the Merchant Service; Laws Relating to the Practical Duties of Master and Mariners.* Boston: Thomas Groom, 1851.
———. *Two Years before the Mast.* New York: Harper and Brothers, 1940.
Donahue, James. *Terrifying Steamboat Stories.* West Bloomfield, Mich.: Altwerger and Mandel, 1991.
Drummond, William Henry. *The Habitant and Other French-Canadian Poems.* New York: Putnam, 1897.
Dunbar, Willis F. *Michigan: A History of the Wolverine State.* Grand Rapids, Mich.: Eerdmans, 1965.
Elliott, James L., *Red Stacks over the Horizon: The Story of the Goodrich Steamboat Line.* Grand Rapids, Mich.: Eerdmans, 1967.
Feltner, Charles E., and Jeri Baron. *Shipwrecks of the Straits of Mackinac.* Dearborn, Mich.: Seajay Publications, 1991.
Fowke, Edith. *Songs of the Great Lakes.* Record album and liner notes. Folkways Record and Service Corp., 1964.
Graham, Robert W. "Drawn by the Lakes." *Michigan History* 78 (January/February 1994): 24–29.
Harlow, Frederick Pease. *The Making of a Sailor: Sea Life Aboard a Yankee Square-Rigger.* Salem, Mass.: Marine Research Society, 1928.
Harold, Steve. *Shipwrecks of the Sleeping Bear.* Traverse City, Mich.: Pioneer Study Center, 1984.
Hartwick, Louis M. *Oceana County Pioneers and Business Men of Today.* Pentwater, Mich.: Pentwater News Steam Printers, 1890.
Hatcher, Harlan. *Lake Erie.* New York: Bobbs-Merrill, 1945.
Havighurst, Walter. *The Long Ships Passing.* New York: Macmillan, 1961.

Hendrix, Glen A. "Songs of Beaver Island." *Journal of Beaver Island History* 2 (1980): 58–111.
Hugill, Stan. *Shanties and Sailors' Songs.* London: Praeger, 1969.
Hullfish, William. *The Canaller's Songbook.* York, Pa.: American Canal and Transportation Center, 1984.
Hyde, Charles K. *The Northern Lights.* Lansing, Mich.: TwoPeninsula Press, 1986.
Keller, James M. *The "Unholy" Apostles.* Chelsea, Mich.: Bookcrafters, 1984.
Lloyd, Albert Lancaster. *Folk Song in England.* London: Lawrence and Wishart, 1967.
Luce, Stephen B. *Naval Songs.* New York: W. A. Pond, 1883.
Masefield, John, ed. *A Sailor's Garland.* London: Methuen, 1906.
McEwen, George M. "Ivan H. Walton, a Pioneer Michigan Folklorist." *Michigan Academician* 2 (1970): 73–77.
Michigan Writers Project. *A Guide to the Wolverine State.* New York: Oxford University Press, 1941.
Peters, Harry B. *Folk Songs out of Wisconsin.* Madison: State Historical Society of Wisconsin, 1977.
Pound, Louise. *American Ballads and Songs.* New York: Scribner, 1922.
Ratigan, William. *Great Lakes Shipwrecks and Survivals.* Grand Rapids, Mich.: Eerdmans, 1960.
Rickaby, Franz. *Ballads and Songs of the Shanty-Boy.* Cambridge: Harvard University Press, 1926.
Sandburg, Carl. *The American Songbag.* New York: Harcourt, Brace, 1927.
Schairbaum, A. W. *A Marine Glossary for the Ship Modeler.* St. Charles, Ill.: AWS Creations, 1990.
Shay, Frank. *Iron Men and Wooden Ships.* New York: Doubleday, Page, 1924.
Sommers, Laurie Kay. *Beaver Island House Party* (book and compact disc). Lansing: Michigan State University Press, 1996.
Swayze, David D. *Shipwreck! A Comprehensive Directory of Over 3,700 Shipwrecks on the Great Lakes.* Boyne City, Mich.: Harbor House Publishers, 1992.
Thompson, Mark L. *Steamboats and Sailors of the Great Lakes.* Detroit: Wayne State University Press, 1991.
Truscott, Charles B. "The Lake's Unique Gospel Ship." *Telescope* 22, no. 5 (1973): 132–38.
Walton, Ivan H. "Folk Singing on Beaver Island." *Midwest Folklore* 2, no. 4 (1952): 243–50.
———. "Sailor Lore of the Lakes." *Michigan History* 19 (Autumn 1935): 355–69.
Whall, W. B. *Ships, Sea Songs, and Shanties.* Glasgow: James Brown and Sons, 1930.
Whittle, D. W., ed. *Memoirs of P. P. Bliss.* New York: A. S. Barnes, 1877.
Wolff, Julius F., Jr. *Lake Superior Shipwrecks.* Duluth, Minn.: Lake Superior Port Cities Inc., 1990.

INDEX OF FIRST LINES

A is for anchor which is sometimes called hook, *91*
A is the anchor of our gallant ship, *90*
All you true feeling Christians, I hope you will draw near, *177*
Another proud and gallant ship, *213*
Attention give both young and old, *216*
Away, haul away, we'll haul away together, *77*
Boney was a warrior, *79*
Brightly beams our Father's mercy, *215*
De cap'n's in de pilot house ringin' de bell, *43*
Come all brave Union sailor lads, *113*
Come all brother sailors, I hope you'll draw nigh, *173*
Come all good people from far and near, and listen to my lay, *225*
Come all ye jolly seamen, *112*
Come all you Beaver Island boys, *175*
Come all you bold sailors who follow the Lakes, *124*
Come all you jolly sailors and listen to my song, *131*
Come all you true-born shanty boys, *152*
Come all you young sailors and landlubbers too, *141*
Come gather 'round me lads, and I'll sing you a little song, *126*
Come listen to me one and all, *217*
Come listen young fellows who follow these Lakes, *121*
Come shipmates and listen, a story I'll tell, *99*
Come, shipmates, listen to my story, *221*
A farmer boy stands on the deck, *47*
Gone was summer with its sunshine, with its mild and favoring gales, *224*
A gray-haired mother knelt in prayer, *179*
Haul on the bo'lin', our bully ship's a-rollin'! *76*
High ho and up she goes, *103*
If ever I follow the ships again, *86*
I just came down from Buffalo, *168*
I'll tol' of wan boat, de scow *Jean La Plante*, *161*
I thought I heard the Old Man say, *49*
In a handy four-master I once took a trip, *71*
In Amsterdam, there lived a maid, *38*
In eighteen eighty-four, upon the first of May, *210*
In eighteen hundred eighty, in October, the sixteenth day, *212*
In the late month of November, upon a low'ring day, *226*
In the year of eighteen eighty, *222*

I shipped aboard a fat old tub, *168*
I suppose that you remember when the *Sephie* she was new, *96*
It's of a stately vessel, a vessel of great fame, *150*
It was on the sixth of April, *117*
I was a handsome nice young man, *109*
I was two weeks at Cleveland, *135*
A long, long time and a very long time, *69*
Loud roared the dreadful doomday, *223*
Loud roared the dreadful thunder, *209*
The mules that walked our fo'c'sle deck, *136*
My boys, if you will listen now, I'll sing you a little song, *188*
My first trip down old Lake Erie, *115*
My seafaring comrades, attend to my lay, *180*
Nigh forty years have passed away, *219*
The night was fair, the sky was clear, *108*
Now sit you down beside me, *139*
Oh, blow the man down, bullies, blow the man down, *58*
Oh, blow ye winds, I long to hear you, *61*
Oh, fare you well, we're homeward bound, *51*
Oh, heave my lads, oh heave and sing, *39*
Oh, poor old Reuben Ranzo, *63*
Oh, roll the cotton down, my boys, *62*
Oh, sad and dismal is the tale, *193*
Oh, sailors, come gather and list to my ditty, *164*
Oh, Sally Brown is very pretty, *34*
Oh, Santa Anna gained the day, *41*
Oh, say, was you ever in Rio Grande? *35*
Oh, Shenandore's a rolling river, *37*
Oh, Tommy's gone, what shall I do? *67*
Oh, we towed out the *Moonlight,* dropped the tug in the gale, *233*
Oh, whiskey is the life of man, *64*
On November first in eighty-nine, *145*
On October twenty-eight, oh, how the wind did scream! *198*
On the eighteenth of December, *111*
On the eighth day of November, *143*
On the nineteenth of May, ninety-four, I suppose you have heard tell, *207*
On the sixth day of November, *228*
On wan dark night on de Lac St. Clair, *157*
Out through the piers at Ludington one dark September day, *178*
De *Rosie Belle Teeneau* was wan vere fine batteau, *158*
Sad and dismal is the tale to you I will relate, *195*
The schooner *Hume* is staunch and strong, *197*
A scow kom sailin' down Lac Sainte Claire, *162*
Scrubber Murphy was the captain of the steamer called *Mohawk, 94*
She's an iron ore vessel, a vessel of fame, *123*
She's a saucy trim packet, a packet of fame, *97*
Since you ask Caruso for it, *127*

The St. Clair River is thirty miles long, *45*
Steaming out of the Straits of Mackinac, *184*
They call me "hanging Johnny," *66*
They may boast of their dreadnaughts and cruisers likewise, *186*
They worked all day, *104*
Up from the poor man's cottage, *201*
We are a band of seamen, *114*
We have heard of many happenings since last year first began, *182*
We leaves Detroit behind us, *96*
We're in a flash packet, a packet of fame, *100*
We shipped aboard the *Kolfage* at Chatham, County Kent, *147*
We've got the rusty mud-hook up, *87*
We wallowed Lake Superior through, *111*
What shall we do with a drunken sailor? *70*
When the Mate calls up all hands, *54*
While running down for Cleveland, *165*
Yim Yonson ship from lumberyard, *166*
You all may bless your happy lot, *204*
You may talk about your pleasure trips, *88*
You pretty girls of Michigan, *102*
You sons of freedom listen to me, *106*

NAME AND SUBJECT INDEX

A. S. Barnes and Company, New York, 215
Africa (schooner), 111–112
Alabama, 62
Alanson Sumner (tug), 108–109
Algonac, Michigan, 220
Allegan, Michigan, 139
Allen (schooner), 191
Allenburg, Ohio, 125
Alice Strong (scow), 165–166
Alpena (side-wheel steamer), 211–213
Alpena, Michigan, 110, 205
Alpena (schooner), 211–213
Amherstburg, Ontario, 44–45
Amsterdam, 36–38
Angus Smith (schooner), 231
Anna M. Peterson (schooner), 231
Antelope (schooner), 14, 202–205
Apostle Islands, Lake Superior, 234
Arizona, 17
Army Signal Corps, 13
Asia (schooner), 208–209
Assinibois (steamer), 14
Atlantic Ocean, 12, 14, 49, 57, 85, 98, 103, 231
Augusta (schooner), 200
Avon Point, Ohio, 135

Bain, Johnnie, 143
Ballads and Songs of the Shanty-Boy, 191
Baltimore, Maryland, 44, 67, 86, 103, 189
Banks of Newfoundland (song), 101
Barcelona, New York, 110
Barclay, Robert Heriot, 105
Baubie, William Edward, 158
Bay City, Michigan, 84, 145–146
Bay State (propeller), 225–226
Beaver Island, 15, 21, 24, 103, 171–189, 219
Beaver Island group, 120–122, 132, 171
Beck, Earl Clifton, 16, 133, 152, 192
Belle Jane Anne (fishing vessel), 206
Belle River, Ontario, 155
Belle Sheridan (schooner), 192, 221–223

Berlin, Michigan, 165
Big Heart River, 155
Big Sable Point, Michigan, 140–142
Big Sable River, Michigan, 140–142
Bird, James, 104–107
Black Ball (sailing packet), 98
Black Ball Line, 57–59
Black River, Ohio, 135
Bliss, P. P., 214–215
Bois Blanc (Bob-Lo) Island, Lake Huron, 55
Bonaparte, Napoleon, 78, 158
Bone, David W., 36, 60, 67
Bonner, William, 220
Boston, Massachusetts, 60
Boston (schooner), 93
Boyce, Harley M., 231–232
Boyd, Samuel, 222
Boyle, Tommy, 172–176
Bradley, Alva, 113
Brooklyn Theater Fire (song), 206
Brown, Fayette, 113
Brown, Wesley "Yankee," 187–189
Brown and Reddington, Cleveland, 119
Bruce Peninsula, Ontario, 142
Buffalo: canal boats, 15, 115, 167–169; coal trade, 198; copper trade, 41; departing from, 54, 228–229; destination, 52, 68, 95, 96, 103, 110, 132–133, 138–139, 197; grain trade, 9, 34, 37, 46–47, 51–52, 187, 231–232; harbor, 65, 77, 116, 211, 223; lightship location, 185–186; lumber, 130; shipbuilding, 144, 199, 225; tugs, 217; waterfront diversions, 52, 59, 114–117; 133, 135, 167–169
Broadway, New York City, 59
Brown, John, 220–221
Buffalo (schooner), 134
Buffalo Express (newspaper), 96, 192
Bundy, Henry, 214
Bunyan, Paul, 13, 187

Burns, Peter, 183
Burnt Cabin Point, Michigan, 112
Byng Inlet, Georgian Bay, 209

Cabot's Head, Ontario, 143
California, 39
Camptown Races (song), 39
Canal Street, Buffalo, 114–115
The Canaller's Songbook, 88
Cape Horn, 10, 39–40, 68–69,
Cape Hurd, Lake Huron, 227
Capstan Bars, 36, 60, 67
Carlton Island, Lake Ontario, 129
Carr, Michael, 217
Cassandra (passenger steamer), 19
Cataract (schooner), 148–149
Central Michigan College of Education, 13
Challen Ecarte, Lake St. Clair, 155
Charlevoix, Michigan, 16, 189
Charlotte (Rochester), New York, 99–100, 221–222
Charlton, John, 195
Chatham, Ontario, 147
Cheboygan, Michigan, 137
Chene Street, Detroit, 164
Chicago: departing from, 119–121, 199, 204; destination, 54–55, 95, 124–125, 177, 200, 210–212; grain trade, 34–35, 46, 51, 191–193, 213, 220–221; harbor, 39, 87, 110, 231; lumber trade, 9, 129, 139–143, 196–197, 224–225; Mormons, 171; Old Black Pete's, 55; sailors' union hall, 15, 64; shipbuilding, 176; waterfront diversions, 172
Chicago Marine Hospital, 70, 232
Chicago River, 140, 200
Chicago Seamen's Benevolent Union, 112
Chieftain (schooner), 84
Christy, Willie, 209
City of Mackinac (schooner), 110–111
Civil War, 9, 65, 119, 140, 200
Clara Youell (canaller), 149–150
Clark Street, Chicago, 140
Cleveland: departing from, 198; destination, 111, 119, 122, 214; home port, 109, 110; ore trade, 9, 41, 112, 123–124, 134; owners, 112, 234; shipbuilding, 15, 110, 113, 119, 228; stone hauling, 135; 165–166; strike, 113; waterfront diversions, 122, 134
Clifton (schooner), 170, 179–185

Clyde, Scotland, 18
Clyde Bank, Scotland, 18
Colcord, Joanna, 39
Cole, Darius, 110
Collar, Helen, 179
Collingwood, Ontario, 208
Colonial (side-wheel steamer), 110
Columbia Yacht Club, Chicago, 110
Conneaut, Ohio, 223
Cove Island, Lake Huron, 143, 227
Craine, Charles, 224
Crawford Line, 225–226
Cumberland (warship), 140
Cumberland's Crew (song), 140
Currier, J., 129

Dagle, Charles, 224
Danger (schooner), 168
Darius Cole (side-wheel steamer), 110–111
David Vance and Company, 231
Davidson's shipyard, Bay City, Michigan, 84
Death's Door, Wisconsin, 120–122
Detour, Michigan, 123
Detroit: building materials trade, 135, 155, 164, 179; departing from, 96, 128, 132; destination, 44, 182, 184; home port, 125; passing, 54; port, 41–42; racing, 110; residence, 19; shipbuilding, 112, 129; surrendered to British, 105
Detroit Free Press, 19, 161
Detroit News, 13
Detroit River, 45, 54, 61, 96, 113, 135, 155, 161–162, 164, 166, 217
Dispatch (schooner), 138–139
Door County Peninsula, Wisconsin, 120
Douglas, Stephen A., 200
Drake, Sir Francis, 231
Dreadnaught (packet), 11, 14, 97–100, 120,
Drummond, William Henry, 156
DuChene, Jean Baptiste, 158–160
Duluth, Minnesota, 103
Dunoon, Scotland, 18
Dykes, Agnes Loudon, 18

E. C. Roberts (timber drogher), 119–122
Eastland (passenger steamer), 200
Ecorse, Michigan, 158–160
Edmund Fitzgerald (freighter), 110
Edward E. Skeele (schooner), 46
Elgin, Oregon, 200
Elk Rapids, Michigan, 174
England, 12, 36, 98, 144

Enterprise (warship), 105
Erie Belle (tug), 104, 226–227
Erie Canal, 15, 115, 129–130, 167–169
Escanaba (tug), 122
Escanaba, Michigan, 121, 127, 186
Evergreen Point, Michigan, 127
Exile (schooner), 122

F. L. Danforth (schooner), 234
Fair Haven, New York, 196
Favorite (tug), 179
Fayette Brown (schooner), 112–114
Fennel, Patrick, 191
Fisher, A. J., 19
Florida (schooner), 110
Flying Cloud (clipper), 11, 161–162
Flying Fish (clipper), 57–58
Folk Songs out of Wisconsin, 206
Forest Queen (steamer), 110
Fort Gratiot (Port Huron) Michigan, 133, 137, 146
Forth and Clyde Canal, Scotland, 18–19
Forty Mile Point, Michigan, 179
Foster, Stephen, 39
Fowke, Edith, 195
Fox Islands, 120–122
French River, Ontario, 208
French-Canadian Verse, 158
Fulton (sloop-barge), 149

Gallagher, Emmett, 179–180, 183
Gallagher, Johnny, 172–174
Gallagher, Owen, 172
Gallagher, Peter, 179
Gallagher, Seamus, 172
Garden Island, Lake Ontario, 129
Garden Peninsula, Michigan, 113
Garson, Dave and Mose, 135
General Gage (warship), 105
Genesee River, New York, 99, 166
George C. Finney (schooner), 124–125
Georgian Bay, 96, 142–143, 147, 208–209, 226
Gilbert Knapp (schooner), 138
Gilbert Mollison (schooner), 213–214
Gillis, William, 228
Girard, William, 224
Glad Tidings (gospel ship), 214
Glass, Joseph, 143
Glencairn (freighter), 179
Goderich, Ontario, 93, 96, 149–150, 179
Good Harbor, Michigan, 104, 213
Goodrich Transportation Company, 211

Gordon, Desmond, 143
Grand Haven, Michigan, 211–212
Grand Island, Lake Superior, 124
Grand Marais, Michigan, 103, 124, 130
Grand Rapids Herald, 13
Grand Traverse Bay, Michigan, 172
Gravelly Bay, Lake Erie, 99–100, 109–110
Gray's Reef, Lake Michigan, 185
Green Bay (schooner), 127
Green Bay, Wisconsin, 120–122, 155, 166
Grosse Pointe, Michigan, 156–158

The Habitant and Other French-Canadian Poems, 156
H. C. Albrecht (lumber hooker), 196
Hall, William B., 99
Hallene, Peter, 224
Halsted Street, Chicago, 95
Hamilton, John, 222
Hamilton, William, 200
Hamlin Lake, Michigan, 140–142
Harlow, Frederick Pease, 64, 65
Harrington, Grace Florence, 19
Harrison, William Henry, 106
Hercules (schooner), 142–143
Heywood, Thomas, 36
Historical Collections of the Great Lakes, Bowling Green State University, Ohio, 20
Hog Island Sound, Lake Michigan, 189
Hong Kong, 58
Houghton, Michigan, 42, 127
Hull, William, 105–106
Hullfish, William, 88
Hume, Thomas, 196
Hunter (schooner), 133
Huron (side-wheel steamer), 110

Idaho (steamer), 228–229
Illinois (side-wheel steamer), 216
Informants: Allers, Charles C., of Beaver Island, 127, 180; Anderson, Harry, of St. Clair, Michigan, 119; Armstrong, E. W., of Port Hope, Ontario, 167–168; Ashley, W. A., of Milwaukee, 65–66, 113, 232; Baker, C. R., of Cleveland, 176; Baker, A. E., of Dunkirk, New York, 30, 78, 101, 104; Baker, Neil, of Cleveland, 113; Banner, Pat, of St. Clair, Michigan, 101; Beaupre, Peter, of Kingston, Ontario, 156; Becker, Carl M. G., of Cleveland, 57, 62, 68; Bonnah, Harvey, of Cleveland, 156; Bonner, Manus J., of Charlevoix,

Informants (*continued*)
Michigan, 39, 89, 178, 211; Bonner, Mrs. Manus J., 219; Bonner, Dan, of Beaver Island, 187; Bonner, Pat, of Beaver Island, 172, 181, 187 ; Bovee, Charles L., of Adams, New York, 100; Boyce, Harley M., of Milwaukee, 232; Brown, John, of Cloud Bay, Ontario, 96, 101; Buzzard, E. J., of Erieau, Ontario, 109; Cardinal, Peter, of Muskegon, Michigan, 156; Cavanaugh, Jeremiah, of Port Dalhousie, Ontario, 99; Chene, Ralph, of Detroit, 156, 164; Churchill, "Billy," of Bronte, Ontario, 138; Clark, William E. "Billy," of Buffalo, 33, 34, 37, 57, 64, 67, 68, 76, 78, 111, 120, 133, 136, 223; Collen, Robert "Brokenback," of Chicago, 15–16, 34, 37, 50, 52, 64, 66, 67, 76, 86, 87, 113, 168; Conkey, A. N., 10; Crockett, T. J., of Port Huron, 119; Delano, Fred M., of Detroit, 162; Dix, James, of Kingston, Ontario, 136; Doesburg, Mrs. Gerrit, 104; Dunn, William R., of Cleveland, 11; Elliott, F. W., of Fairport, Ohio, 113, 125, 156; Ericksen, Henry, of Milwaukee, 49, 71; Gallagher, Arthur, of Beaver Island, 15; Gallagher, Dominick, of Beaver Island, 172; Gallagher, Rose, of Beaver Island, 15; Gallino, A. P., of Port Huron, 144–146, 206; Galusha, John "Yankee," of Minerva, New York, 88; Garrett, Dan, of Escanaba, Michigan, 156, 186; Glass, James, 142; Graham, Colin, of Kincardine, Ontario, 226; Graham, Malcolm, of Goderich, Ontario, 93; Green, John W., of Beaver Island, 116, 120, 133, 172, 176; Hayes, John E., of Port Huron, Michigan, 42, 112, 198; Hare, Al, of Port Credit, Ontario, 136, 195; Head, William, of Picton, Ontario, 113, 130, 136, 138, 195; Hubbard, C. H., of Milwaukee, 113; Hudgins, Nelson, of Picton, Ontario, 195; Hylant, Thomas, of Buffalo, 33, 40, 46; Jacobson, S. C., of Waukegan, Illinois, 136, 156, 166, 232; Johnson, Martin, of Traverse City, Michigan, 134; Joys, Carol, of Milwaukee, 34, 65–66, 96, 133–135; Kelley, William, of Cleveland, 113; Kelly, Timothy, of Manitowoc, Wisconsin, 65–66; Kendall, Earl, of Marysville, Michigan, 42; Kendall, Harvey, of Marysville, Michigan, 41–44; La Roche, Israel, of Wolfe Island, Ontario, 202, 220; Leach, Charles, of St. Clair, Michigan, 11, 46; Leach, George, of St. Clair, Michigan, 46; Leaman, James M., of Milwaukee, 232; Mahaffey, Frank, of Port Colborne, Ontario, 44, 112–113; Malloy, John, of Beaver Island, 173; McCannell, James, 14, 16; McCauley, Mary, 176; McConnell, Henry, of Picton, Ontario, 114; McCarthy, Jim, of Port Huron, 45; McDonald, Grafton, of Marine City, Michigan, 42; McDonald, John "Red," of Goderich, Ontario, 142, 147–149; McDonald, Malcomb, of Goderich, Ontario, 113; McDonough, Pat 175; MacIvor, Norman "Beachie," of Goderich, Ontario, 96, 110, 115, 138, 149–150; MacLeod, Duncan, of Buffalo, 223; McLoud, David, of Port Colborne, Ontario, 64; Millard, Charles, of Sarnia, Ontario, 40; Monroe, John "Young," 152–153; Morrison, Charles, of St. Joseph, Michigan, 134; Murphy, Frank, 45; Murray, William, of White Lake, Michigan, 134, 156, 220; Navin, Edward, "Ned" of Cobourg, Ontario, 113, 167–168, 202; Nicholas, William of Chicago, 196; Nye, Pearl R., of Akron, Ohio, 88; O'Donnel, Mike, 175; Oertling, Henry, of Milwaukee, 115; Parmalee, George and Harry, of Waukegan, Illinois, 33, 63, 78; Parsons, John S., of Oswego, New York, 36, 39, 75, 76, 97, 113, 123, 124, 165, 202, 210, 222, 225; Peckham, Ben, of Oswego, New York, 34, 108, 202, 213, 216, 225; Peckham, Thomas, of Oswego, New York, 108, 202, 210, 225; Perry, John, 224; Preston, William, of Grand Haven, Michigan, 113; Ray, J. Sylvester "Ves," of Port Huron, 45, 110, 111, 120, 139–142, 206; Putnam, James, of Port Huron, 156; Reid, Robert, of Red Bay, Ontario, 147; Reid, Mrs. Robert, of Red Bay, Ontario, 208–209; Remington, Dave, of Kincardine, Ontario, 226; Rice, Mrs. James, of Grand Rapids, Michigan, 104; Roddy, Frankie "Francie," of Beaver Island, 172–173, 217; Rolsing, Iver, of Buffalo, 92–93; Secord, C. D., of Cleveland, 42, 134; Small, William J., of Port Huron, Michigan, 45, 140, 144, 206;

Sullivan, Butch, 167; Thomas, Alfred, of Toronto, 136; Thomas, Walter "Doc," of Bronte, Ontario, 138, 195; Walkingthaw, Captain, of Port Colborne, Ontario, 85; Wright, Walter B., of Oberlin, Ohio, 89
Ile aux Galets (Skillagalee), Lake Michigan, 87–89, 92, 120–122, 132, 142, 219
Independence (tug), 98
Isaac G. Jenkins (schooner), 220–221
Isabella County, Michigan, 13
Peach Island, Lake St. Clair, 158
Isle Bob-Lo, Lake Huron, 55
Ives, Burl, 16

Jackson Mining Company, 113
J. H. Rutter (schooner), 190
J. N. Carter (schooner), 226–227
James G. Worts (schooner), 100–101
Jean Francois de Nantes (French hauling song), 78
Jean La Plante (scow), 161–162
Jeanie Deans (side-wheel steamer), 18
Jennie P. King (bark), 137–139
John Bentely (schooner), 97–100
John Bigler (timber drogher), 14, 119, 125, 129–135, 223
John Brown and Co., shipbuilders, 18
John C. Kolfage (schooner), 147–149
John M. Nicol (steamer), 44
Jones, James M., 129
Joseph Sellwood (freighter), 89
Julia B. Merrill (schooner), 231
Julia Dean (brig), 219–220
Julie Plante (scow) 155–158, 161–162, 166

Kalamazoo River, Michigan, 139
Kate Williams (tug), 122
Kelly's Island, Lake Erie, 135, 165
Keweenaw Peninsula, Michigan, 41
Kilsyth, Scotland, 18
Kilty, Peter, 178
Kincardine, Ontario, 226–227
Kingston Volunteers, 106
Knight, Frankie, 143

Lac St. Pierre, Ontario, 155–156
Lachine Canal, Ontario, 155–157
Lady Elgin (passenger steamer), 14, 199–202
Lake St. Clair, 45, 110–111, 147–148, 151–152, 155–158, 161, 162, 166
Lansing, Michigan, 13
Lansing Shoal, 186

Lavinda (schooner), 139–142
Lizzie A. Law (schooner), 233–234
Lawrence (warship), 105–107
Library of Congress, 16, 88
Little Bay de Noc, Lake Michigan, 186
Little Bear Creek, Ontario, 155, 162
Liverpool, 10, 15, 57–60, 68, 101
Lomax, Alan, 16
London, 59, 68
Lonely Island, Georgian Bay, 208
Long, John, 191
Long Point, Ontario, 54, 133, 228
Look 'n' See (scow), 162–164
Lookout (sailboat), 172–175
Lowell (propeller), 145–146
Lozon, Joe, 160
Lucy Smith (steam barge), 87–89
Ludington, Michigan, 13–14, 140, 144, 178, 224,
Lyman Davis (schooner), 56
Lynn, Dan, 205–208
Lyrics and Songs, 192

MacCosh, Jack, 147
Mackinaw City, Michigan, 15, 186
Mackinaw boats, 163
MacLeod, J. C., 223
MacLeod, R. R., 223
Maguire, Shandy, 191
The Making of a Sailor, 64
M. J. Cummings (schooner), 209–211
Maggie Hunter (canaller), 194–196, 223
Malott, Darius Nelson, 200
Malloy, Dan, 173, 175
Manistee, Michigan, 89
Manitoba, 19
Manitou Islands, Lake Michigan, 132, 198–199
Manitoulin Island, Georgian Bay, 208–209
Manitowoc, Wisconsin, 196
Maple Leaf (schooner), 133
Marcotte, Pete, 159
Marine City, Michigan, 41
Mariposa (steamer), 228
Marquette, Michigan, 103, 111, 120, 123, 130, 216
Marquette and Bessemer No. 2 (car ferry), 223
Masefield, John, 33, 36,
Mattie (fishing boat), 189
McAddams, John, 216
McCauley, Frank, 176, 178, 180, 186, 187–188
McDonald, John, 147–149

McDonough, Anthony, 183
McEwen, George M., 17, 20
McKay, Hector, 143
McKee, Cal, 133, 135
McQuarie, Jimmie, 142–143
McSherry, James, 222
McSherry, James, Jr., 222
Menominee, Wisconsin, 155
Merrick, M. F., 125
Merrimac (warship), 140
Mersey, England, 98
Mexico, 41
Miami Canal, Ohio, 154
Michigan Folklore Society, 16
Michigan Island, Lake Superior, 230, 234
Midrech Bay, Lake St. Clair, 155
Milwaukee: grain trade, 34, 45, 65, 95, 96, 231–234; lumber trade, 130–135; Mormons, 171; coal trade, 198; harbor, 210, 228; shipbuilding 230
Milwaukee Fire (song), 206
Milwaukee Union Guards, 199–200
Minch (schooner), 122
Minch, Peter G., 198
Miner, Charles, 106
Minnie Battle (schooner), 125
Minnie Corlett (schooner), 224
Mobile, 44, 60, 62, 68
Moffett, Joseph, 113–114
Mohawk (schooner), 93–95
Monroe, Michigan, 162
Mont Line, 118, 125–127
Montcalm (schooner), 125
Monterey, Mexico, 41
Monticello (schooner), 125
Montmorency (schooner), 125
Montpelier (schooner), 125
Montreal, Ontario, 155–157
Moody, Dwight L., 214
Moonlight (schooner), 230–234
Moore, Charles, 224
Moran, John V. (propeller), 44
Moran, Sam, 123–124
Morgan, "Blinky," 93
Mormons, 171, 219
Morrison, Christina Ann, 208–209
Moscow, 79
Mount Pleasant, Michigan, 13
Munuscong (Mud) Lake, 44
Murphy, Henry "Scrubber," 90–95
Muskegon, Michigan, 15, 101, 186, 196, 211

Muskegon (steamer), 211

Napanee River, Ontario, 99
Nelson, Fred, 10
Nettie Fly (scow), 23, 164–165
New Orleans, Louisiana, 60, 62, 68
New York City, 15, 57, 59–60, 67, 78–79, 98, 103
New York State, 187–189
New York State Barge Canal, 96
Newhall House Fire (song), 206
Niagara (brig), 105–107
Niagara (tug), 125–126
Niagara Falls (escarpment), 99, 166
Niagara River, 51, 166, 219
Nixon, Frank, 194–195
Northern Islander (newspaper), 219
Northerner (side-wheel steamer), 110

Oceana County Pioneers, 224
O'Donnell, Peter, 120, 133, 146
Old Betsie dune, Michigan, 140–142
Old Half Moon (brig), 111
Oliver Cromwell (barge), 144–146
Olson (tug), 217–219
Oriole, 119, 216
Oswego, New York: canallers, 123, 191–196; departing from, 210; home port, 100, 124, 213, 220; ships built, 209; tugs, 107–108; waterfront, 34, 36, 50
Oswego Palladium-Times, 220
Otis, John, 220
Our Son (schooner), 10, 14
Owen Sound, Ontario, 208–209

Paradise Street, Liverpool, 58–60
Parker, Billy, 141
Parry Sound, Ontario, 142–143, 208
Parsons, Thomas, 202
Patch, Sam, 166
Pentwater, Michigan, 224
Pere Marquette 17 (car ferry), 178
Pere Marquette 18 (car ferry), 177–179
Perry, Oliver Hazard, 105–107
Persian (canaller), 191–194
Peters, Harry B., 206
Pettigrew, Herb, 147
Point Abino, Ontario, 139
Point aux Barques, Michigan, 112, 133–134
Port Burwell, Ontario, 104, 147, 149
Port Colborne, Ontario, 109, 133
Port Credit, Ontario, 195

Port Dalhousie, Ontario, 32, 99–100, 125, 136, 210
Point Edward, Ontario, 147
Port Huron, Michigan, 10, 54, 110, 112, 126, 140–141, 144–145, 205–207
Port Maitland, Ontario, 228
Point Pelee, Ontario, 54, 63, 87, 89, 137, 158
Port Sanilac, Michigan, 132, 146
Port Stanley, Ontario, 223
Porter (schooner), 233
Portes des Mortes passage, Wisconsin, 120
Presque Isle, Michigan, 123–125, 132, 194
Presque Isle, Ontario, 107–109
Preston, Jack, 125
Princess Royal (warship), 11

Quebec, Ontario, 130

Rape of Lucrece, 36
Ratcliffe Highway, London, 59
Red River, Manitoba, 19
Red Rock, Ontario, 143
Republic (schooner), 125–126
Rickaby, Franz, 191
Rio Grande, 34–36, 68
River Clyde, Scotland 18
Robert Emmet (tug), 132
Robertson, F. L., 119
Rochester (Charlotte) New York, 99, 135, 166, 221,
Roddy, Andrew, 172–173
Roll and Go: Songs of the American Sailorman, 39
Rondeau, Ontario, 134
Rood and Smith's Elevator, Cleveland, 133
Root, Frank, 228
Rorke, Sara Eliza, 195
Rosebush, Michigan, 13
Rosie Belle Teeneau (scow), 158–161
Rothesay, Scotland, 18
Rouge River, Michigan, 164
Runge, Herman, 19
Ryan, Mike, 222

Sacramento River, 39–40
Saginaw, Michigan, 152
Saginaw Bay, Michigan, 122–125, 146, 179, 184, 191
Saginaw River, Michigan, 145
St. Anne's Island, Lake St. Clair, 155
St. Clair Flats, 45, 133–134, 147, 163
St. Clair River, 45, 61, 155, 164
St. Helena, 79

St. Ignace, Michigan, 74, 187
St. Lawrence River, 129–130, 155
St. Mary's River, 44, 126
Sam Patch (scow), 166
Sam Ward (side-wheel steamer), 41–44
San Francisco Bay, 39, 69
Sand Beach, Michigan, 144, 206–208
Sandburg, Carl, 13, 16
Sand Point, Michigan, 122
Sanilac County, Michigan, 205
Santa Anna, Antonio Lopez de, 40–41
Santa Paula, California, 20
Sarnia, Ontario, 128, 142–143, 147–149, 155
Sault Ste. Marie, 91, 123, 208
Savage, J. N., 208
Schenectady, New York, 169
Scotland, 18
Sephie (schooner), 96–97, 128
Shannon, Harvey, 120
Sharpe, George, 195
Shay, Frank, 14
Sheboygan, Wisconsin, 178
Sheboygan (side-wheel steamer), 232
Shenandoah Valley, Virginia, 36
Shied, Joe, 183
Ships, Sea Songs and Shanties, 36
Singapore, 68
Sleeping Bear Point, Michigan, 140–142
Snider, C. H. J., 195
Songs of the Michigan Lumberjacks, 152
South Haven, Michigan, 15, 127
South Manitou Island, Lake Michigan, 140–142, 213
Southampton, Ontario, 149
Southerner (warship), 11
Souvenir (schooner), 224–225
Spanish Armada, 231
State of New York (schooner), 110
Stewart, John, 221
Stone, Alex, 176
Straits of Mackinac, 51–52, 55, 132, 137, 140–142, 145, 179, 182, 184, 191, 219, 234
Strang, James Jesse, 171, 219
Sturgeon Bay, Wisconsin, 179
Sugar Island, 123
Sullivan, Daniel, 191, 194
Superior (steamer), 176
Swallow Tail (sailing packet), 98
Sweepstakes (schooner), 133
Sydesharn River, 155

Tawas City, Michigan, 145
Thames River, Ontario, 147, 155, 162
Thayer, Thomas, 224
Thomas Hume (schooner), 196–199
Thompson (tug), 205–207
Thompson, Stith, 16–17, 21
Three Bells (schooner), 103–104
Thunder Bay, Michigan, 122, 142
Thunder Bay Island, Lake Huron, 123, 125, 132
Three Sisters (schooner), 168
Tinkiss, Duncan A., 208–209
Titanic (passenger steamer), 19
Toledo, Ohio, 110, 139, 162
Toledo Blade (newspaper), 13
Tonawanda, New York, 129–130, 139–140
Toronto, 99–100, 194–195, 222
Toronto Evening Telegram, 222
Tourangeau, Jules, 159
Traverse City, Michigan, 172–174
Turpin, Charlie, 111
Twin Points, Wisconsin, 166
Twin River Point, Michigan, 176
Twilight (schooner), 122–124
The *Two Orphans* (song), 206

University of Chicago, 13
University of Illinois, 13
University of Michigan, 17
University of Michigan Bentley Historical Library, 17
University of Michigan College of Engineering, 13
Upper Peninsula, Michigan, 125
U.S. Lighthouse Board, 185
U.S. Lightship 57 (light vessel), 185
U.S. Lightship 98 (light vessel), 185–186

V. H. Ketcham (schooner-barge), 73
Vernon (propeller), 176–177, 184
Vick (tug), 147
Vienna (schooner), 148–149

W. H. Gilcher (freighter), 197–199
Walker (tug), 123–124
Walkerville, Ontario, 160
Walton, Lynn, 12, 17
Walton, Mildred (Hallett), 13, 17
Walton, Nicholas, 12
Walton, Sue, 17
War of 1812, 57, 104–107
Ward, Eber Brock, 41
Ward Line, 41–44
Ward, Sam, 41
Washington Island, Wisconsin, 120
Waterloo, 79, 98
Waugoschance Point (Wobble Shanks), Michigan, 132, 142
Welland Canal, 99–101, 109, 115, 123, 124, 129–130, 167
Weller's Bay, 222–223
Western Reserve (freighter), 197–198
Whall, W. B., 36
Whitcomb, Fred, 224
Whittle, D. W., 215
Whitefish Bay, Michigan, 124, 198
William Shupe (schooner), 205–208
Wilson, E. S., 219
Wilson, Loudon G., 18–22, 104, 134
Windmill Point, Ontario, 217
Windsor, Ontario, 155, 226
Winnetka, Illinois, 200
Wm. H. Stevens (schooner), 42, 44
Winnipeg, 115
Woods, A. J., 224
Work, Henry C., 200
World War I, 13, 96
W. S. Lyons, (schooner), 124
Wyandotte, Michigan, 110, 159
Wyoming (propeller), 112

Young, Brigham, 219

Titles in the Great Lakes Books Series

Freshwater Fury: Yarns and Reminiscences of the Greatest Storm in Inland Navigation, by Frank Barcus, 1986 (reprint)

Call It North Country: The Story of Upper Michigan, by John Bartlow Martin, 1986 (reprint)

The Land of the Crooked Tree, by U. P. Hedrick, 1986 (reprint)

Michigan Place Names, by Walter Romig, 1986 (reprint)

Luke Karamazov, by Conrad Hilberry, 1987

The Late, Great Lakes: An Environmental History, by William Ashworth, 1987 (reprint)

Great Pages of Michigan History from the Detroit Free Press, 1987

Waiting for the Morning Train: An American Boyhood, by Bruce Catton, 1987 (reprint)

Michigan Voices: Our State's History in the Words of the People Who Lived It, compiled and edited by Joe Grimm, 1987

Danny and the Boys, Being Some Legends of Hungry Hollow, by Robert Traver, 1987 (reprint)

Hanging On, or How to Get through a Depression and Enjoy Life, by Edmund G. Love, 1987 (reprint)

The Situation in Flushing, by Edmund G. Love, 1987 (reprint)

A Small Bequest, by Edmund G. Love, 1987 (reprint)

The Saginaw Paul Bunyan, by James Stevens, 1987 (reprint)

The Ambassador Bridge: A Monument to Progress, by Philip P. Mason, 1988

Let the Drum Beat: A History of the Detroit Light Guard, by Stanley D. Solvick, 1988

An Afternoon in Waterloo Park, by Gerald Dumas, 1988 (reprint)

Contemporary Michigan Poetry: Poems from the Third Coast, edited by Michael Delp, Conrad Hilberry and Herbert Scott, 1988

Over the Graves of Horses, by Michael Delp, 1988

Wolf in Sheep's Clothing: The Search for a Child Killer, by Tommy McIntyre, 1988

Copper-Toed Boots, by Marguerite de Angeli, 1989 (reprint)

Detroit Images: Photographs of the Renaissance City, edited by John J. Bukowczyk and Douglas Aikenhead, with Peter Slavcheff, 1989

Hangdog Reef: Poems Sailing the Great Lakes, by Stephen Tudor, 1989

Detroit: City of Race and Class Violence, revised edition, by B. J. Widick, 1989

Deep Woods Frontier: A History of Logging in Northern Michigan, by Theodore J. Karamanski, 1989

Orvie, The Dictator of Dearborn, by David L. Good, 1989

Seasons of Grace: A History of the Catholic Archdiocese of Detroit, by Leslie Woodcock Tentler, 1990

The Pottery of John Foster: Form and Meaning, by Gordon and Elizabeth Orear, 1990

The Diary of Bishop Frederic Baraga: First Bishop of Marquette, Michigan, edited by Regis M. Walling and Rev. N. Daniel Rupp, 1990

Walnut Pickles and Watermelon Cake: A Century of Michigan Cooking, by Larry B. Massie and Priscilla Massie, 1990

The Making of Michigan, 1820–1860: A Pioneer Anthology, edited by Justin L. Kestenbaum, 1990

America's Favorite Homes: A Guide to Popular Early Twentieth-Century Homes, by Robert Schweitzer and Michael W. R. Davis, 1990

Beyond the Model T: The Other Ventures of Henry Ford, by Ford R. Bryan, 1990

Life after the Line, by Josie Kearns, 1990

Michigan Lumbertowns: Lumbermen and Laborers in Saginaw, Bay City, and Muskegon, 1870–1905, by Jeremy W. Kilar, 1990

Detroit Kids Catalog: The Hometown Tourist, by Ellyce Field, 1990

Waiting for the News, by Leo Litwak, 1990 (reprint)

Detroit Perspectives, edited by Wilma Wood Henrickson, 1991

Life on the Great Lakes: A Wheelsman's Story, by Fred W. Dutton, edited by William Donohue Ellis, 1991

Copper Country Journal: The Diary of Schoolmaster Henry Hobart, 1863–1864, by Henry Hobart, edited by Philip P. Mason, 1991

John Jacob Astor: Business and Finance in the Early Republic, by John Denis Haeger, 1991

Survival and Regeneration: Detroit's American Indian Community, by Edmund J. Danziger, Jr., 1991

Steamboats and Sailors of the Great Lakes, by Mark L. Thompson, 1991

Cobb Would Have Caught It: The Golden Age of Baseball in Detroit, by Richard Bak, 1991

Michigan in Literature, by Clarence Andrews, 1992

Under the Influence of Water: Poems, Essays, and Stories, by Michael Delp, 1992

The Country Kitchen, by Della T. Lutes, 1992 (reprint)

The Making of a Mining District: Keweenaw Native Copper 1500–1870, by David J. Krause, 1992

Kids Catalog of Michigan Adventures, by Ellyce Field, 1993

Henry's Lieutenants, by Ford R. Bryan, 1993

Historic Highway Bridges of Michigan, by Charles K. Hyde, 1993

Lake Erie and Lake St. Clair Handbook, by Stanley J. Bolsenga and Charles E. Herndendorf, 1993

Queen of the Lakes, by Mark Thompson, 1994

Iron Fleet: The Great Lakes in World War II, by George J. Joachim, 1994

Turkey Stearnes and the Detroit Stars: The Negro Leagues in Detroit, 1919–1933, by Richard Bak, 1994

Pontiac and the Indian Uprising, by Howard H. Peckham, 1994 (reprint)

Charting the Inland Seas: A History of the U.S. Lake Survey, by Arthur M. Woodford, 1994 (reprint)

Ojibwa Narratives of Charles and Charlotte Kawbawgam and Jacques LePique, 1893–1895. Recorded with Notes by Homer H. Kidder, edited by Arthur P. Bourgeois, 1994, co-published with the Marquette County Historical Society

Strangers and Sojourners: A History of Michigan's Keweenaw Peninsula, by Arthur W. Thurner, 1994

Win Some, Lose Some: G. Mennen Williams and the New Democrats, by Helen Washburn Berthelot, 1995

Sarkis, by Gordon and Elizabeth Orear, 1995

The Northern Lights: Lighthouses of the Upper Great Lakes, by Charles K. Hyde, 1995 (reprint)

Kids Catalog of Michigan Adventures, second edition, by Ellyce Field, 1995

Rumrunning and the Roaring Twenties: Prohibition on the Michigan- Ontario Waterway, by Philip P. Mason, 1995

In the Wilderness with the Red Indians, by E. R. Baierlein, translated by Anita Z. Boldt, edited by Harold W. Moll, 1996

Elmwood Endures: History of a Detroit Cemetery, by Michael Franck, 1996

Master of Precision: Henry M. Leland, by Mrs. Wilfred C. Leland with Minnie Dubbs Millbrook, 1996 (reprint)

Haul-Out: New and Selected Poems, by Stephen Tudor, 1996

Kids Catalog of Michigan Adventures, third edition, by Ellyce Field, 1997

Beyond the Model T: The Other Ventures of Henry Ford, revised edition, by Ford R. Bryan, 1997

Young Henry Ford: A Picture History of the First Forty Years, by Sidney Olson, 1997 (reprint)

The Coast of Nowhere: Meditations on Rivers, Lakes and Streams, by Michael Delp, 1997

From Saginaw Valley to Tin Pan Alley: Saginaw's Contribution to American Popular Music, 1890–1955, by R. Grant Smith, 1998

The Long Winter Ends, by Newton G. Thomas, 1998 (reprint)

Bridging the River of Hatred: The Pioneering Efforts of Detroit Police Commissioner George Edwards, by Mary M. Stolberg, 1998

Toast of the Town: The Life and Times of Sunnie Wilson, by Sunnie Wilson with John Cohassey, 1998

These Men Have Seen Hard Service: The First Michigan Sharpshooters in the Civil War, by Raymond J. Herek, 1998

A Place for Summer: One Hundred Years at Michigan and Trumbull, by Richard Bak, 1998

Early Midwestern Travel Narratives: An Annotated Bibliography, 1634–1850, by Robert R. Hubach, 1998 (reprint)

All-American Anarchist: Joseph A. Labadie and the Labor Movement, by Carlotta R. Anderson, 1998

Michigan in the Novel, 1816–1996: An Annotated Bibliography, by Robert Beasecker, 1998

"Time by Moments Steals Away": The 1848 Journal of Ruth Douglass, by Robert L. Root, Jr., 1998

The Detroit Tigers: A Pictorial Celebration of the Greatest Players and Moments in Tigers' History, updated edition, by William M. Anderson, 1999

Father Abraham's Children: Michigan Episodes in the Civil War, by Frank B. Woodford, 1999 (reprint)

Letter from Washington, 1863–1865, by Lois Bryan Adams, edited and with an introduction by Evelyn Leasher, 1999

Wonderful Power: The Story of Ancient Copper Working in the Lake Superior Basin, by Susan R. Martin, 1999

A Sailor's Logbook: A Season aboard Great Lakes Freighters, by Mark L. Thompson, 1999

Huron: The Seasons of a Great Lake, by Napier Shelton, 1999

Tin Stackers: The History of the Pittsburgh Steamship Company, by Al Miller, 1999

Art in Detroit Public Places, revised edition, text by Dennis Nawrocki, photographs by David Clements, 1999

Brewed in Detroit: Breweries and Beers Since 1830, by Peter H. Blum, 1999

Detroit Kids Catalog: A Family Guide for the 21st Century, by Ellyce Field, 2000

"Expanding the Frontiers of Civil Rights": Michigan, 1948–1968, by Sidney Fine, 2000

Graveyard of the Lakes, by Mark L. Thompson, 2000

Enterprising Images: The Goodridge Brothers, African American Photographers, 1847–1922, by John Vincent Jezierski, 2000

New Poems from the Third Coast: Contemporary Michigan Poetry, edited by Michael Delp, Conrad Hilberry, and Josie Kearns, 2000

Arab Detroit: From Margin to Mainstream, edited by Nabeel Abraham and Andrew Shryock, 2000

The Sandstone Architecture of the Lake Superior Region, by Kathryn Bishop Eckert, 2000

Looking Beyond Race: The Life of Otis Milton Smith, by Otis Milton Smith and Mary M. Stolberg, 2000

Mail by the Pail, by Colin Bergel, illustrated by Mark Koenig, 2000

Great Lakes Journey: A New Look at America's Freshwater Coast, by William Ashworth, 2000

A Life in the Balance: The Memoirs of Stanley J. Winkelman, by Stanley J. Winkelman, 2000

Schooner Passage: Sailing Ships and the Lake Michigan Frontier, by Theodore J. Karamanski, 2000

The Outdoor Museum: The Magic of Michigan's Marshall M. Fredericks, by Marcy Heller Fisher, illustrated by Christine Collins Woomer, 2001

Detroit in Its World Setting: A Three Hundred Year Chronology, 1701–2001, edited by David Lee Poremba, 2001

Frontier Metropolis: Picturing Early Detroit, 1701–1838, by Brian Leigh Dunnigan, 2001

Michigan Remembered: Photographs from the Farm Security Administration and the Office of War Information, 1936–1943, edited by Constance B. Schulz, with Introductory Essays by Constance B. Schulz and William H. Mulligan, Jr., 2001

This Is Detroit, 1701–2001, by Arthur M. Woodford, 2001

History of the Finns in Michigan, by Armas K. E. Holmio, translated by Ellen M. Ryynanen, 2001

Angels in the Architecture: A Photographic Elegy to an American Asylum, by Heidi Johnson, 2001

Uppermost Canada: The Western District and the Detroit Frontier, 1800–1850, by R. Alan Douglas, 2001

The Iron Hunter, by Chase S. Osborn, 2002

Windjammers: Songs of the Great Lakes Sailors, by Ivan H. Walton with Joe Grimm, 2002

A NOTE ON THE RECORDINGS

These recordings span more than twenty years and a range of technologies. They reflect the uneven capabilities of the equipment and Ivan H. Walton's informants. The first and last two recordings on this disc are not from the field but from a program Walton organized at the University of Michigan in 1955. The interviewer on some of the recordings is folklorist Alan Lomax, whom Walton introduced to some of his informants. The recordings were copied onto reel-to-reel tape and then onto cassettes in the Walton audio archives at the University of Michigan's Bentley Historical Library. The selections on this disc were chosen by Lee Murdock and Joe Grimm. Murdock and Mark Karney of Norwest Communications, Barrington, Illinois, edited the recordings and eliminated many of the technical imperfections.

This CD was published with the assistance of a fund established by Thelma Gray James of Wayne State University for the publication of folklore and English studies.

1. Opening remarks; Walton, folklore program at University of Michigan, Ann Arbor, July 1955. (1:24)
2. "The Gallagher Boys"; sung by John W. Green, story by Dominick Gallagher, Lomax interviewing, Beaver Island, Michigan, August 1938. (7:07)
3. "The *Clifton*'s Crew"; sung by Patrick Bonner, Lomax interviewing, Beaver Island, Michigan, August 25, 1938. (5:21)
4. "The Fisherman Yankee Brown"; sung by Dan Bonner, Lomax interviewing, Beaver Island, Michigan, August 25, 1938. (3:18)
5. "The Gallant Tommy Boyle"; sung by Pat McDonough, Beaver Island, Michigan, August 25, 1938. (3:31)
6. "The Smugglers of Buffalo"; sung by John W. Green, Beaver Island, Michigan, August 26, 1938. (1:51)
7. "James Bird"; sung by John W. Green, Beaver Island, Michigan, August 26, 1938. (3:12)
8. The Timber Drogher *Bigler*"; sung by Asa M. Trueblood, Lomax interviewing, St. Ignace, Michigan, September 7, 1938. (3:19)
9. "The Old Barge *Oliver Cromwell*"; sung by John Gallino, Walton interviewing, Port Huron, Michigan, September 2, 1938. (5:12)
10. "Scrubber Murphy," "The Crack Schooner *Moonlight*," "The Old Mont Line"; testing his balky recording equipment, Walton sang several fragments, as one might record notes, preserving melodies that do not appear to have been recorded elsewhere. Port Huron, Michigan, September 1, 1938. (1:19)
11. "The *E. C. Roberts*"; sung by Captain James Putnam, Walton interviewing, Port Huron, Michigan, September 1, 1938. (3:59)

12. "The Red Iron Ore," "The Timber Drogher *Bigler*," "The Wood Scow *Julie Plante*"; sung by Harry Barney of Algonac, Michigan, Walton interviewing, Port Huron, Michigan, September 1, 1938. (6:03)
13. "The Ill-Fated *Persian*"; sung by John W. Green, Walton interviewing, Beaver Island, Michigan, July 1959. (4:14)
14. "Bound Away on the *Twilight*"; sung by Ed Vandenberg, University of Michigan, Ann Arbor, July 1955. (5:34)
15. "The Schooner *Thomas Hume*"; sung by Ed Vandenberg, University of Michigan, Ann Arbor, July 1955. (3:20)

© 2002 Wayne State University Press